FANATIC

BOOKS BY JIM GORANT

FIT FOR GOLF
(with Boris Kuzmic)

FANATIC

FANATIC

TEN THINGS
ALL SPORTS FANS
SHOULD DO
BEFORE THEY
DIE

JIM GORANT

HOUGHTON MIFFLIN COMPANY

BOSTON ▪ NEW YORK

2007

For information about permission to reproduce selections
from this book, write to Permissions, Houghton Mifflin Company,
215 Park Avenue South, New York, New York 10003.

Visit our Web site: www.houghtonmifflinbooks.com.

Library of Congress Cataloging-in-Publication Data
Gorant, Jim.
Fanatic : ten things all sports fans should do
before they die / Jim Gorant.
p. cm.
Includes index.
ISBN-13: 978-0-618-61298-7
ISBN-10: 0-618-61298-x
1. Gorant, Jim. 2. Sports spectators — United States
3. Sports — Sociological aspects. I. Title. II. Title: Ten
things all sports fans should do before they die.
GV715.G67 2007
796 — dc22 2006033831

Printed in the United States of America

Book design by Victoria Hartman

QUM 10 9 8 7 6 5 4 3 2 1

Most names and some identifying details of the people who appear
in this book have been changed in order to protect the privacy of those
involved. For narrative purposes, the book contains some composite
characters, transferred dialogue, and condensed scenes. In writing chapter 8 I used *The 100-Yard War* by Greg Emmanuel (John Wiley & Sons,
2004) as a reference, and for chapter 9 I used *Mudbaths and Bloodbaths*
by Gary D'Amato and Cliff Christl (Prairie Oak Press, 1997).

Photo credits: page 81: Harry How/Getty Images; page 127: AFP Collec-
tion/Getty Images; page 148: Jonathan Daniel/Getty Images; page 165:
Tom Pidgeon/Getty Images; page 184: Joe Malecki; page 205: Travis Lind-
quist/Getty Images. All other images were taken by the author.

For my mother,
LUCY TSANGARIS GORANT
October 12, 1942, to June 24, 2004

★

CONTENTS

INTRODUCTION

WHADDAYA SAY, PATRIOTS?" I don't say anything. He shouts again, "What do you say, Patriots?" His face is now so close, I can see the blondish stubble of his beard reemerging after that morning's shave, and if I chose to I could give a fairly detailed accounting of his dental work. I don't choose to.

At this proximity, our faces are like mirror images, but they're quite different. Mine is clean and largely expressionless, save the raised eyebrow. His is painted with a primal combination of blue, red, and silver, and twisted into an expression, of what, exactly? Pain, anger, enthusiasm? I can't say. Nor can I say why he's chosen to ask me this question. Has he mistaken me for a fellow Patriots fan?

It is the Friday before Super Bowl XXXIX, which this year features the Philadelphia Eagles and the New England Patriots, and we are at The Landing in downtown Jacksonville, a sort of outdoor mall and plaza that has already become the alcohol-fueled core of the three-day pregame party both sets of fans will take part in.

Almost everyone here has some sort of identifying mark, whether it's a hat, T-shirt, team jersey, or otherwise. Two guys with actual Eagles football helmets drink their beer through straws. Dozens of grown men in green face-paint high-five each other upon passing. Those who don't are local residents who've come down to join the party or check out the scene. I, in contrast, have nothing on that would indicate I'm for either team. I'm as neutral as neutral can be. Maybe that's why this guy has chosen to get in my face. He needs me to declare my allegiance one way or the other. Friend or foe? I don't know, but I do know that as the question hangs there between us a palpable tension grows. He's shirtless. He's drunk. He's right in my face.

The reason I'm nose to nose with the face-painter is because I'm an idiot. Not in the same way that he's an idiot, exactly, but an idiot nonetheless. Ever since I was, maybe, five, I've been addicted to sports. I played them all. I watched them all. Football, baseball, basketball, hockey, tennis, golf, badminton, pro wrestling—for chrissakes, my brother and I followed Australian Rules football on ESPN before the network could afford real programming. I've watched not just the Grey Cup, the Canadian Football League version of the Super Bowl, but regular-season games as well; at one point I could name the starting lineup of the Montreal Alouettes.

I was never a total stat nerd, but by second grade I'd mastered the calculus of scoring a tennis match. By third grade, I could tell you all the divisions and conferences of all the major sports, how their playoffs worked, where the wildcard teams came from, and how to calculate who had the home-field advantage. By fourth I understood that "questionable" meant a player had a 50 percent chance of playing, while "doubtful" dropped the odds to 25 percent.

Most kids pined for Christmas; I loved early spring and midfall. In spring, baseball returned, basketball and hockey moved into the playoffs, and college basketball reached its seasonal climax. In October, the NFL was going strong, college football bustled with rivalries and showdowns, baseball played out its bittersweet endgame, and the NBA and NHL began to rev up. The virtual orgy of sports was—and still is—a sports fanatic's dream come true.

Growing up in northern New Jersey I developed deeply felt regional allegiances. Giants, Yankees, Rangers, Knicks. (This was a typical trend along the Connecticut–Westchester–New Jersey axis. East of Manhattan lay Met, Jet, Islander territory, although the arrival of the Nets and the Devils and the Jets' move to Jersey have muddled the picture in recent years.) College football: Penn State. College basketball: uncommitted. I loved them all.

In 1976 I was nine years old and the Giants signed Larry Csonka, fresh from his disastrous stint in the World Football League. Csonka was not the player he'd been as the centerpiece of the great Miami Dolphins teams of the early to mid-1970s, but the Giants had been so bad for so long that anything that had even the slightest crumb of success clinging to it was welcomed like an ice cube in a European restaurant. No surprise then that when I found out the Zonk, as my dad called him, would be signing autographs at a local car dealership, I forced my mom to haul me over there.

I still have the autograph – "Thanks for visiting DeMassi Cadillac" scribbled across a glossy black-and-white photo of the Zonk, who smiles out from under his comically twisted nose and cheesy *Magnum, P.I* mustache – but I remember little about the meeting with the future Hall of Famer. He sat on a chrome barstool with a black leather seat and wore a sport jacket—which threw me. I think I was expecting him to be in uniform. It was the first time I'd ever met a professional athlete, and I'd never imagined them as real people with lives off the field; somehow they didn't exist to me in any way but the way in which I always encountered them, suited up and ready to play. He asked my name. I can't remember but I must have responded because the autograph reads "To Jim," although it's possible that in my shell-shocked muteness my mother responded for me. My father, who'd once seen Csonka in a restaurant, had talked about the size of his thighs, but what caught my attention were his hands. Meaty, tangled, snarled, and powerful, they were hands that knew things. They had held on to footballs at the bottom of ruthless piles, had led the charge on countless devastating forearm shivers, and had been held aloft in the ultimate triumph.

The mildly homoerotic undertones of the exchange were lost on me then, but the larger picture was not. I came away thinking three things: Larry Csonka was my favorite football player; there could be nothing greater in the world than to be a professional athlete; sports were awesome. The meeting had such an impact on me, in fact, that as the legend goes, my family was awakened several times over the next few weeks by the sound of my voice ringing out in the deepest part of the night. They were used to me talking in my sleep (a childhood affliction I eventually outgrew), but this was different. There were variations, but the content usually went something like this: "Csonka off the left side. He breaks a tackle at the 20. He's at the 10, the 5, touchdown!"

The number of Saturdays and Sundays that I spent between the ages of ten and twenty-five watching sports from before lunch until well after dinner are countless. Ohio State vs. Michigan? Sure. Who cares that I don't know anyone who went to either school and have hardly set foot in either state? That hasn't stopped me from not only watching the annual matchup dozens of times, but actually looking forward to it. In fact, by the time I got to college, coming across such a game was a bonus. In those carefree days my friends and I would happily settle in for a filler game like the Citadel vs. VMI. The more obscure, in some ways, the better. And while I thought my hours of fandom would have reached a peak in college, it was in my early twenties that my sports jones really took off. I lived in a quintessential bachelor pad outside New York City with two guys I'd known since childhood, and we watched sports just about every night and in nonstop doses on the weekend. Sometimes, to get out, we'd visit friends and watch with them. There's many a well-built seat cushion out there that's been permanently marked with the imprint of my ass thanks to my inability to carry on without knowing whether the Seahawks or the Cards prevailed in the second game of some meaningless Sunday doubleheader.

What's truly extraordinary about it all is that we weren't out of the ordinary. Every guy I knew was—and to a large degree still is—obsessed with sports. When we were done watching for the day, we regrouped and went out to a bar, where 90 percent of the guys in the room kept one eye on the young women who would very soon be rejecting their come-ons and the other eye on the ubiquitous ring of TVs that provided the flickering light by which we lived—sports.

The downside—isn't there always one?—was that I suffered an increasing degree of guilt and self-loathing. It was one thing when I was a teen, but as I got older sports just didn't seem like serious enough business for intelligent men to spend so much time watching, thinking about, and debating. Never mind the whole aspect of idolatry, the fawning reverence paid to the athletes, the emotional swings, the blind loyalty to an entity that neither knew nor cared the least about me. I loved the games, but I hated that I could become so involved that I would sulk for a night if my team lost.

I began distancing myself from the sheer tribal call of sport. I forced myself to stop referring to the teams I rooted for as "we." I got rid of any jersey and even T-shirt I owned with a team name or logo on it. I intellectualized about how I was drawn to the games by the people, the story lines, the suspense of a live, unfolding drama. I did everything but stop watching.

Marriage and fatherhood changed the equation but did not alter the sum total. I have a lot less free time these days—so the sheer volume of watching has gone down, but the interest has not waned. It wasn't that long ago that we went on an overnight visit to my in-laws' house. They are immigrants and intellectuals who know little about and care almost nothing for sports, and I've always felt particularly sensitive around them. So although my alma mater was playing a game that in the context of the moment was very important, I resisted the temptation to break away from the conversation so I could turn on the TV and check the score. But late that night, I could bear it no longer. I slipped out of the warm bed where my wife lay sleeping, tiptoed past the closed door of my in-laws' bedroom, and made my way down the stairs. There in the darkness of the living room, with the volume turned all the way down, I cut open a vein and let the scores that run across the bottom of the ESPN screen flow directly into my bloodstream.

It may come as a surprise, then, that when I became a writer, I intentionally avoided becoming a sportswriter. I was afraid that, as often happens, taking something that was previously fun and turning it into a job would make it tedious. I don't know for sure if that would have happened to me, but there's no shortage of bitter, jaded, and cynical sportswriters out there.

As it happened, though, in 1998 I started playing golf in earnest and then writing about it. Eventually I was offered a job at *Sports Illustrated*, and that's how I wound up at the 2004 Masters. One night at the tournament I went to dinner with some colleagues from the magazine and a few people from one of the golf-equipment manufacturers. Somehow the conversation came around to the Kentucky Derby. One of our group confessed, "I've never been to the Derby." *Never been!* People at the table were shocked. "If there's only one sporting event you ever go to, it should be the Derby," a senior member of the group advised.

"Yeah," said someone else. "The Derby and the Masters."

"Actually," another wizened diner claimed, "there are five events every sports fan should attend: the Derby, the Masters, the Final Four, the Super Bowl, and Wimbledon." Huzzahs ensued. The conversation broke off into splinter groups of two and three. Names percolated up from the accumulated chatter: the Olympics, the World Cup, the World Series, a day game at Wrigley, a night game at Fenway, a December game at Lambeau. I remained silent through it all. Other than a singular World Series game and this, my first Masters, I'd never been to any of the events mentioned. I was happy when the conversation turned to another topic.

But something about the subject registered deep within me, and I dog-eared the page in my brain where it was stored. A few weeks later I was sitting at my desk when the list of five must-see sports events returned to me. I wrote them down. I did a little research. Some history, some scheduling. It occurred to me that a person could take one year and knock off the whole menu. I pondered that for a few seconds, then let the topic die.

The list sat on my desk among other scraps of paper. One day during a cleanup effort, I came across it and reread it. I thought about it some more. Were those the five? My dinner companions that night had noted others. I could think of more myself. And why limit the list to five? Why not ten? I began to bring it up in conversation with friends and colleagues: If you could go to any ten sports events, what would they be? I cross-referenced the lists. I doodled them while riding home on the train. It became a thing for me to think about when I had nothing else on my mind.

Eventually, I realized that my growing obsession about what was on the list was simply a way of masking the obvious: I wanted to go. I'd seen virtually all of them on TV, sure, but I'd never been to them. How could that be? I was a sports nut. I was the kind of guy these things were made for. I knew the Super Bowl was special, the game of games, I'd been watching it for years, but I couldn't say how or why. What was different about being there live? Certainly there was a lot on the line for the two teams, but didn't it go beyond that? I didn't know. I'd never been. They had built it, but I hadn't come.

When I tuned in now, I couldn't help but notice the crowd. There was something going on just outside the spotlight that called to me. I had once been the sort of fan who would shout at televisions and get in heated arguments with supporters of other teams. The kind of guy who bought season tickets and rode a wave of adrenaline through the game. I had, it pained me to admit, once painted my face for a college basketball game. Now I was a sports professor. No less addicted to the action, but watching it all from an intellectual distance. I didn't know where I had gone off the track or if I wanted to go back, but it suddenly became very clear to me that the answers were out there, on the road, in the stands, at the games.

Like my dedication to sports itself, the idea of going to all the events on my list became something of a compulsion — albeit a preposterous one. A person with a full-time job, a wife who works, and two young kids doesn't just take off on ten trips over the course of a year to watch sports. As I pictured it, though, this would be more than a series of boondoggles. It would be a journey on which I'd hope to find some common thread between them all, a sort of Rosetta stone of sport that explained why I and so many people like me were addicted to the games. I didn't want to accept the now-clichéd conclusions of those who had gone before me. I wanted to start with those conclusions as questions and move beyond them, finding new answers, asking new questions.

On a more personal level, I'd be attempting to come to grips with two mysteries: my own growing need to go to these events and how my relationship to sports had changed from passionate participant to distant viewer. I hoped to gain some understanding of why these games held me so enraptured. Maybe I could once and for all put the whole topic behind me or at least accept my weakness and get back to loving sports without feeling bad about it.

My children had now reached the age where they were starting to play sports and query me about them. When they saw me watching a game they no longer ran off to play but lingered before the screen and asked questions. My wife had always encouraged me to teach them about sports, because she never knew much about them and she felt that put her at a disadvantage. I've been reluctant, though, because of my own mixed feelings about my habit, as if teaching them about sports was like teaching them to smoke. But I couldn't avoid the topic any longer. I needed to figure out how I was going to present sports to them and what role sports would play in our ongoing relationships.

Moreover, I'd recently lost my sixty-one-year-old mother to cancer, an event that left me feeling lost and vulnerable. I was thirty-seven years old and for the first time in a long time the future held a destabilizing uncertainty. My life was only getting more complex.

In the end, it was less a feeling of wanting to go than of having to go. It was now or never. What would I find? Who would I meet? What would I discover about sports, about others, about myself? What would I do when a shirtless maniac got in my face and screamed, "Whaddaya say, Patriots?"

1 ★ The Super Bowl

Philadelphia Eagles vs. New England Patriots

Jacksonville, Florida, Feb. 4–6, 2005

GOOD MORNING, LADIES and gentlemen, we're now ready to begin boarding American Airlines flight 2481, departing La Guardia at 6:30 A.M. for Jacksonville . . . and the Super Bowl!" A solitary voice in the corner of the boarding area musters a sagging "woohoo," but otherwise the only reaction is the shuffling of the first-class passengers as they prepare for their courtesy boarding. I am concerned.

Not because there's so little enthusiasm. I assume that, like me, most of the people gathered here have been up since four or four thirty, an hour of awakening that effectively kills cheeriness of almost any sort and certainly snuffs out the kind of "big game" rowdiness our gate agent was attempting to rally. Neither am I unnerved by the snow that's falling through the still-dark sky and the sight of deicing fluid being sprayed liberally onto our plane's wings. What's bothering me right now is the sight of my old college roommate, Raphael, walking across the terminal.

It's not that he's unexpected. I had gotten a late start on my Super Bowl planning, and hotel rooms within a one-hour drive of the stadium were hard to come by — "I have nothing," my travel agent told me. I knew that Raf's parents lived about twenty minutes outside of Jacksonville, so I dropped him an e-mail: "You going to the Super Bowl?" I asked innocently enough.

"I'm thinking about it," he responded. "You?"

"Yes, but I don't have a ticket to the game or a place to stay yet."

"If I can get a ticket I'll go, and you can stay with me at my parents' house," came his reply. I felt a little guilty, because that was, of course, exactly what I was hoping he would say, but I rationalized it in two ways. First, even if I had already booked a hotel room right next to the stadium, I still would have checked in with Raf to see if he was going to be in town during the game, and second, all I did was ask if he was going. I didn't say, "Why don't you go?" or, "You should go." I just asked. He easily could have said no. Right?

In truth, I knew he wouldn't, because among many other things — intelligent, funny, generous — Raphael is the type of guy who's drawn to a happening. He likes to go to things for the very I-was-thereness of the experience. He's the kind of guy you see at a baseball game sitting behind home plate talking on his cell phone, waving his hands wildly. You don't have to be a skilled lip reader to tell he's saying, "Can ya see me? Can ya see me?"

In a way, that made him a perfect companion, because if you believe the experts, many of the people who fill the stands at a Super Bowl couldn't care less about the game. They're there for the spectacle. Although I think of myself as a much better sports fan than Raphael, more dedicated and knowledgeable, I have to admit I'm here largely for the same reason. After years of hearing about the Super Bowl and regarding the NFL as my own form of Sunday worship, I want to see what all the fuss is about. If I have to squeeze a little hospitality out of a friend in that pursuit, then so be it. Still, as the game approaches, my misgivings about using Rafi get worse. I've managed to finagle a media credential, but it's becoming clear that tickets are going to cost Raf at least $1,500. What if he took a few days off work, left his wife and two kids behind for the weekend, and then couldn't even get a ticket to the game? What's more, I have the sense he's expecting me to show him some sort of great time. I can get him into the *Sports Illustrated* Super Bowl gala — at least I think I can — and there is a charity golf event that sounds welcoming, but that's it. Will that be enough to make it worth the trip for him?

These anxieties whirl around my head as I see Raphael approaching the gate. Born in America of Palestinian descent, he's dark-skinned, with black hair and huge brown eyes that rarely fail to give away what he's thinking. He wears a brown suede jacket and has a thumb hooked over jeans that are pulled up a hair too high. When he walks, he bends his knees a bit too much, giving him an odd, birdlike gait. In his other hand he carries a large brown shopping bag with red streamers cascading out of the top. He moves forward with his head tilted down slightly, and I can see him scanning the space with his eyes. I let out a simple "Raf," and without moving his head his eyes dart toward me. He smiles and lifts his chin in a reverse nod. He slumps into one of the molded plastic chairs next to me. "This four thirty shit is too early," he says by way of greeting.

Raphael is from the same Brooklyn neighborhood as John Travolta's character in *Saturday Night Fever*, and he has a little of that Tony Manero edge Travolta had in the movie. When we were much younger, we capped many a night out in the neighborhood at the very same White Castle where Tony and his friends wound up drunk and obnoxious at 3:00 A.M. We spend a minute exchanging how's the family type chatter, and then I ask, "What's the ticket situation?"

"My guy says everything's going for at least two thousand, but he thinks it should come down on Saturday."

I am very concerned.

★ Welcome to Jacksonville! Just outside the gate, two senior citizens in red shirts are waiting for us. One of them pulls a finger gun out of an imaginary holster, points, and yells, "Welcome to Jacksonville!" in a raspy twang. As we stand there for a moment and get our bearings, we realize he does this for everyone who comes off the plane, with such energy and enthusiasm that I wonder about the wisdom of self-medicating. Raphael makes a goofy face, draws his own finger gun, then mimics, "Welcome to Jacksonville," in his best southern accent. "What the fuck is that?" he says with a laugh.

It isn't long before we realize the shouter is no aberration. He's part of Jacksonville's effort to be "the little host city that could," as one colleague put it. As we walk along, every gate has a Super Bowl poster, there are Super Bowl banners everywhere, and every store and kiosk is overflowing with Super Bowl junk. Posted at regular intervals along the way are more red-shirted greeters who shout, "Welcome to Jacksonville!"

In the main concourse a thick-waisted guy with a receding hairline stands on a temporary platform behind a huge synthesizer, singing Jimmy Buffett tunes to prerecorded music. Beyond him, a tableful of red shirts hand out information kits, complete with downtown maps, event schedules, brochures, and the official *SuperGuide*. Raphael flips through a packet and asks, "What, there's no game ticket?" The red shirts giggle and then shoo us along.

Down the escalator in the baggage claim area yet more greeters await. As people gather, two of them break into song, belting out a tune I assume must be self-composed, since it consists of only three words. You guessed it, "Welcome . . . to . . . Jacksonville." While Raphael waits for his bag, I make my way to the Avis counter, where I'm greeted by a smiling man who welcomes me to Jacksonville.

Near the baggage carousel we notice a small commotion surrounding a short, unshaven guy in a T-shirt and baseball cap. "That's Chris Moneymaker," Raphael tells me. "He won the World Series of Poker." All right! We've been off the plane only ten minutes and we already have our first celebrity sighting. That's got to be worth something. Raphael knows who the guy is, and he seems legitimately excited, that's got to be worth, what, a hundred bucks I figure. Assuming he spends $2,000 on a ticket, we only need another twenty little coincidences like this before he'll have gotten his money's worth.

As we make our way out the door, another guy with a keyboard is setting up in the corner, and outside, along the taxi stand, a steel-drum band is in full swing. I don't know for sure, but I'm guessing the Jacksonville airport is not normally quite this verdant with live music. I'm as happy to be here as anyone, but between the music, the constant barrage of superenergized welcomes, and the scrubbed, officially logoed patina on everything, the airport experience is a little overwhelming.

I'm hoping this is not a sign of what the entire weekend will be like. So far this is the sports equivalent of a corporate retreat, where overenthusiastic consultants cheerlead you through a series of dull, scripted activities. It's starting to feel like a dreadful mistake. Could it be that the Super Bowl is actually one of the ten things all sports fans should avoid?

★ By late afternoon we have regrouped, decompressed, and made our way to downtown Jacksonville. A good part of the downtown on either side of the Saint Johns River has been shut down for the week, including a few of the bridges. We come across ESPN's outdoor studio, where a *SportsCenter* broadcast is taking place. At home I certainly watch my share of the show, but seeing it live is as exciting as, well, watching a few guys sit at a desk and read. This does not stop hundreds of rabid fans from gathering around the set and shouting on cue when some producer waves his arms at them to indicate that they've returned from commercial and it's once again time to make the world believe that we're all in a state of perpetual excitement at the sight of Dan Patrick. The worst part is that the scene is so lame I can't even rate it as high as the Moneymaker sighting. Maybe fifty bucks for the whole cast.

As we cross a parking lot to enter a building, Stuart Scott and another guy step out of a truck and head for the same door. As we approach I see Raphael staring. "Stuart Scott," I whisper. "From ESPN." He nods and gives Scott the big stare, which is made all the more obvious since he and Scott reach the door at the same moment. Both reach for the handle, but Raf defers and Scott pulls the door open. The guy he's with is lagging behind, so Raphael steps through the open door. As I follow, Scott looks at his buddy and says, "Believe that. This motherfucker thinks *I'm* here to open the door for *him*." I resist the temptation to say something back, which is good because across the lobby there's another door. Raphael holds it open for me and after I pass through he continues to hold it for Scott and his pal, nodding and grinning as he does. Now Scott is all smiles and personality. "Ah, there you go," he says, laughing. "You got me back, you got me back." I'm tempted to value this as equal to the Moneymaker encounter — $100 — but the fact that he was such a prick makes it a better story, worth maybe $150.

We're doing well with the celebrities. Earlier today we'd seen Deion Sanders, former Eagles and Patriots wide receiver Irving Fryar, and the diminutive star of many bad comedies, Rob Schneider. The toughest of them is Schneider. I mean, I loved *Deuce Bigalow* as much as the next guy, but could I possibly count him as a $300 value? Three times the worth of a poker player for a guy who's been on the cast of *Saturday Night Live* and starred in actual Hollywood productions? Seems fair.

At any rate, the real action seems to be far from the ESPN compound, on the other side of the river. As we walk across the bridge we can see, off to the left, The Landing, an outdoor plaza that's jammed with people. To the right, two streets run along the river for about a mile from the bridge to the foot of Alltel Stadium. Both these streets — Water and Bay — have been closed down and turned into the world's biggest block party. Bay Street in particular is lined with white tents, making it look like some sort of Bedouin outpost along the banks of the Saint Johns.

Raphael and I head into the fray, and discover that it is an international bazaar of beer and food, everything from Greek, Spanish, Italian, Thai, and Chinese to domestic favorites like barbecue and seafood. And since the game will pit the Philadelphia Eagles against the New England Patriots, there are Philly cheesesteaks and New England clam chowder.

On every other block stand three-story-tall stanchions with massive speakers mounted at the top, which crank out party music from 9:00 A.M. to midnight. The Super Bowl, it seems, has a soundtrack. It adds to the raucous vibe and full-on unruliness that has come with the official waving of the open-container laws and sound ordinances.

Nowhere is this more evident than at The Landing. Upon entering the circular center of the mall, we come across two guys in full Patriots regalia. The first is dressed in a Captain America outfit, complete with fake muscles. The costume already uses the Patriots color scheme and he has further modified it with Patriots emblems. His buddy has a blue-and-red-dyed Mohawk, his face painted to match, a Patriots jersey, and those puffy red, white, and blue zebra-striped workout pants. He carries a Patriots flag as well. One by one people come up to have their picture taken with the pair.

I approach the face painter with the zebra pants. "What brings you to Jacksonville?" I ask. He looks at me for a second to see if I'm serious, then smiles and begins to recite his resumé with the practiced smoothness of an MBA graduate. "I was the Patriots Fan of the Year in 1999. I moved one mile from the stadium so I could tailgate in my backyard and walk to the games." He stops to look into a camera and smile for a picture. "My house is full of Patriots stuff. I've got a ceiling fan in my TV room" — another picture — "and the blades of the fan are shaped like football helmets. You should check out my" — picture — "Web sites, www .patriotnation.com and www.mikeschuster.com. And I'm in that new MasterCard commercial too. Have you seen" — picture — "that one, it's a salute to the fans? There's a shot of me right in the beginning in full war paint."

That's a lot to digest, and now that I finally have a chance to speak I'm not sure what to say. Schuster turns back to me from another photo op and I blurt out what seems like the most obvious question: "This isn't full war paint?" Schuster laughs and turns back toward the cameras. He has something to add, but before he can an eagle emerges.

This is a guy in a head-to-toe eagle costume, complete with football helmet. He could be the Eagles official mascot, and he's certainly on par with Schuster and his buddy. Upon meeting up, the three of them feign some fisticuffs, then line up together to a symphony of flashes. Like a group of mall Santas coming back from a coffee break, the eagle steps off to one side, where a line of Philly fans immediately forms, while Schuster and Co. go back to their own line of Patriots fans. At least no one's peeing on Schuster's leg and whispering the names of Power Rangers in his ear.

These guys are only a small part of the scene at The Landing. The rest of the circle is ringed with restaurants and bars, each of which has an outdoor seating area. The restaurants are jammed, and long lines snake out of every door, the longest coming from Hooters. The people at the tables have all turned their chairs to face the center of the circle, as if they were looking at a fountain, except instead of flowing waters they're staring out at a geyser of people.

Upstairs, the rail that borders the entire second-floor patio is lined with revelers who lean on their elbows, sipping drinks and watching the action below. The two staircases that lead up there are also packed with railhangers. Within this circular plaza there's actually a two-step drop into a smaller circle at the center, so between the balcony, the street level, and the two inner rings you get an amphitheater effect. You also get something of a Dante's *Inferno* effect, in which everyone assumes that the truest sinners reside a level below them at the center of the action. This is not an entirely erroneous assumption.

The air is filled with the sounds of a party, the talking, the laughter, the crash of beer bottles being dropped onto the sidewalk. Random shouts rise above the clamor. "You guys suck!" crows one passionate fan. Shooter girls in cowboy hats and boots roam through, calling their wares, "Tequila, whiskey, Jäger." The most striking thing by far, though, is the near-constant singing.

The Patriots and Eagles are two wildly different clubs. The subdued, team-oriented Patriots are playing in their third Super Bowl in four years, while the star-driven, trash-talking Eagles lost the only Super Bowl they ever played in twenty-four years earlier and haven't won an NFL Championship since 1960. Each team's fans, I'm quickly learning, are as different as the squads they root for. The Patriots fans are no less accomplished in the quaffing of alcohol, but they tend to be more reserved. Maybe they're jaded because they've been here so often. Maybe it's their starchy New England reserve. The Philly fans, on the other hand, are louder, more buoyant, and far more plentiful. I would say that their behavior reflects the gritty urban resolve of their city, but there's one problem: They sing like the cast of a Rodgers and Hart musical.

Their anthem is the Eagles fight song, a simple and cloying little ditty invented by a few hard-core fans. The lyrics:

> Fly Eagles fly,
> On the road to victory
> Fight Eagles fight
> Score a touchdown one, two, three
> Hit 'em low, hit 'em high
> And we'll watch our Eagles fly
> Fly Eagles fly
> On the road to victory
> E-A-G-L-E-S, Eagles!!!

What may account for the song's success is the ease with which it's memorized, which not only locks it into your brain after maybe three repetitions, but allows the singers to move on to the job of learning the accompanying dance. This includes arm flapping, and making a chopping motion at the knees during the "hit 'em low" line and another at about eye level for the "hit 'em high" refrain. The truly advanced help out their fellow rooters by actually forming the letters with their bodies for the spelling test that comes in the last line.

Here at The Landing, all the Eagles songs start the same way, with just one or two voices. Others who are nearby quickly join in, and as the singing gets louder, more hear and more join in so that the sound spreads up around the circular layout like a dishtowel being sucked up into a tornado, until it rings out from all sides. When they tire of the fight song, the Philly faithful also have the T.O. song, an homage to Terrell Owens, the Eagles' braying showboat of a wide receiver. The lyrics for this one:

> Teeee Ooooo
> T O
> T O
> T O
> Teeee Ooooo
> Teeee Ooooo

The Patriots fans, nowhere nearly as well-rehearsed, have been noticeably quiet. Once or twice they muster a "Let's go Pats" chant, but it fades before ever getting full lung support. It's so embarrassing an effort, in fact, that it leads to the Eagles fans showering them with a chant of "Assholes, assholes . . ." To my surprise, they don't try to spell it. All the singing and chanting adds to the frat-party vibe that seems to have spread throughout the jam of humanity packed into The Landing. At times it feels like it's impossible to move, although many people are trying to do just that, traversing from one identical side of the circle to the other, like teenagers cruising the strip.

A guy who's been standing next to me at the edge of the first circle (Suicides and Grafters?) without saying a word for twenty minutes pulls out a cell phone. When whomever he's calling picks up, he says, "Now I know what they mean about the Super Bowl. Ain't no party like the Super Bowl, man, celebrities, thousands of people. Unbelievable."

I'm tempted to point out three things. First, I've been at The Landing for about two hours and haven't seen any celebrities. Second, he's not actually "partying," he's just sort of standing around watching other people party, sort of secondhand partying. And third, there's probably someone on the balcony above (Hoarders and Wasters?) looking down at us, two dullards standing around sipping beer, telling someone back home how crazy the party is. It's as if we're all there to validate one another's experience, staring back across the circle, raising our glasses to the sky and shouting into the void, "You guys having fun? We're having fun." There is a strained quality to the experience, as if everyone feels like they have to have a good time because they spent so much to be here and, well, because this is the Super Bowl, dammit! As a party, we are the sound of two hands clapping. And if ever that applause becomes too dim, we can pick up our cell phones and bounce the experience off someone back home.

★ Raphael and I make our way to a bar just off The Landing's main circle. Raphael has a handful of cousins who live in the area, and a few of them are coming down to meet us, so we settle in for the wait. As I order a beer, Raphael surveys the drinks menu before finally choosing an appletini. During the course of the evening I've seen a lot of people wearing long beaded necklaces, and now just across from us there seems to be a fevered negotiation going on over the five or six strands some guy has around his neck. At last he hands one over to the two women he's talking to, and in an instant they whip up their shirts. A cheer goes up from the crowd. Digital cameras flash to life.

Raphael, too, seems to have shed his inhibitions. By the time his cousins arrive he's on his third appletini. As breasts and cameras flash all around us, the night devolves into a tumult of drinking, dancing, and trash talking. I have conversations with fans of both teams. Some rattle off in-depth analyses of each team, which, as far as they're concerned, lead to only one logical conclusion: their favorite winning. Others just spew a loud roar followed by some variation of the idea, *We're gonna kill 'em.* I watch as these fans taunt each other about the game, then high-five, wish each other luck, and move on. There are a few times I get the sense that things might turn violent, but they never do.

By nine thirty Raphael is on his eighth 'tini and feeling no pain, but he's still got it together and he's there with his cousins, so I feel all right going out for a little walk to see what's happening. Outside, the circle is more crowded than before, though I didn't think that was possible. About a block away from the center of it all, I take a minute to call home. While I'm talking with my wife, I get a call waiting. It's Raphael. "They kicked me out," he says.

"Who?"

"Some guy in the bar, he said 'You're too drunk, you've got to go, and he made me leave.'"

"Where are you?

"Right in front of the bar."

"I'll be right there." When I arrive, Raphael is indeed right out front, bent over at the waist, leaning on a metal railing. "Hey, let's go," I say. It's then I get an idea of how bad off we are. He raises himself up with great effort, teetering and exhaling loudly when he finally makes it to an upright position. He takes two steps forward and lurches wildly to the side, crashing into a small table. I grab him before he falls, and try to steer him around the circle and back toward our car, which is parked across the river, about a mile of crowded streets away.

Raphael is not a small person, so even with my arm hooked through his it takes a lot of pushing and pulling to keep him on a wobbly course, and we proceed like some drunken version of the *Laverne & Shirley* opening sequence, schlemieling and schlemazling our way out of The Landing. At one point we approach three police officers, and I'm afraid they'll stop us and issue some sort of public drunkenness ticket. Before I can decide if I should consider an alternate route, one of them spots us and begins shaking his head. I give him a smile and nod, trying to show that at least one of us is reasonably sober. "Look at this one," he says as we go by. "Get him home. Get him home."

That's the plan, but not half a block later, Raphael says he needs to sit. As luck would have it we're passing a little alley that has a bench. I steer Raf back there and he plops down, shoulders slumped, head in hands. I walk back to the main thoroughfare to buy him a water, and as I do the sky over the river erupts in fireworks. As part of its party plan, Jacksonville has been shooting off impressive pyrotechnic displays every night of Super Bowl week. Stretching along the river from the stadium to The Landing, the colorful explosions reflect off the water and the glass high-rises of downtown.

I watch for a minute before returning to Raphael. As I walk up the alley there's a pretty blond woman standing about twenty feet away, staring at him with a horrified look. She sees me and, sensing that I'm with him, smiles weakly and says, "Um, your friend just puked on his shoes."

How do you respond to that? "Thanks," I say. I give Raf the water. He takes a sip, spits, and sits up.

"I'm all right. I'm all right," he says. With that he lurches forward and heaves onto the brick path in front of him. I turn around and catch another glimpse of the fireworks lighting up the sky behind me and notice that they're strikingly similar to the little starbursts of appletini exploding across the ground.

★ On Saturday morning, Raf's hooded eyelids tell last night's story all over again. I don't know what I was expecting, but the Super Bowl festivities were far different than I'd imagined. When I was eight, my father took me to my first football game, the New York Giants vs. the San Diego Chargers at Shea Stadium. I was already a huge Giants fan. I'd watched dozens of games at home on the couch and knew the rules and players. What impressed me, though, were the colors, the sounds, the smell of the cigar smoke. I was amazed that you could order a hot dog and that people would pass it down without taking a bite or pass the money back to the vendor without stealing some. I couldn't believe how loud my father could clap. He had this way of cupping his hands — still does — that makes a sound like someone slamming together two pieces of wood. I remember specifically that a little-known Giants wide receiver, Danny Buggs, almost returned a kickoff for a touchdown.

Most of all, though, I remember that the Giants, who were terrible for most of the '60s and '70s, won, because as it turned out, it was the team's first home win in two years. In the aftermath, people were going absolutely nuts. Grown men were crying. Complete strangers hugged each other. Pure, sheer joy engulfed the building. From that day on I became, not by choice but by inference, a purist. The games have always been about the game for me. I've gone to my share of tailgates, but I was never there for the party. I'll drink a beer or two during the game but couldn't care less if they ended beer sales altogether. After seeing, at eight, the reaction to that meaningless Giants victory, nothing could ever be more exciting than what takes place on the field.

I guess I imagined that people who made a pilgrimage to the Super Bowl had a similar worldview. Sure there would be some extracurricular activity, but for the most part, the fans who were there would be all about the game. The bars, I thought, would be filled with earnest men who sipped beverages while discussing strategies and players and how long they'd been fans. The pregame tension would make it impossible for anything too raucous to bubble up. Now, with the benefit of one night of Super Bowl partying behind me, it seems obvious that the pregame buildup would be little more than Mardi Gras in the shadow of a stadium. In hindsight, I am a little embarrassed by my naiveté.

Perhaps it's that I was born too late (or I'm living in the past). As bigtime sporting events go, the Super Bowl is incredibly young, having come into being in 1967 as a lightly regarded showdown between the old and established National Football League and the upstart American Football League. Frankly, the AFL was considered a bit of a joke by NFL fans, but it had become a serious business, and as part of a gradual merger the leagues agreed to a game between their respective champions. It would eventually be called the Super Bowl. In that first matchup, when the NFL Packers met the AFL Chiefs, tickets cost only $10, and even then the game could only fill 61,946 of the 94,000 seats in Los Angeles's Memorial Coliseum. There was no pregame show, no celebrity anthemeer, and two college marching bands performed at halftime.

It wasn't until the AFL Jets, led by the brash Joe Namath, beat the NFL's Colts in Super Bowl III — just before the leagues completed a merger into what we now know as the NFL — that the game gained any real cultural purchase and the new league realized they had something on their hands. Besides notoriety and credibility for the AFL teams, Broadway Joe had brought women, expanding the audience beyond just sports fans and proving that others would tune in if there was something for them to watch. The following year the first celebrity replaced the marching bands as halftime entertainment — assuming for a moment that one is willing to consider Carol Channing a celebrity. Ticket demand, viewership, and the cost of commercial airtime all went up. Over the next ten years the pregame acts grew, special guests to toss the coin were introduced, and the halftime show became more and more elaborate, skewing toward big production numbers that brought to mind the opening ceremony at the Olympics. The Super Bowl was the proverbial snowball rolling down the mountain, and there was no bottom in sight.

Then, Super Bowl XXV featured the popular boy band New Kids on the Block at halftime and ushered in a new era; it was now a given that intermission would be a pop concert featuring a megastar. The numbers, if they can be believed, have gone into the stratosphere. The game is broadcast in 234 countries, and more than 90 million Americans tune in every year (45 percent of them are women). The ten most-watched TV shows of all time are Super Bowls. Face value for the cheapest ticket in the house is around $600, and commercial time sells for up to $2.5 million for a thirty-second spot.

The rise, over a relatively short period of time, is astounding, but two truths drive the ascent. First, the Super Bowl is one of the few events, along with presidential elections, the Oscars, or some massive tragedy, that our entire culture sits up and takes notice of. Second, at its heart, it is still a football game.

★ Along the way, *Sports Illustrated* got in the act by throwing a gala party in the host city during Super Bowl week. Tickets to this year's *SI* bash are said to cost $750, and word is they're being scalped for as much as $1,500. What these parties turn on — what makes people want to be at them at all and what gets them press — is which and how many celebrities show up. On this night alone, *Playboy* and *Maxim* are also throwing bashes, so the competition to get the most A-list celebs and to make the crowd you're trying to woo feel like they're actually a part of some grand happening is intense.

Of course, I'd assumed all along that I'd be welcome at the party, seeing as I work at the magazine. And in fact a few weeks earlier I'd e-mailed a very nice woman in our PR department, and she assured me I'd be put on the list. I thought about asking if that allowed me to bring a guest, but I was afraid the answer would be no, so I didn't ask. Whenever the subject of the party had come up with Raf, I'd just nod and say, "Yeah, it's supposed to be a great time." The party is a major component of my value-added plan, and I suddenly realize that my scheme for getting in lacks a certain creativity: I'd figured I'd just show up and hope for the best. Worst-case scenario — play dumb. They couldn't turn me away, could they?

So when we approach the entrance to the party, held in a huge tent on Jax Beach, I am considerably more nervous than I let on. I can see velvet ropes holding back several hundred people, all of them wielding cameras and autograph books. I'm not sure if anyone mistakes us for celebrities as we go past because the walkway is flooded with the blinding white light of a movie set. While the lights guarantee that we can't see the fans, it ensures that they'll see us get sent away if we aren't allowed into the party, adding public humiliation to the personal and professional uppercut I am certain I am about to take.

Once we emerge from the halo we arrive at a desk with two computers and two women. There are a few people checking in in front of us so we wait. As we do, a limo pulls up to the tent. Out steps Lynn Swann and four women. As Swann walks up the red-carpeted ramp and into the party, a small band of photographers and reporters previously loafing around next to the carpet snap to life. A virtual bank of lights clicks on. Local newsmen fuss with their hair. Flashes pop. Swann graciously stops and gives the TV guys a few quotes, then disappears into the room.

Meanwhile, Raf and I arrive at the front of the line. "Name," the girl behind the desk says. I give her my name and she clicks away at her keyboard as if she works for an airline and I just asked for an upgrade. At last she looks up. "Okay," she says, giving me the yellow wristband that says I am cool and wanted. Then she looks at Raf. "Name." Raf hesitates. I jump in. "He's with me."

"Oh," she replies, looking back at her screen. Again she types, this time as if I wanted a vegetarian kosher meal. I swallow hard and give Raf a quick nod, as if to say, it's cool, this is how it's supposed to work. She tries to get the attention of a colleague who seems to be running the show, but that woman is shouting into her walkie-talkie and making it clear she doesn't want to be bothered. At last she looks back at her screen and says, "Oh, you work for *Sports Illustrated*?" Yes, I say. "Um, okay, then, just go ahead."

I exhale.

Rafi and I turn and head for the red carpet Lynn Swann just walked up, but before we get there, we are stopped by a guy in a red blazer and redirected up a second ramp that runs behind the bank of media people. As humiliations go, I am happier to suffer this one than if we'd been turned away with our tails between our legs.

Inside, the tent is about the size of a football field and it's kind of crowded. Not crowded like The Landing, but there are a lot of people. Three podiums rise above the crowd, and on each one a model in a bikini dances provocatively to thumping music. The party is, I remember, to celebrate this year's Swimsuit Issue. (Almost without fail, the first question you're asked when you tell someone you work for *SI* is, "Do you get to work on the Swimsuit Issue?" The second is, "Do you know Rick Reilly?") Within the room, the crowd has separated into three main groups. At the front, near speakers so loud you can actually feel your sternum rattle, there's a collection of club kids, in their funky pants and mismatched country club attire. They are crowded into a small dance area, thumping and grinding away to the music. Those who don't dance, bop in place at the edges of the floor, mouthing the lyrics.

Toward the middle of the room, people in more-traditional party attire — suits, cocktail dresses, sport jackets — drink, chat, and occasionally make embarrassing attempts at dancing. This crowd is peppered with celebs. You never know who'll pop up. Oh, there's gold medal sprinter Michael Johnson ($500). That tall guy rising above the crowd? Former Washington Redskin Joe Jacoby ($100). The curvy blonde drawing stares? Former *SI* cover girl Vendela ($150).

The back of the room holds the gawkers and the stiffs. The gawkers stay near the door, and they run and strain to see who's coming every time the lights power on. The stiffs are mostly middle-age white guys who've forgotten how to loosen up and have fun. They stand with their arms crossed, watching the girls dance. When they get self-conscious about standing there not doing anything — not talking, not drinking, not really having fun — they check their cell phones, as if they're just waiting for a call, or might have just missed a call. The message is that there are people out there who might want to talk to them.

Rafi and I make our rounds, mocking the guy with the silver jacket that looks like tinfoil and scoffing at the Paris Hilton knock-offs dancing together. There's someone famous, although we don't know who, and that woman with the implants and the skimpy dress who has seven guys drooling over her has a wedgie. We almost walk smack-dab into Tom Arnold ($200), the former Mr. Roseanne, at the time the host of a sports show. Arnold is on his way out, and as he passes flashbulb row, the lights come on. Arnold quickly smoothes his hair, looks into the lens, and offers up a few quips.

There's a little tremor in the crowd and we turn to see fallen '90s superstar rapper MC Hammer ($300) heading toward us. As he goes by, Raf reaches out to tap him on the shoulder. One of Hammer's two bodyguards quickly pushes Raf's arm away before he can make contact. As the man sang: "Can't touch this."

Having followed Hammer's progress, we figure out that there's a roped-off VIP section, which we try to sneak into without luck, so instead we head for the food. At the back of the room they're serving up high-end hors d'oeuvres in lieu of dinner. We sample the mini steak sandwiches, get a few bites of some sort of pâté on toast, and then come to the garlic mashed potatoes, which are being served in martini glasses, the very sight of which makes Rafi gag.

I fall into conversation with a guy in black pants and a floral shirt that covers a tremendous beer gut. He turns out to be Tim Tickner, a member of the Jax Beach town council, who was given the tickets as a courtesy. His wife, a plump woman in a beige dress, is a gawker, dashing off toward the door every time someone enters, whether the klieg lights flash on or not. Tickner says that, in general, the "fans have been great," although he does point out that there is "a big difference between what you see downtown and here." But what does he think of the party overall, I ask. "Well," he says, smacking his gums and looking across the room, "they seem to be doing all right with the celebrities."

The closest I come to a football fan is a short man named Ron, who must be sixty and is trim, forthright, and stands bolt-straight. That along with his wavy brown-gray hair makes him look like Jack La Lanne's younger brother. Ron is here with a group of about six guys, and he doesn't know where they got their tickets or how much they paid, but one of them used to work for the Patriots and he set it all up. Ron went to last year's Super Bowl as well, and this year they're even staying at the Pats' team hotel, which he thinks "will be fun if they win."

"Been a Pats fan for long?"

"Yeah," he responds.

"How long?"

"Um, how long have they been a franchise?"

"I think about forty years," I say, slightly surprised that he doesn't know.

"Yeah," he says, "that sounds good."

Within moments Kanye West is introduced, and as he bounds onto the stage the party turns into more of a concert. As the show goes on, Raf and I find ourselves at the back of the room, looking around dumbly, arms folded across our chests. For a moment I feel awkward and painfully aware of how foolish I look. Instinctively I pull out my cell phone and check to see if I have any messages.

★ Game Day. We are in an RV park about two blocks from the stadium, although it's an RV park only in that there are RVs parked on it. In actuality, it's a fenced-in grass-covered field that has been appropriated for the big game. We are here to see our college friend Billy.

Billy is one of those guys who started losing his hair at eighteen, has always had narrow, rounded shoulders and a little bulge around his waist, and he's an accountant. All of which means he's had the fading hairline, sagging body, and career of some middle-management schlub since he was twenty-two. From the time we were in college he always swore he'd be the last guy to marry, and that has proven true. Over the years, he's gone through a string of women who can only be described as far too nice and far too good-looking to be spending their time with him. In each case they stay with him for three or four years, watching as he shrugs off increasing pressure to restore their honor, and then finally, after the last ultimatum has been ignored, they dump him. He moves on without much regret. Some of them have even come back for a second stint, convinced he'd changed or matured or whatever, only to once again end up disappointed.

Part of his unwillingness to settle down is his appetite for a good time. He's Falstaffian in his capacity to drink and make merry, carrying on like some twenty-year-old who has no greater worry in the world than next week's macroeconomics midterm. No surprise he's here, then, raging with a group of similarly minded party boys he's befriended over the years. About ten of them are crashing at the home of a divorced colleague who lives with his twelve-year-old son. It's a real guys' weekend. In a move that shows both his intelligence and his experience, Billy has rented a limo for the duration so they won't have to worry about driving or parking.

As it turns out, Jacksonville has so few cabs and limos that the city imported cars and drivers from all over the state for game week. Billy's guy is from Tampa, and "he has no idea where he's going," Billy shouts over another rendition of the Eagles fight song. "We get in the car and tell him we want to go someplace, and he takes out all these maps and starts asking us what it's near."

Another faction of Billy's contingent has avoided such troubles — along with the costs and hassles of finding hotels and booking flights — by caravaning down in a fleet of RVs, which is how we've ended up drinking Miller Lites in what is usually a vacant lot. Next to the vehicles, they've set out a bunch of lawn chairs, a radio, and a series of coolers. A variety of shapes, sizes, and colors, these coolers are arranged in a circle, so that they appear to me like some sort of campfire Stonehenge. I'm certain that with a little more time I could figure out "what it all means." Instead, I find myself sitting around with six or eight guys I don't know particularly well sipping beer and shooting the shit.

They are the kind of hard-core fans who wear jerseys to the game and tuck their jeans into their workboots. I see my former self in them — the kid who ran around the yard screaming when Bucky Dent hit a home run to win a one-game playoff against the Red Sox in '78, who threw a glass against the wall when the Giants lost to the 49ers on a seventy-eight-yard touchdown in the waning seconds of a game, and who once painted his face for a college basketball game. I envy them. They're here for the Eagles and nothing else — well, maybe the Eagles and the beer. They were up all night drinking and here they are by early afternoon back at it again. Even Billy is watering himself liberally despite staying out until 7:00 A.M. Of course, the last hour and a half of that was spent trying to direct the limo driver back to the house.

One of the guys I'm talking to says Billy might actually be getting close to marrying his current girlfriend, after only four years of making her suffer. I must know more. "So what's up," I say, "you finally going to pull the trigger or what?"

"Huh?" he says, looking confused.

"Kathy," says his buddy.

"Oh." Billy grunts, waving his hand. "Whatever." He takes a big swig of beer.

Another guy has sold a bunch of stocks from his kids' college savings account to come up with the $2,500 for his tickets. He's hoping to make it back with a big bet on the Eagles, but he gets into a shouting match on the phone with his bookie. Not a good sign. Billy got his tickets for $2,200 through a friend's sister, who works for an NFL corporate partner.

Despite the solemn intensity of our little group, there is a different feeling in the air today. Back at The Landing, people were literally dancing in the street, boogying to Motown classics belted out over the omnipresent sound system. Moreover, there exists that sort of big-game thrum, the palpable rise in metabolism that comes from some combination of anticipation, expectation, and flat-out energy. Chanting and singing have reached a new level. People randomly high-five each other and let out bloody guttural screams.

The revelry, though, is mixed. As we head for the game, Rafi finally admits defeat in his quest for a ticket. The virtual throng of long-suffering Eagles fans has created a seller's market, and prices range as high as $4,000 a ticket. There are hundreds of people walking the streets holding up "I need tickets" signs. Some people have painted it onto shirts and hats. One guy carries an inflatable sex doll that holds a sign saying "I need tickets." Another stands next to one of the main thoroughfares, waving twenty $100 bills fanned out like it's the world's best rummy hand ever. "Who's selling, who's selling, who's selling?" he sings.

"For $3,000," Raf reasons, "I can buy myself a flat-screen HDTV and watch all the games I want."

Now I don't have to feel bad that he spent a bundle just to go to the game, but I do regret that I dragged him down here and now he's not even going. Instead he's decided to watch at a sports bar out at the beach with his cousin. It is an awkward moment as we part outside the stadium.

★ Inside, the sense of separation only gets more acute. There are still two hours until kickoff, and I have nowhere to go and no one to talk to. I spend some time peering over the fence that sets off the NFL's corporate tailgate. Lucky executives with no connection to either team eat, drink, and mingle. On a large stage, a cover band jams out a decent version of the old Kansas hit "Carry On Wayward Son." As I take in the goings-on, the song rattles to a conclusion and the lead singer grabs the mike and yells, "Thank you Super Bowl, we are Kansas." That's when it hits me: I'm at the Super Bowl. Only the Super Bowl can turn a band like Kansas — admittedly past their prime, but still — into a sideshow diversion. The group should not feel bad, though, because the three-ring circus inside the stadium will turn even bigger-name acts into a revolving wheel of disposable pregame fodder.

Concert over, I continue wandering. In a men's room, twelve guys are lined up using the facilities. Somehow, based on some sort of telepathy or unseen (by me) hand signal, they break into the E-A-G-L-E-S chant in midstream. It's an impressive if slightly unnerving display of spirit and togetherness.

Like all the seats, mine is covered by a blue cushion with the

Super Bowl XXXIX logo on it. A zippered pouch hangs off the front of the cushion. Inside it is a small flashlight, a folded-up card, and a mini–satellite radio with earphones, with which you can pick up four different versions of the game broadcast: the ones from Philly and Boston radio stations, Fox's national coverage, and a Hispanic station. Since I'm officially here as a member of the media, I also get a box dinner (a turkey sandwich, two 3 Musketeers bars, and a Pepsi).

It's too early to eat, so I head off to wander about the stadium. I'm at the Super Bowl, but somehow I feel more like a fourteen-year-old at the mall on a Friday night. I finally settle on a small patch of grass just inside the entry gates. There's a guy sitting a few feet away from me. He wears a green and-white-striped rugby shirt with a green turtleneck underneath, an Eagles cap, and large, black-framed glasses. The hat is not one of these modern types, with the bent brim that sits low on the wearer's head, but an older kind, with a foam front that rides high and makes his head look taller than it is. Somehow the hat, his shiny white sneakers, which appear to be brand-new, and the glasses work together to give the guy a childlike appearance.

We start out talking about cell phones, because I'm having a hard time getting reception. After a little while, I ask what he thinks will happen today in the game. "Oh," he says, looking directly at me, his blue eyes distorted behind the thick lenses. "We got depth, composure, and confidence, but not arrogance. It took us a long time to get here, and we know how hard it is to make it. Our hunger, drive, and desire will lead us to victory."

This speech springs from his mouth fully formed, without hesitation, as if he'd memorized it earlier just in case anyone should ask. I'm intrigued. Turns out, Jimmy Kepran has lived and died by Philadelphia sports for most of his fifty-two years. When Jimmy was a kid his dad would take him and his brother to Eagles, Phillies, Flyers, and Sixers games. He went to college about an hour outside Philly, so he could stay close to the teams and the city he loved. In 1978 he and his brother bought season tickets for the Eagles. Within a year, he was transferred out of town and spent the next five years living in Chicago and St. Louis, but he never gave up his seat. He'd come back for two games a year. When he finally moved home in the mid-'80s, that ticket was waiting for him, but his time away had caused him to miss out on the Eagles' only other Super Bowl appearance. In 1981 he watched from St. Louis while his brother attended the game.

This time his brother had stayed home, but once the Eagles made it, "there was never a doubt I would come," he says. "It's a dream come true." And you can imagine little Jimmy over the years dreaming of exactly this. In the dream, though, his brother is probably here, as are his father and uncle, who together witnessed the last and only Eagles title win, the 1960 NFL Championship. Jimmy exhales after a moment of silence, then adds wistfully, "I'm here for a lot of people."

We talk until the Florida A&M marching band begins to assemble on the grass next to us, making it impossible to hear. We shake hands and nod our goodbyes. All the way back up to section 404, Jimmy's words are with me: "I'm here for a lot of people."

Settling in, I look around to get my bearings. The seats are quickly filling up and the energy of the street begins to spread through the stadium. The ends of the structure are lower than the middle, which means that from this height I can actually look down out of the stadium. To both the left and right I can see the river bending around downtown. As dusk takes over, the water reflects a strange orange light and long strings of white outline the cruise ships tied up along the shore. The night is cool, perhaps forty-seven degrees, and expected to drop to the low forties, with winds gusting to 15 mph, making it feel cold, certainly too cold for the light clothes I'm wearing, even three layers' worth. All of it together — the energy, the glow, the height, and the wind — makes me incredibly aware that I'm alone. Everyone I've met in the last few days has been here with someone. A wife, a father, a group of friends. Even Jimmy Kepran carries with him a list of ghosts and memories. What he lacks in companionship he makes up for in passion. I don't care about these teams and I no longer have Rafi at my side — and I'm realizing those two things are musts.

It's the first profound difference between being here and all those times I watched at home. From my couch I could watch the Super Bowl, any game, really, by myself and have a complete experience. At the scene, though, something more is required. Hereafter, the action on the field plays out at a remove, through the filter of my own isolation, as if I'm watching through a scrim. I'm there, but not totally part of what's going on.

A portable stage is rolled out and a few hundred hired fans in pastel sweaters charge out onto the field. They crowd around the stage, bouncing and sizzling like drops of water on a hot pan. Pregame acts roll by like widgets on a conveyor belt: Gretchen Wilson, the Charlie Daniels Band, Earth, Wind & Fire, the Black Eyed Peas, and Alicia Keys. When they finally start rolling out the World War II and Iraq veterans and the Armed Forces Chorus, I decide it's time to break into a 3 Musketeers. I feel pretty safe in this since it's usually some overhyped diva who sings the national anthem, and there are none yet in sight. To my surprise, the NFL has decided to play the patriotism card and the Armed Forces Chorus is there to sing the anthem. There's nothing wrong with that, except that I'm now forced to stand and sing while palming a half-eaten chocolate bar.

Still, the power and familiarity of the anthem reminds everyone why we're here and restores the energy drained by the long-winded pregame festivities. There is a legitimate roar, and even though the crowd is less than half-filled with Pats and Eagles fans, noticeable animosity fills the air. A fat, older guy in an Eagles jersey stands up and starts yelling at the field. Two rows in front of him, a gentleman of a similar age with a Pats jersey and silver hair parted on the side stands and begins giving it right back to him. "You guys are gonna fly, all right. We're gonna toss you right out of here."

"Tom Brady is going down," replies Eagle guy. "Going down."

This is what it's all about. All the talking and analysis, all the celebrity hoopla, all the drinking and carrying on are over. This is, at last, a football game. A big fat glorious one with everything on the line and two great teams on the field. Eagles fans of course take it as an opportunity to sing. At least here in the bowl-like setting of the stadium, with a solid twenty thousand or so voices singing along, the "Fly Eagles Fly" song sounds less like a pep rally ditty and more like a deep, reverberating military march.

The players line up for the kickoff. The whistle blows. The crowd, instinctively, rises to their feet, and I rise with them. The noise, a gale blowing through a tunnel, builds to a crescendo, and then the ball is rising, soaring through the air. The sound dissipates, loses its unanimity, as people break off to root for their individual outcomes and discuss their own observations.

As the game proceeds the intensity does not falter. In the early going the crowd hangs on every play, gasping or cheering for every yard gained or pass that falls to the ground incomplete. Philly receiver Terrell Owens makes a few big catches, and after each one, the Eagles fans break into the T.O. song, which is also more impressive in a full stadium, bringing to mind one of those haunting chants you hear resounding through European soccer games just before the fans start burning flags in the aisles and go stampeding through the local village smashing people with broken bottles and closed fists.

It is the greatest football event ever, until it is not. At the end of the first quarter, the telecast goes off to commercial, and the public-address announcer comes on the loud speaker. "Welcome, ladies and gentlemen. It's now time for a rehearsal of our halftime festivities. It's a two-part show. The first part will take place on the field, while the second part will take place in the stands. Your role is essential in transforming the entire stadium into a work of art. First locate the flashlight and colored card in the pocket of your seat pad. Don't worry if you don't have a card, not everyone gets one, it's part of the effect. When the scoreboard says GO LIGHT, turn on your flashlight. When it says GO CARD, hold up your card. Ready? Here we go!"

The announcer then says "go light" and the words flash on the scoreboard. I look around, and I can't find one person holding up their flashlight. In fact, the dive into the pocket has led many people to discover their satellite radio for the first time, and far more have taken them out and are trying to figure out how to use them. The guy in front of me is making a call on his cell phone, as are many others. Most people sit and chat. The two older guys — the fat one and the silver-haired one — have rekindled their Pats-Eagles debate. The rehearsal for our part in the halftime show is a complete failure. I fret for the quality of the "work of art" we will produce.

At halftime the teams leave the field and workers roll out an even bigger stage and four light towers. Once they're in place the pastel sweaters come storming out and fill in around the stage. Around me the crowd has once again gone off on a mental walkabout, making calls, playing with their flashlights (now!) and chitchatting. Perhaps they're thinking about the other ways they could've spent $3,000. The PA announcer introduces Paul McCartney. One person in my row claps. If the people at the Super Bowl don't care much about the game, they care less about the all-star pregame and halftime shows.

Suddenly a figure in a red shirt appears on the stage and the music thunders to life. From here in Row W there's no way to tell if it's Paul McCartney or the apostle Paul, except that he's playing his guitar lefty and he's singing "Live and Let Die." Almost immediately, people around me start pulling out cell phones and holding them up in the air. Is it possible that the person on the other end of the line doesn't have a TV?

During the climax of the song, a huge burst of flames squirts from the top of the speaker towers. The pyrotechnics bring a roar from the crowd and I admit I like them, too, but mostly because they send a wave of heat up the stadium that feels awesome. As Sir Paul wraps up with "Hey Jude," it's time for our collective star turn. First come the lights, then we follow the scoreboard's cue to hold up the cards. When we do, it reveals that we've spelled out the words to the song's refrain — Na, Na, Na, Na — in red, white, and blue letters. This, I imagine, helps the home audience sing along in case they've forgotten the lyrics. For those folks in Philly, who need help with the T.O. song, I'm sure it is a welcome development.

The coolest effect occurs after the show is over. With the music done and the lights still down, the stadium is filled with smoke from the pyrotechnics. Many in the stands continue to shine their flashlights, creating a sort of eerie panorama of little specs of white swaying in the bluish smoke. In an instant, though, the stage folds up and disappears, the stadium lights snap back on, and the bright green field once again shines up. It's a jarring conversion, like walking out of a movie theater into a bright sunny afternoon. The entertainment has been more impressive and engaging than it is on TV, during which, frankly, I usually walk away and get something to eat, but if anyone thinks the halftime show isn't a distraction from the game, all he needs to see is that field. It makes plain how dramatic a shift is necessary to go from one form of entertainment to the other in less than thirty seconds.

★ With about seven minutes left, the Eagles are driving for a score that will cut the lead to three when the Patriots intercept a pass. Almost immediately the tension drains from the stadium. The energy drops, the noise level plummets, and people are less focused on the field. With about five minutes left, people begin to leave. "This sucks," yells the fat Philly guy, to which his silver-haired friend responds by standing up and clapping. The only drama anyone seems to care about is whether or not the Eagles will cover the spread.

The odd thing is that the game is far from over. In the aftermath, most of the analysis and discussion will focus on how the Eagles blew their chance for a comeback in the final two minutes. But in the stadium, the game was over well before then. Hardly anyone seemed to notice how the Eagles mismanaged the clock. "Score to cover," one Eagle fan yells as his team approaches the goal line in the final minute.

By the time I work my way to the gates for the long walk back to my car, it's nearly an hour after the game has ended. The streets around the stadium are still crowded, but the atmosphere is more like a Fourth of July parade now. It's less intense and more purposeful than pregame. There is still singing, but now it's the Patriots fans who have found their voice. In a mocking cadence they change the lyrics of the T.O. song to "Three Oh," a reference to the fact that the Pats have played in three of the last four Super Bowls and won them all. (It should actually be "Three One," since the team lost the '86 Super Bowl to the Bears, but that doesn't really rhyme.)

Between choruses, the streets are filled with the sound of vindication. "Oh, I'm so sick of that song," shouts one Patriots lover, echoing a thought many of us have had over the last few days. "They just didn't know how to act," decides another. "Classless."

As I make my way back through downtown Jax, the crowds siphon off into parking lots, hotels, bars. I call Rafi but there's no answer. I get Billy and he gives me the name of a bar where he and his crew plan to reunite. It's on my way, but when I get there I can't find the motivation to go in. I have nothing to celebrate, nothing to mourn, and I've already partied far more than I imagined I would this weekend. For a minute I stand there looking through the window, watching the crowds gather. The Patriots fans celebrate with a back-slapping, high-fiving exuberance. That's to be expected.

What surprises me though are the Eagles fans. Some have gone muttering off into the night, but many more have remained on the town, looking to wring a few more hours of pleasure out of their trip. They are deflated and disappointed — and not always behaving particularly well — but they're still having fun. Why not? They've spent a lot of money and put out even more in hope and frustration and lung power over the previous twenty-four Super Bowl–less seasons just to get here. Maybe that's why it's better that the game is such a big "event": It allows us a chance to indulge the bounds of our fervor, but also to rise above our own involvement and enjoy it in a broader way.

Yeah, my team lost, but I'm at the freakin' Super Bowl!

I, too, am glad to have come. If I return, I will be with friends and my team will be playing. But whenever and wherever I watch the Super Bowl next year and the year after that, it will be more than an overanalyzed hype-fest flickering through the TV. It will be a few days spent with an old friend I don't see much anymore. A party that stretches for miles, a taste, a scene, a feeling. An annoying song, sung by a band of drunken fools, that I can't get out of my head.

February 17–20, 2005

Daytona Beach, Florida

I T IS A SUNNY but cool Florida afternoon as I approach Exit 87 on Route 95 North — Daytona Beach. I've spent the better part of the morning fighting a battle that doesn't show any signs of waning. On the one hand, I'm resisting the temptation to give in to clichéd characterizations of the South. On the other, I'm about to attend my first NASCAR event, cultural crucible of simple truths, reductive politics, and cloying jingoism, all things I find particularly distasteful. At the moment, the clichés are winning. As I approach the exit, on either side of the highway emerge two gargantuan fields packed with RVs. Accordioned within a mélange of Harley billboards and fireworks ads, they give the impression that all the trailer parks that were ever swept away in tornadoes had been suddenly dropped in one place. At the bottom of the exit ramp a sign reads: "Speedway 2 mi., Dog track 1 mi." It might as well say "Welcome to The South."

The cultural shock is too great, so I reach out for the first thing I see that seems familiar: Denny's. It's about 10:00 A.M. and the place is packed, mostly with retirees in windbreakers and middle-age guys who trend toward some sort of racing-themed T-shirt tucked into denim shorts and a belt with at least a cell phone clipped onto it, if not a cell phone and a multi-tool. The hostess shows me to a booth, where I order some breakfast. The talk seems to be mostly race chatter — parking tips, favorites, start times — although the older couple one table over is discussing a rather intricate series of upcoming doctor appointments. Another silver-haired fellow sports a T-shirt with a picture of Mark Martin's Viagra-sponsored car sprawled across the back, a bold, self-confident statement that I imagine makes him pretty popular around the retirement community.

The ordinariness of my fellow diners and their prattle makes me realize what I've known all along: The people of NASCAR are just regular folks. This does not exactly qualify as a revelation, especially since in one of my first jobs I wrote about boating and fishing, so I've spent my share of afternoons drifting along backwaters with good ol' boys and never had anything but a good time with them. Within the context of the moment, it does, however, soothe my nerves. If anything, I'm a little too quick to meld right into my surroundings. After I finish my eggs, the waitress asks, "Honey, would you like another Coke?" I don't answer "Yes, please," as I normally would, but instead come out with, "That'd be all right," letting the Ls roll just a little so they start to resemble Ws. The combined effect is to make me feel like those tourists in New York City who are afraid to ride the subway: Because they've never been down there, they imagine it as some dark scary place with thieves and murderers lurking behind every pillar. Once they actually try it, they realize it's not anything like what they've seen on TV. In fact it's relatively safe and efficient and for the most part filled with normal people on their way to and from work.

There is a reason for my unusual anxiety, though: my accommodations. A few weeks earlier, I'd been doing some research on a NASCAR-related Web site when I stumbled across a bulletin board listing.

Topic: DAYTONA 500
Posted by: REDREB
Date: JANUARY 15, 2004
SEE DAYTONA 500 FROM TE COMFORT OF A RV IN THE GREEN SPECIALTY AREA. THE 4 DAYS OF RACING INCLUDE ROOM & BOARD, TICKETS IN A 32FT MOTOR HOME. GREEN AREA IS ON TURN FOUR 60FT FROM TRACK. WE LEAVE ORLANDO WED. NIGHT FEB 11 AND RETURN SUNDAY EVENING. $800. CALL FOR DETAILS.

Camping out in an RV sixty feet from the track? I had to do it. There was only one problem: The listing was for the '04 race, and had not been renewed for '05. Perhaps the poster just hadn't found time yet to update it. I took a chance and fired off a quick note to the address.

Bull's-eye. A few days later, REDREB wrote back saying the berth in his RV was available for this year's race. It was mine if I wanted it. Over the next week or two we hammered out the details by e-mail. Then one day my phone rang and on the other end was Rod Harrison: REDREB. He'd called to introduce himself and make some final arrangements.

He spoke quickly, chewing off the end of his words. His voice was clear but definitely possessed a Florida accent, more of a clipped, twangy thing than the swooping drawl of other southeastern states. The conversation didn't last more than a few minutes but swirled around my head for hours afterward. Two things in particular struck me. First, before he asked what I liked to eat, he asked what kind of beer I drink. Second, when we went to exchange cell phone numbers he said, "Hold on, I'm in my truck and I don't got a pen. Jenny" — he yelled this into what I could only imagine as a humid Florida afternoon — "you got a pen?"

As I hung up, an image of them popped into my head, Rod and Jenny, barreling down some featureless interstate in a red pickup with rust spots on the doors. The side windows are open, and there's a Confederate flag painted in the back window. Maybe a hound sleeps in the bed. Rod sits in the driver's seat, with a hand casually flipped over the wheel. He's got big Elvis sideburns, and a chain runs from his belt to his wallet. Between his legs sits a Slurpee cup, into which he occasionally spits the brown-black offal of his Skoal. Jenny sits across from him with her legs tucked under herself, wearing a pair of denim cutoffs and a red-and-white checkered shirt tied in front to expose her belly. In searching for the pen, she sweeps through empty Bud cans that roll around like tumbleweeds, ketchup-stained Hardee's wrappers, and yellowing copies of USA Today.

Well, maybe that's not right. Maybe I'm being too harsh, jumping to conclusions, but I can't help myself. The clichés are winning. In a few hours I'll be sharing a very small living area with these people and their guests — eating, showering, sleeping —

and the most persistent frame of reference I have for imagining them is *Deliverance*.

At first I was excited about the prospects of bunking with the REDREBs because it would solve my Super Bowl problem: I may not yet have a passion for NASCAR, but I would certainly have companionship for the Daytona 500. The only hitch was that I had no idea who my companions would be. Were they the sort who'd be up all night chugging Jack Daniels from the bottle and hooting at the stars? Would they exist on a diet of Bud and microwaved burritos? In search of clues, I went back to the original post. Suddenly the misspellings (TH instead of THE?) and questionable syntax (*A* RV?) jump out at me. How could I have missed them before?

Ultimately, though, they tell me nothing. The answers to my questions are unknowable and that has fed my unease. As comforting as it is, a Denny's full of clean-cut guys in Dale Earnhardt shirts and a Grand Slam can't change the reality of it.

What I find in Space 927 of the "green" RV section does nothing to quell my fears: the saddest little RV in the entire lot. Perhaps it simply suffers by comparison — it's surrounded by much bigger, newer rigs — but I don't think so. It's one of those all-in-one models, in which the cab melts right into the body so that it looks like a big shoebox on wheels. Mid-'70s vintage. The off-white exterior is highlighted by a horizontal stripe that seems as if it was once the color of dark chocolate but has now faded to a shade closer to caramel. A huge retrofit awning hangs off the side, casting shadows on the ground and making the body look smaller and more pathetic, like a little kid wearing a hat that's too big. The ladder that leads up the back to the roof is not a trim, factory-installed number, but a store-bought aluminum thing held in place by a system of bungee cords and duct tape. Shit-brown industrial carpet covers the ground under the awning.

As I stand there, one thought runs through my head: Where can I get a hotel room? There's nothing local, but I'm certain I could find something in Orlando. Before I found Rod's listing, I'd considered Orlando but hesitated because it was an *hour* away from the track. Now I tell myself, Orlando is *only* an hour away. As I ponder my options, the little RV begins to shake. A groan emerges from the sagging undercarriage. *Someone is moving around in there.* My mind rushes. What do I do? What rough beast slouches toward the sunlit Florida afternoon? It's too late. The shaking stops. The handle turns. The door swings open and slams against the side of the vehicle.

★ On the drive up from the airport, I had tried to put any misgivings about my lodgings out of my mind by focusing on the race. The Super Bowl had been something of a culminating event for me. I had grown up on the NFL. It had nourished me from my post-toddler years all the way to adulthood. I didn't need to look up the game's history. I knew it. I'd absorbed it like Vitamin D — it was, seemingly, in the very sun that shone down on me. (Thanks to NFL Films, I'd never missed my RDA of John Facenda's voice.)

Daytona was a different story. I knew a bit about NASCAR, but just enough to reinforce the stereotypes and preconceptions of someone Rush Limbaugh would classify as a New York media elite. It wasn't a case of complete ignorance so much as one of a little knowledge being a dangerous thing. As a kid I had seen the sport's gleaming, logo-festooned cars zip around asphalt circles enough that my brother and I had picked our favorite drivers: Always one to play the odds, I rooted for the Allisons, Bobby and Donnie, while my brother cheered on Buddy Baker. Whose guy won, though, was strictly a function of what lap they were on when we turned off the TV (or, more likely, changed the channel), because we almost never watched an entire race.

NASCAR is, quite famously, a legacy of bootleggers. Country boys who ran backwoods stills during Prohibition and delivered their home-cooked hooch in supercharged cars that could outrun the heat. Think *The Dukes of Hazzard* without the dental hygiene. When they weren't running booze, these guys often emerged from hiding to duel for bragging rights on the road.

The phenomenon was national, but two particular hot spots were the mountains of North Carolina, where small tracks began to pop up, and the beach at Daytona, where the wide, flat, hard-packed sand had long been a favorite spot for speed trials. Nothing really became formalized until 1947, when a mechanic from Daytona named Bill France organized a meeting of racing promoters, car and track owners, drivers, and mechanics from as far away as Massachusetts and Ohio. Over four days, they mapped out a set of rules and a schedule of races and formed an organization that would tally the standings, award championships, and keep the sport's records. They called the organization the National Association for Stock Car Auto Racing, or NASCAR.

The sport grew, and in the mid-'50s France decided to take a chance on his real dream. He raised $3 million to build a track as big as any other in the world, a 2.5-mile tri oval he called Daytona International Speedway. In 1959 the track hosted the first Daytona 500, which Lee Petty won in a photo finish that took three days to decide.

The France family still maintains control of the track and they still run NASCAR, the annual Daytona 500 has become the sport's Super Bowl, and four generations of Pettys have made a living racing cars. The most famous of them was Lee's son, Richard, who became known as "the King" during a career in which he won two hundred races, including seven Daytona 500s.

In my mind, this entire prologue has set the stage for my visit to the Daytona 500, but nothing could prepare me for the actual race.

★ The sound of a NASCAR race is unique: a whine mixed with a roar, a jet at takeoff undercut by one hundred dump trucks rumbling past. As the cars come out of turn one at the opposite end of the track, they offer a distant scream, one thousand hair dryers being turned on at once. It grows louder as the bright specks crawl up the backstretch. They reach turn three, appearing larger, and the sound explodes. It's ten thousand hair dryers. Now twenty thousand. In the artificial light that floods the track, the cars seem not just to shine, but to glow. As they ride up the high banks of turn four, they are so close that it appears as if I could reach out and pluck one right off the asphalt, like a Matchbox. Splayed across the vertical wall, it is not so much the law of gravity they seem to be defying as those of time and space: They're going so fast and yet they're impossibly close to one another. And still they maneuver, passing, switching lanes, pouring on the gas. The track seems wide enough for two, but then three squeeze across and sometimes four. There's no way not to cringe.

Then they sweep down out of turn four and the sensation literally hits you: The impact of forty-three cars going by at 200 mph is not just theoretical. My chest vibrates, my eyelashes flutter, and a tingle passes through my arms and legs. I haven't moved but I feel like I've stepped back, as if I've been shoved. The sensation passes and the cars Doppler by, sprinting down the front stretch. This is not the NASCAR you see on TV. This is the surprising thrill of the real thing.

It is Friday night and what we're watching are not actually cars but modified pickups, which run in something called the Crafts man Truck Series, the sport's version of Double A ball. (The Triple-A Busch Series races 750 horsepower cars on Saturdays, and the The Show, aka the Nextel Cup Series, takes place on Sundays in 850-horsepower cars.) Because of their less aerodynamic shape, the trucks are actually harder to drive and therefore more volatile on the track. I have not come to see a crash, but what appears to be the sheer inevitability of one keeps my eyes bolted to the action. For the first four laps, each time the trucks barrel through turn four I involuntarily let fly with a "holy shit."

My awe is well-founded because on the tenth lap it happens. As the pack steams around the corner in front of us, some element in its horizontal formation suddenly goes vertical. It's not even something you consciously notice, just a slight misalignment that registers deep in your brain, and then in an instant there's chaos. Smoke steams off the wall, cars swerve, collisions ring out, debris flies in the air, the crowd "oohs," the reactions and countermoves are impossible to track. The momentum is unstoppable. The majority of the trucks rush on down the track. The smoke lifts away. The pavement clears. One truck rolls backward onto the grass. An-

other skids down the blacktop on its hood, sparks flying everywhere, before it rolls back onto its wheels.

There is a kind of silence. The roar of the other thirty-six trucks
has not subsided, but for the moment you don't hear it, and almost
no one in the place looks at them either. All attention falls on the
steaming wreck. I have one arm wrapped around my head and one
foot lifted off the ground as if bracing for an impact. I feel a tug
on my arm, and there is Rod dancing beside me. "I told you!" he
shouts. "I told you this was the spot!" I put my hand on my forehead and shake my head.

"These trucks are crazy!" He hoots and slaps me on the back.

Rod and I have become fast friends. After he opened the door
to the RV this afternoon, we stared at each other across the bursting coolers and plastic tables that make up his alfresco dining area,
faces frozen in mutual distrust. "Jim?" he asked, speaking first.

"Rod?"

A big smile creased his face. "We been wondering when you
were gonna make it," he said, stepping toward me and extending a
meaty paw. After that we spent the afternoon in the boatlike surroundings of the RV — the paneled walls, the brass, bell-shaped
lights, the cramped, creaky interior — trading life histories and
racing stories. Rod is not the scary redneck I'd feared, though he
does have a bit of the good ol' boy about him. "This is a great spot,"
he told me minutes after we met. "We're right off turn four here,
where all the crashes happen."

About sixty, with a sweep of white hair, a fluffy mustache, and
bright blue eyes, he looks like a working man's version of Captain
Kangaroo. When he speaks you can see he's missing a few teeth on
the left side of his mouth and that one of his front teeth is graying.
He has the stooped, pained gait and thick forearms of someone
who's worked hard for a long time. He speaks quickly and has a
habit of smacking his lips together — like someone tasting soup to
see if it needs more salt — while searching for a word or idea. He
does this somewhat frequently, because he's the kind of storyteller
who believes no anecdote can be separated from its own history.
So the story of how he came to meet his current wife begets the

story of his own stint driving racecars, which begets the story of how he once delayed an Apollo launch, which in turn explains why he talks in such quick bursts.

Sorted out and reassembled, the chronology begins in the early '60s, when Rod was working for TWA. At the time, the airline had the maintenance contract at Kennedy Space Center. Rod ran the main control board, where all forty-five safety checkpoints had to call in via intercom before a launch. When Rod first got the gig, this rundown took six minutes, an unacceptable length of time, which led to the launch delay. By the time he left, it could get done in less than a minute, an improvement achieved mostly through fast talk.

He left because he and a friend had been running drag races on the weekends, and they thought they could make it as professional drivers. So he took a six-month sabbatical. They traveled throughout the Southeast and did pretty well, he says. "There was no money in it back then. If we won, we got maybe $200, but more likely a stack of tires or something. We did it for six months, lost maybe ten grand, but I was young and" — he pauses, smacks his lips, and runs his hand down the side of his face — "it was something to do."

By the time he made it home, TWA had lost the NASA contract, so Rod went off to work for a friend who was head of custodial services at the not-yet-opened Disney World. The rush to finish the place in time was brutal. Rod and many of his coworkers lived in a nearby hotel, sleeping for three hours a night. The pace led to the dissolution of his first marriage, but the park opened on schedule — barely. "The night before we opened, we were pouring concrete," he says.

Disney was where he met Jenny. An olive-skinned Latina who wears her long black hair pulled back in a ponytail, Jenny is warm and welcoming but also clearly a no-nonsense type. A Bronx refugee, she speaks directly, emphatically, and holds your eye without blinking. She spends a lot of time discussing the various labor-management disputes at the House of Mouse, and how she told so-and-so what she was or was not going to do. She's a good counterbalance to Rod, who's got a bit of a mischievous side that comes out in his devilish, gray-toothed smile and needling sense of humor.

When I ask how they met, they take turns relaying the story. Jenny, who's been a waitress at Disney since it opened, says, "My manager was on vacation. He was the sub" — Rod had by then been transferred into the restaurants — "and he was real tough."

"She hated me," Ron interjects, flashing the gray tooth.

"I was trying to be nice," she shoots back. "After a week, he called me into the office. I thought I was going to get fired because we had just not gotten along. He asked me if I liked my job, if I had kids, and did I want to go to Daytona with him one weekend? And that was it," she says. "I mean that was it. He didn't speak to me again."

"I was playing hard to get," Rod says.

"Finally, about a month later, I asked him to a party," Jenny continues, "but I had a lot of doubts. At that time the ratio of women to men working at Disney was like 30 to 1. I didn't want to be part of that harem. He was living in an apartment with two other guys and they had a scoreboard above the bedroom door . . ."

"It was just a chalkboard . . ."

"Same thing. I told him, I better not be on there."

The last member of our party is José, who has been coming to Daytona with Rod and Jenny for almost fifteen years. He has a thin mustache that sits below permanently flared nostrils, and jet-black hair that's longer in front so that it falls down over his temples like a pair of drapes. He is quiet, spending a lot of time on his cell with his girlfriend and going off for long walks by himself. Every time his phone rings, Rod and Jenny tease him, rolling their eyes and saying things like "There's sweetie" and "Uh-oh, it's been twenty minutes, what's wrong now?" José takes these jabs in a good-natured manner that includes a big laugh, during which he throws his head back and opens his mouth wide, revealing an abundance of silver dental work.

Another transplanted New Yorker who waits tables at Disney, he moved to Florida right out of high school. "I didn't like the cold," he tells me as he reflexively runs his thumb and middle finger back over his skull to sweep the hair out of his eyes. He is also a committed race fan. He seems to know the names of most of the drivers just by the numbers on their cars, and he has a working knowledge of the rivalries, grudges, and history of the sport.

The four of us are now on top of the RV, watching the sparkling trucks career around the track. The same cold snap that froze me at the Super Bowl is still lingering; the temperature is in the mid-forties. Rod wears a sweatshirt that says "Big Dog" on the front and a baseball cap with a Road Runner patch on it, while Jenny sports a red, white, and black Dale Earnhardt windbreaker. We witness seven or eight crashes (I lose count) and as the trucks cross the finish line, one last collision mars the course. Even as they are cleaning up the wreckage — towing away the trucks, blowing the debris off the track — fireworks light up the sky.

Back inside the trailer, we drink our last beers and rehash the action. Rod tells the story of when he bought the RV, which of course requires a full history of the previous RV and his houseboat, which was basically an RV on the water. This one he acquired from a friend who worked at a used-car lot. This friend brought the RV in to work one day with hopes of selling it, but it was such an eyesore his boss told him to have it off the lot by the end of the day. The guy called Rod, who wasn't in the market but came to look anyway, and ended up buying it for $1,500 in cash. He paid two guys to spend two days cleaning it. Finally, with great trepidation, he brought it home. "She takes one step onto it, looks around, and says, 'It's filthy.'" Even now, years later, he can't take it. His eyes light up and he cackles, rocking back and forth. "Two days cleaning it and, 'It's filthy.' I thought, 'If she only knew.'"

With that last laugh, everyone agrees it's time for sleep. Rod and Jenny crash on the dinette, which converts to a double bed, and José gets the couch right next to them. I have the back bedroom to myself. The huge lights around the track illuminate it. Like the Super Bowl, Daytona has a massive public-address system and the speakers that snake throughout the place provide play-by-play during the race and high-decibel music the rest of the time. At midnight, it finally goes quiet. For the first time, I notice three frosted bottles on the nightstand. There's Japanese writing on the labels and fake flowers carefully arranged in each. As I drift off, I hear the slightest symphony of snoring from the other room. It's not exactly *The Waltons,* but it ain't *Hee Haw* either.

★ Noriega. I can't help but think about the former Panamanian dictator who was known as Pineapple Face.

The night was brutal. An RV kept in Florida is not, understandably, well weatherproofed, so the windows around my bed were draftier than one of Jennifer Lopez's dresses. Around 5:00 A.M. I finally discovered a way to jam my pillow into the window frame to cut the inflow of cold air down to gale force, and I was able to drift off to sleep. But any thoughts I have about lingering in bed to make up for lost time come to an abrupt halt at eight o'clock sharp. That is when the PA system kicks back on.

Instead of music, it replays the broadcasts of famous finishes of Daytona 500s past ("As they come into the final turn, it's Petty by half a car length . . ."), which really just amounts to someone screaming through a loudspeaker. Isn't this how the U.S. Army attempted to flush Noriega out of his compound after he'd barricaded himself inside? They aimed gigantic speakers at it and cranked a steady diet of rock music (Twisted Sister, if memory serves) and pro-American propaganda to weaken his will and break his spirit.

Perhaps brainwashing connects these big sporting events. So far beer and the constant barrage of nostalgia and party tunes piped through a centralized sound system are the only constants. Whatever the motivation, the programming (or reprogramming) forces me out of bed. The rest of the crew continues to snooze in the dim light of the main cabin, so I dress quickly and head outside. As I descend the steps of the RV I almost trip on a fresh copy of the *Daytona Beach News Journal.* I don't think much about it as I head off to explore the infield. I'd gotten a basic lay of the land yesterday, but not a chance to really look around.

Before I even make it to the end of our aisle I spot license plates from California, Indiana, Massachusetts, Michigan, Montana, New York, Virginia, West Virginia, and Ontario, Canada. And it's not just the locations that are notable but the rigs themselves. Compared with our little *Brady Bunch* special, the majority of the RVs in the lot are bigger, newer, fancier; minicondos on wheels, really. The most popular model is not even an RV, in my mind. It's one of those decked-out buses rock bands use to tour the country. There are hundreds of them. Their generators hum as the people inside microwave breakfast and watch DVDs.

It's then I notice that all the RVs have newspapers waiting outside. It hits me: There's newspaper delivery inside the track. And that's not all. Garbage trucks make their way up and down the aisles, collecting trash. A tanker truck also makes the rounds: For $20 he'll pump out a holding tank. Long-bedded golf carts sell bags of ice. Food concessions sizzle and smoke everywhere, custom tractor-trailers contain little shops that sell officially licensed goods ranging from shot glasses to baby bottles, and low concrete buildings marked "restrooms" and "showers" pop up with comforting regularity. Before the weekend is out, I will catch a news report about a flu outbreak spreading through the infield. We are a population unto ourselves, complete with our own social services, public works, and germ networks. This is not a sporting event so much as a community. Call it Speedway City.

As the morning warms, the citizens of Speedway City emerge. The parking spaces are wide enough that most of the RVs have a small yard, set up with tables and chairs and barbecue grills. Old men sit in lawn chairs outside their rigs, smoking cigars and talking politics. Grills pop with the sound of bacon. Dogs sniff along the edge of the family plot. Teenagers throw footballs and Frisbees. At a concession truck that houses a slot-car racing track, ten-year-olds try to impress their dads by refusing to slow down in the turns, kicking the dusty ground when their little model Chevys and Dodges inevitably fly off the track.

All right, I change my mind. This is not a metropolis so much as a small town. Of the '50s. Not Speedway City but Speedwayville. There's even a picturesque boardwalk. A boardwalk? It runs along the lake, on which there is a ramp and a slalom course, and three times a day there are waterskiing shows. That's how much space there is inside a 2.5-mile tri-oval.

I find my way to pit row. Today's race, the Busch Series Hershey's Take 5 300 (say that five times), doesn't start until 1:00 P.M. I arrive early, and there's little yet to see, so I wander into something called the Fan Zone, a large brick-paved area with various buildings and attractions. I get something to eat and sit at a table.

Next to me, two guys in their mid-thirties sit drinking extralarge coffees. One of them reads the paper while the other fiddles with his BlackBerry. "This food's actually not that bad," I say. The guy reading the paper explains that it should be good since this whole setup is brand-new — the café, the concert stage behind us, the gigantic gift shop, the bays where you can look through Plexiglas into the garages to watch teams working on their cars, and even the viewing area, where you can see NASCAR engineers certifying that those cars meet race specs.

"Pretty cushy," I say.

"Keeps gettin' nicer every year," he answers. This, I infer from the way he says it and because he's wearing Jimmie Johnson gear, is a good thing. Johnson is a prototype driver of the new NASCAR — talented, polished, civilized, family oriented, and good-looking — in a sport that claims 40 percent of its fans are female. "Thirty years ago," the guy says as we discuss that issue, "you couldn't bring a woman in the infield. Now you got fifteen-year-old girls walking around by themselves."

That's a far cry from the good ol' days. Thirty or forty years ago, the circuit's heroes, from Petty to Junior Johnson to the Intimidator, Dale Earnhardt, were counterculture icons who represented some lingering defiance of southern culture and a hypermacho example of American rugged individualism: Marlboro men with steering wheels. The stars and the sport itself clung to its image as a band of rough-and-tumble bootleggers and rednecks who lived hard, drove hard, and made their own rules. It has been a key part of the sport's appeal. NASCAR's breakthrough moment came when

Donnie and Bobby Allison fought with Cale Yarborough after a final-lap crash in the 1979 Daytona 500. There was a major snowstorm along the East Coast and with nothing else to do, the shut-in masses witnessed the fight live on TV. The image of those three boys duking it out like characters from a Western was water-cooler fodder for the next week and NASCAR's popularity jumped.

It was no better in the stands. As the stories go, the people who came to the 500 were as hard-core as the drivers. "I heard stories about guys bringing girlfriends back in the day, and it never turned out good," adds the guy with the BlackBerry. Rod, too, has stories. Drinking, betting, fighting, and worse. Back then, they didn't yell "Show us your tits." They went up and forcibly exposed them.

I've certainly seen nothing to make me think the 500 is anything but a wholesome family event, but there is still some undercurrent of the old days in the air. The hot rumor of the week has Michelin attempting to break up Goodyear's monopoly as a tire supplier. The competition could bring more innovation and more money into the sport, but there is a problem: Michelin is a French company. And that's the crux of NASCAR at the start of the twenty-first century. It wants to be an international sport that welcomes women and children along with all the beer-drinking men, but it's stuck on its own provincialism. At its heart it's still attached to those old southern roots, dripping with cornball patriotism and xenophobia.

How else do you explain why Jeff Gordon, a laid-back, photogenic Californian, who has been the most successful driver of the last decade, has not been embraced by traditional NASCAR fans? Instead they've labeled him a pretty boy and a shill. Meanwhile, Dale Earnhardt Jr. has won only a handful of times. He's as good-looking and sponsor-savvy as anyone, but he speaks with a drawl and has inherited his father's blue-collar edge and fan base. He is by far the circuit's most popular driver.

★ My eyes have become trained to pick out a certain shade of blue. I can find it among the 200-mph scramble of colors and numbers and shifting glints of reflected light. It is the color of the #5 car driven by Kyle Busch, and it has become the focus of my afternoon.

I watched most of the IROC race from the pit area to get a different perspective, but I've returned to the RV. In the heat of the afternoon, the trip back was far different. Speedwayville had a different feel. The stands across the track were full. The lawn chairs had been joined by inflatable pools, an army of coolers, and more bars than a prison. Some of the bars are pretty elaborate, with hanging glass-holders, leather stools, neon lights, and inflatable palm trees. The people who populate these impromptu watering holes come in the full variety of the Lord's blessings. There is no shortage of tattooed, pierced twenty-somethings, but there are fewer shirtless dudes in cowboy hats than I would have imagined. Most of the people wear some race-related garb that features a driver's number and his main sponsor, with women disproportionately opting for the half shirt, even when they really shouldn't. And there are plenty of colorful T-shirts: "Drive it like you stole it"; "If you lick it, it will come"; "The Biker Ministry of Jesus Christ."

Among this younger generation is a good mix of older folks. White-haired stoics who perch atop their rolling retirement homes, looking through binoculars and taking pulls at tall, sweaty glasses of indiscernible liquids. They are joined by the swollen-bellied know-it-alls who kick the world's virtual tires and talk about all the times they've seen the same thing, only different. And there are still plenty of kids, many of them trailed by clean-cut guys in T-shirts and cargo shorts — the famed NASCAR dads of electoral demographics.

José, it turns out, is one of them. He's been divorced for more than a decade but has a twelve-year-old son, who is also a race fan. He sees the boy as much as he can, he says, because he wants more than anything to be a good dad. "I made a mistake twelve years ago," he says, referring to his marriage, "and now I want to make something good come out of it."

José stands next to me now as the cars zip around the track. Rod and Jenny sit on fold-out lawn chairs behind us. Rod has introduced me to the receiver, which is basically a one-way walkie-talkie. Plug in a set of headphones, turn the dial, and you can tune in the in-car communications of the drivers. Not only between the driver and his crew chief but also with his spotter, who stands on a platform high above the track and feeds his driver information about what's happening around him.

Somehow or other I've settled in on the channel assigned to Kyle Busch, a nineteen-year-old who's in his second year on the Busch tour and a Nextel Cup rookie, and the younger brother of 2004 Nextel Cup champ Kurt Busch. His #5 car is a bright blue with yellow accents, so besides watching the battle at the front of the pack, as the cars roar up the backstretch, I also keep my eyes out for the flash of blue that lets me know what has happened to Busch in the far turns.

Now I'm watching two races. The one for the lead, and Kyle Busch's race within the race. As it turns out, he's a good guy to watch. By the time I zoom in on him, he's running in the middle of the pack. But as he relays to his pit, the car is strong I listen in as his spotter tells him he has room high. Lets him know when he's got room below him on the track. Gives him tips on who's got the good line — "Stick with the 99." Over the course of twenty or twenty-five laps, he works his way to the front, and runs in the top five for quite a while. And then he dings his right side trying to maneuver through two other cars that have crashed on the track.

The repair costs him two laps. But he doesn't quit. Back on the track, he's miles behind but falls into the same easy rhythm with his spotter, who feeds him his lap times: "You're running almost a second faster than the leaders." He eventually works his way back onto the lead lap. As he bobs and weaves among the other cars, goes up and back, as the steady drone of his spotter fills my ears, I find that I'm forming a bond with Kyle Busch. I'm rooting for him. I'm in his camp. No doubt, his demeanor is part of it. He's calm and positive. After the accident, there's no cursing or whining, he just asks what happened because he didn't actually see it all. "Let's see if we can't win this thing," he says when he finally gets back on the lead lap, and I think, Why not? Come on, Kyle, you can do it.

Between the crashes, the battle for lead, and following Busch, I can't believe how fast 120 laps go by. It doesn't end well for our hero — he commits a rules infraction that sets him back too far to recover — but to this day, a year and half later, I check the race results in the newspaper on Monday mornings, and I always look to see how Kyle Busch did.

★ "I'm sick of Vegas," Ron says. It's early evening and we're spread out around the inside of the RV watching *COPS: Las Vegas*. After the Busch race ended there was a notable sense of deflation. It seemed there was little left to do but eat dinner and sleep. We dined on tacos, sitting around the tiny table like a sitcom family, reliving moments from the day's events and laughing. The generator hummed in the background, but the noise was forgiven since it powered the heater that kept us warm.

Dinner done, we spread out across the interior of the cabin. With the artificial heat, the lingering smell of the tacos, and the furry upholstery, the place feels incredibly warm and close, in a good way. Like we're all snuggled into a four-person sleeping bag on a cold rainy day. José's cell phone rings and as he crosses the cabin to answer, Jenny says, "Tell her I said hi." Rod makes little kissing noises and watches José's face for a reaction, shooting a quick glance my way and smiling conspiratorially.

As we watch the show, Rod has been talking about Vegas. All the times they've been there, his favorite places, his best memories. They are in fact going out to Vegas the following week; it's just one of a handful of places they regularly visit that makes their idea of getaways sound like the itinerary of a Spring Break party planner. They're regulars here in Daytona and in New Orleans (pre-Katrina) and Key West, especially when there's something big happening: a race, Mardi Gras, the Fashion First festival. After the debauchery of the Super Bowl, I'm beginning to feel as if I've tapped into this subset of adults who travel the country in search of street parties during which the normal rules of everyday society seem not to apply. Certain events and places attract them like bugs to a zapper: the Super Bowl, Daytona, Vegas, Burning Man, Lake of the Ozarks, etc. I've entered their ranks as part of a one-year adventure, but these people spend their entire lives chasing the good times. It's like a permanently embedded party class.

In some ways, Rod and Jenny don't seem to fit in. Yes, they live the life and their stories are filled with tales of drunkenness, highlighted with the occasional scene of violence or nudity. But Rod and Jenny don't seem to actually drink much, if at all, and there is a prevailing sweetness to them. Their favorite tales are inevitably about people. The attendant at the parking lot in New Orleans where they leave the RV every year. Jenny befriended him by serving him doughnuts and coffee every morning. The two boys who they helped gather beads at a Mardi Gras parade only to be later invited into their grandmother's house as a thank-you for being nice to the kids.

Then there's the Daytona clan. This is a group of fellow campers who've surrounded them for the nine years they've been in this spot. "It's like family," says Jenny. "We send each other Christmas cards and talk on the phone, and we know every year we're all going to get together here, and we all look forward to it."

Rod tells me that the place to catch a little flavor of the way things used to be is the orange parking section at the end of the track. There you can get a parking spot for the week for $710 and pitch a tent, which means the area draws those on a budget — college students, party mavens, out-of-work pipe fitters, bikers, self-proclaimed rednecks. The walk over is marked with a party atmosphere. Night has fallen and the metabolism has gone up. Groups of twenty-blank-year-olds move in packs, mostly guys but occasionally a few women. Gangs ride in the back of pickups, swigging from long-neck bottles. It's Saturday night at Speedwayville, and the cows have not yet come home.

Inside the orange area the feeling is totally different. A haphazard agglomeration of pickups, spray-painted vans, broken-down cars, and beat-up campers sprawls across the ground. The smoke and smell from the open fires and the tents give it the feeling of a Civil War encampment, rebel yells echoing across the landscape. Elsewhere around the track, the RVs have platforms on top, ranging from simple flat areas with a railing around them to elaborate perches with bars and TVs. Here in the orange area the platforms take on the look and feel of dorm room lofts and high school science-fair projects. There are wooden stages built right into the beds of trucks. Odd freestanding metal constructions that straddle cars. And all sorts of creaky, teetering contraptions bolted to the tops of unidentifiable vehicles.

Everywhere, music cranks from small parties and the smell of pot wafts, especially from one encampment made up of giant Grateful Dead banners. In another open tent I watch for a minute while one girl dirty-dances with a shirtless dude as three other guys watch, passing a bottle around. It's an oddly enchanting scene, but at the same time it looks and feels like one of those crime reenactments you see on *Dateline* or *20/20*. I can almost hear the Stone Phillips voiceover, but I don't want to stick around for the "after."

As I round one corner, I see a young boy and a man sitting on tiny stools around a huge fire. The guy weighs probably four hundred pounds. His belly hangs out from under a white sleeveless T-shirt and his shorts disappear into the creases where his thighs meet his waist. I say hi but he just stares at me, so I move on. It is not exactly a vision of Sheriff Andy and Opie, but it brings me face to face (once again) with the issue of fathers. When it comes to men and sports, it's a hard topic to ignore.

For many men, sports is not just a gift they get from their dads, it's a lasting bond, a way to communicate, to reassert their connection and express their emotions without saying so in so many words. Call it *Field of Dreams* syndrome. I know my own attachment to football comes from my dad. Some of my earliest memories are of watching Giants games with him on the couch in our family room. My sister, brother, and I would race to get the spot right next to him, the unhappy losers lining up in a row one or two spots removed. My dad was an active watcher. He yelled at the screen. He clapped. He stood. And when those terrible Giants teams of the '70s drove him past the point of reason, he screamed. He had a lot of hobbies and interests, but nothing moved him to this kind of passion but football, and that certainly had an impact.

Still, I don't think that fully explains the headfirst dive I took into sports fanaticism. Sure, I still talk to my dad about sports and we still play golf together, but we talk about many other things as well. Sports is definitely part of our relationship but it's not the only thing. There has to be something else.

★ The Daytona 500 does not start until 2:00 P.M., but by 9:00 A.M. the unlucky souls who don't have a rolling palace in the infield have begun hauling their coolers up the long flights of steps in the grandstands. Rod says that they used to bring giant coolers and set up shop for the whole day, but it got so that people couldn't get in and out of their seats, so now they are limited to six-pack coolers. Beer drinking is serious business among NASCAR fans, not because they drink more or in some less appealing way than other sports fans, but because it means more.

A good friend who's a longtime race fan told me a story about two guys he'd gone to a race with. One was an Earnhardt Jr. fan and thus drank only the brand of beer that sponsored him, Budweiser. The other guy was a Rusty Wallace fan and therefore partook of that driver's main patron, Miller Lite. When the Wallace guy ran out of Miller, the Earnhardt guy kindly offered him a Bud. No thank you, said the Wallace guy. Couldn't do it. Couldn't drink the other guy's brew. That's loyalty.

That's also one of the reasons advertisers love NASCAR. It's the reason the pits are an onslaught of bright-colored corporate logos and brand names. And why NASCAR drivers never get new tires, they "pop on a fresh set of Goodyears." Their crews never perform well, but "the [name of sponsor] team really kicked it up a notch." This constant hard sell is such a part of the culture that fans tolerate the name-dropping and the logos in a way they never would in sports like football and baseball. (Can you imagine Peyton Manning telling John Madden he delivered the Wilson like a FedEx Priority Overnight?)

There are tradeoffs, though. Like access. Hours before the biggest race of the season, hundreds of fans holding pit passes roam around the pit area, talking to team members setting up equipment, checking out the gear, leaning on stacks of tires. Beyond the pit (you can walk right through) hundreds more mill about on the grass and the track. One guy is actually lying down on the black-and-white checkerboard of the start/finish line.

Up close the race surface is more gray than black. The incline is greater than I imagined, too; I don't need to crawl up it but it's close. And the corners are even steeper. I look down the front-stretch, trying to get an idea of what it would look like rushing by at 200 mph. In some way I had thought of Daytona like racing's version of Augusta National, a pristine and perfect setting for the game's ultimate competition. But as I look down the track all I see are swales and hollows and little mounds. The surface is cracked and patched and uneven. This is not a manicured garden but a battered and lumpy interstate, which only makes the achievement of negotiating it that much more impressive.

In between the track and the pits, a stage has been rolled out for the prerace festivities, and all morning long a steady stream of military bands, glee clubs, and local marching bands have been playing every patriotic song ever written: "God Bless America," "God Bless the USA," "America the Beautiful," and "American Soldier." The mayor of Daytona comes out to make a speech, and it somehow seems odd that a local politician is welcoming people from all over the world to the International Speedway. When she's followed by a city councilman, the whole thing takes on the feeling of a county fair.

As race time approaches, the local talent gets pushed aside in favor of bigger-name acts. Former POW Jessica Lynch takes a bow, then–Boston Red Sox centerfielder Johnny Damon is there, and actor Ashton Kutcher holds a ceremonial title as well. And since this is NASCAR, a boxy brown UPS truck takes a ceremonial lap for some promotional purpose or other.

The pits, however, continue to crawl with regular folks. As teams roll out huge lockers of equipment, they have to shout "Excuse me" to pass. Pit crews stretch and loosen up as spectators almost trip over them. One guy is loading giant tanks of fuel onto a rack but some random fan is sitting where the canister is supposed to go, oblivious. Finally, the fuel loader gets his attention and politely asks if he would move. There is no other sport where you can get this kind of access to the playing field and the players. It's the equivalent of sitting on the bench a half hour before the Super Bowl.

Pretty soon the cars start rolling out, and I can touch them as they go by. Then the drivers get introduced, strutting past in color-coordinated jumpsuits. I keep waiting for security personnel to usher us to our seats, but none materialize. So I stand right behind the thigh-high concrete wall that separates the pit from pit road and watch the drivers' parade, in which NASCAR's finest are driven around the track in convertibles as they wave from the backseat like homecoming queens. Some of them, to my surprise, are as coifed and tanned as any belle of the ball.

As I stand there, two people sweep past very quickly and a third bumps me as he tries to get by. I turn and find myself face to face with actor Matthew McConaughey (shortish, balding), this year's Grand Marshal. The national anthem begins, and a short burst of fireworks go off as Vanessa Williams sings "and the rockets' red glare," bringing a cheer from the crowd. As the final notes play, Air Force jets zip overhead. It's then that McConaughey is introduced, and since this is NASCAR, there's a plug for his upcoming movie. He forgoes his smooth Hollywood speech patterns to announce "Gentlemen, start your engines" in a full Texas twang. I wait to hear the roar of the motors and see the cars fall in behind the pace car before I head back to the RV.

★ Step, step, step, backstretch, pole, Jumbotron, reset, turn two. I am an old pro now, watching races from atop Rod's RV. With my earphones on (I'm again tuned in to Kyle Bush) and the receiver standing on the ground next to me, I watch the cars scream through turn three, then take three little steps that rotate me to the left so I can track them as they go by. When they disappear down the backstretch, I glance up at the pole, which is actually a tower next to the start/finish line. White lights display the numbers of the cars from first place to seventeenth. After checking the pole to see if anyone has changed position, I peek left at one of the Jumbotrons that face the grandstand and catch the pack heading into turn one. At this point, I can't keep turning left or the wire from the headphones will wrap around my body, so I quickly pirouette back to the right, at which point the cars are just about coming back into view out of turn two and up the backstretch.

It's a dance, really, and one with a comforting metronomic rhythm. Almost like a typewriter that *clack, clack, clacks* across the page then zips back to the start. Every second or third lap I take a moment while the cars are in the far turn to swig my beer or pull the headphones off one ear and trade comments with one of my rooftop cowatchers. "Did you see Stewart get stuck in the high line?" or "What happened to Earnhardt there?" Otherwise, the steady beat lulls me into a trance, and before I know it ten, twenty, thirty laps go by. Little bursts of excitement spice the proceedings when there's passing or pit stops or close calls. Until something goes wrong, then the whole thing erupts in a barrage of swerving and smoke and car parts and the smell of burned rubber.

Yet even these things are more predictable than one would imagine. Rod calls it the 50/50 Theory. "All the good stuff happens in the first fifty laps and the last fifty," he explains. "In the beginning they're all fighting for position and seeing who's got what kinda car. At the end, they're all trying to win it. Anything happens in between is just an accident. That's when I go for a nap." He flashes his gray-tooth smile.

When he goes down for his nap today I follow him. I've been incessantly checking the weather all afternoon. I'm supposed to fly out at about nine this evening, but a massive snowstorm, not unlike the one that forced so many people to stay inside and watch the '79 500, is heading for the Northeast. It's predicted to hit New York around ten, which means the chances of my flight being delayed, rerouted, or outright canceled are pretty good. My only option is a 6:00 P.M. flight, which should get me in before the snow, but I'd have to leave with about twenty laps left in the race in order to make it.

I've been flip-flopping all day about what to do, but in the end, missing work on Monday is not an option, so I book myself on the earlier flight and head back up to the top of the RV with José to catch as much of the action as I can. With about sixty laps to go, Rod and Jenny call us down from the top of the RV. There on the little plastic picnic tables is a massive surf and turf meal. "We couldn't have you eating airline food," Jenny says.

In the center of the 200-mph cultural whirlwind that is the Great American Race, a good ol' boy, a transplanted New Yorker, a NASCAR dad, and a member of the New York media elite enjoy filet mignon and lobster tails. There's laughter and teasing. When we're done, I go up for one last look at the track and then exchange hugs, slaps on the back, and phone numbers. "You've got a friend in Orlando," Rod says as I pull away.

Outside the track the race is an eerie howl, and as I get on the highway I tune in the broadcast on the radio. I'm hoping for an uneventful ending to this race, so I won't have missed anything, but from the description on the radio I can tell something's going to give. There's a lot of aggressive driving and no one's backing down. It's make-or-break time.

Sure enough, with sixteen laps left, there's a massive pileup in turn four. I'm expecting a wave of disappointment to sweep over me as I listen to hear who was involved, but instead I get a picture in my head. There's José leaning over the edge of the RV, calling back the names of the drivers involved. Jenny cranes to see if her beloved Earnhardt Jr. is still going. And Rod leaps in the air, headphones askew, shouting, "You see that? You see that? I tol' ya. This is the place."

3 ★ The Final Four

April 2–4, 2005

St. Louis, Missouri

I WAS A SENIOR in high school on April 1, 1985, when I arrived home to find an acceptance letter in my mailbox from Villanova University. The timing was interesting, since that day, Villanova's men's basketball team was at the center of the sports world. The unheralded and unranked team that had squeaked into the NCAA tournament with a 19-10 record had somehow gone on an unprecedented run, winning five straight games. That night, they were playing for the national championship.

Led by their fiery meatball of a coach, Rollie Massimino, and their wheelchair-bound, ALS-afflicted trainer, Jake Nevin, they were the ultimate Cinderella, and a huge portion of the country had adopted them. As fun as it was to watch their tense, low-scoring games and see them make it this far, everyone knew there was no glass slipper coming. The opponent that night was Georgetown, the defending national champions, who were led by the imposing John Thompson and future NBA players Patrick Ewing, David Wingate, and Reggie Williams. The Hoyas were 30-2 during the season and ranked number one in the country, and they had beaten Villanova twice during the regular season. No one gave Nova even the slightest chance at victory. Massimino himself said, "To win, we need to play the perfect game."

And that's just about what happened. Villanova went on to hit 78 percent of its shots, including nine of ten in the second half, and won the game 66–64, providing one of the craziest upsets in the history of March Madness. The Wildcats are still the lowest-seeded team ever to win, and they still hold the tournament record for shooting percentage in a game.

Like most people, I was blown away by the victory, but the funny thing for me was that I'd been rooting for both teams throughout the tournament. For Villanova because it was one of two schools I was hoping to attend. (I didn't get into the other, which made it an easy decision.) And for Georgetown because, like most people, I assumed Nova would get knocked out early, and I needed someone to root for after that. Also, I loved Patrick Ewing. I thought he was intense and passionate. I loved the way he blocked shots and tried to dunk every time he touched the ball, and I didn't like the way he was treated by other teams' fans (including Villanova's). It was somehow considered funny to throw bananas at him and hold up signs saying: "Patrick can you read this?"

So I would have found a silver lining either way, but it was hard not to get wrapped up in Villanova's David-and-Goliath moment. The NCAA tournament has been around since 1939, but it wasn't until the advent of first the thirty-two-team field in 1975 and then the full-blown sixty-four-team field in 1985 that it became the pre-eminent event in college sports. Football is bigger and makes more money, but its championship is muddied by its reliance on opinions, polls, and contrived matchups in a diluted slew of bowl games.

The basketball tournament, which includes the winners of all thirty-one Division I conferences and the next best thirty-four "at large" teams in the country is democratic and egalitarian, at least on the surface, and that appeals to us as a nation. Even more, it's an all-inclusive free-for-all that's known for its unpredictability, a trait that's reinforced in an annual haul of upsets that loan the event a justifiable aura of excitement based on the notion that anything can happen. In that atmosphere, the prospect of winning it all, even for the best teams, is slim, like catching smoke. Hence the name March Madness and the resulting insanity that enveloped Villanova and its home city of Philadelphia when the team won.

The team's celebratory parade in central Philly was sheer pandemonium. TV showed clips of the mayhem on campus, which was shut down for two days because the streets were so clogged with traffic as people rushed to join the party. The overall good feeling it gave you to think that sometimes the little guy can still win over incredible odds was, in short, what always has made and will continue to make sports great.

When I arrived on campus the following fall, school spirit was at fever pitch. During the summer, Massimino had spurned an offer to jump to the NBA, and that loyalty only raised the level of enthusiasm. Freshman orientation meetings would turn into pep rallies, with spontaneous "NO-VA, NO-VA" chants breaking out any time there was a quiet moment or sometimes even in the middle of a presentation. The numbers 66 and 64, representing the final score, became near sacred. People chanted them. Wore them on shirts. Hung banners from dorm room windows with just those four digits.

And there were the stories. Stories of parties and celebrations. Of the massive food fight that took place in the main cafeteria the night Nova eliminated Memphis State from the Final Four. Of eighteen-hour, all-night drives from Philadelphia to Lexington, Kentucky, to catch the final game, scalping tickets, sleeping in cars or on hotel room floors of people you didn't even know. And of going temporarily insane after the win. Of not sleeping for forty-eight hours, not going to class for a week, not ever before or ever since seeing anything like what you saw that week. We freshmen couldn't get enough of it. We pictured ourselves living out our own version of what had become the ultimate college experience: not graduation, but the post–national championship near-riot.

A funny thing happened during the next four years, though. We got sick of the stories. We became the class that had *just missed* the big win. Every time we went to a big party or thought we did something fun, we heard the stories. The phrase "It was good, but nothing like when we won the championship" hung over our heads. Even in my junior year when Villanova went on another unlikely run and made it to the Elite Eight, we could not escape the ghosts of 1985.

I realized I needed to go back in time. To relive in some way the moment I missed. I needed to go to the Final Four.

★ Under a perfect blue sky, crowds of revelers jam into Laclede's Landing, St. Louis's cobblestoned version of the French Quarter. There is no want for local color — among the jugglers, street performers on stilts, and music blaring from the DJ booth situated at the main intersection flow streams of Carolina blue, Louisville red, Michigan State green, and Illinois orange — especially Illinois orange. The Mississippi sluices by in the background but the aura of frivolity in the early spring air floats on a different liquid: beer. This is, after all, the home of Anheuser-Busch.

As I walk among these people, I study their faces. I'm looking for someone in particular. Someone of the right age and type who seems approachable. I'm still on a high from Daytona. I had such a good time with my hosts that I'm now testing a theory that what makes these iconic events stand apart is not just the magnitude of the game, but the company you keep during it.

Ideally, Villanova would have made the Final Four, and I could have hooked up with my old college buddies and finally had the experience we missed twenty years ago. It almost worked out, as Nova made the Sweet Sixteen without their best player before losing by one point to the eventual champions. With Nova out of the mix, so was my old gang. The next best option was to hook up with students from one of the schools who did make it: North Carolina, Illinois, Louisville, and Michigan State. I would, in essence, embed myself among them. These people would be my troops. Their victories would be mine; their defeats would cut me. I would share in their joy, call them by their nicknames, high-five them after dunks, hit on their girlfriends . . .

The Internet had worked well in helping find Rod Harrison. There was a hitch this time, though: I wouldn't know which teams were in the Final Four until five days before the event. I would have to act fast. I also had to hope that at least one of the schools was within reasonable driving distance of St. Louis, because the drive would be a major part of the experience. That locked-in, shoulder-rubbing car time would nurture our budding relationship.

On a Sunday night the teams were set, and I rushed to the computer. A MapQuest search told me that the Illinois and Louisville campuses offered the shortest drives to St. Louis — about two hours from Illinois and three from Louisville. The extra hour would be important for bonding, so I targeted Louisville. I went onto the message board of a fan Web site and posted what I thought was a very mature and reasonable message: LOOKING FOR A RIDE FROM LOUISVILLE TO ST. LOUIS FOR THE FINAL FOUR. WILLING TO PAY FOR GAS.

I got back three or four messages that all seemed to say the same thing:

DUDE/BUD/PLAYA, GREAT. WE'VE GOT A SPOT FOR YOU IN OUR CAMARO/VW BUS/TRICKED-OUT CELLICA, RIGHT NEXT TO THE KEG/BONG/KIDNAPPED 15-YEAR-OLD. WE'LL BE LEAVING AT MIDNIGHT DIRECTLY FROM THE FRAT HOUSE/BAR/NIGHTCLUB. CAN YOU PAY THE GAS MONEY UP-FRONT?

So then I had another idea. I would fly directly to St. Louis, head out into the gathering masses, and find a group of guys to call my own. Preferably a group in which all the members were at least twenty-one and did not have lawyers for fathers. Perhaps I should have bought a copy of *Cosmo* for the plane ride, because I underestimated how difficult it is to meet nice young men.

After trolling the arena without luck, I've now taken up a spot inside a bar called the Study Hall, where a sign in the window proclaims that they're "Expanding minds one drink at a time." So far I've been ignored by a group of frat boys led by one wearing a hardhat with a miniature barbecue grill bolted to it (the Weber grill was a show of support for Illinois head coach Bruce Weber), flat-out rejected by three nerds who thought I was stalking them (I sort of was), and failed to ingratiate myself with a bunch of latter-day preppies in khakis, white oxfords, and light blue bow ties.

Most of the people I approach stop listening once it becomes clear I don't have tickets to sell. Finally, though, I maneuver myself over to a rail where three Michigan State fans lean silently. All are dressed in green from head to toe, including their shoes. One — a tall, thin fellow with floppy brown hair — has the letters *MSU* painted in green and white on each cheek and across his forehead. The second, who has perfected that tousled just-out-of-bed look, wears a sleeveless shirt that showcases big green and white Ms painted on each shoulder. The third guy has not wasted any time carefully painting letters. Instead, in some sort of artistic hara-kiri, he has turned a can of green spray paint on himself. His entire face and all his hair are Michigan State green, making the whites of his eyes seem to jump out of his head like cue balls. To round out the look, he wears one of those huge green foam fingers.

I've moved in on this group because, well, they're already a little drunk, and I can't help but think that helps my odds. But how to approach them? I scroll through the options. "You guys in town for the game?" Stupid. "Think you'll win?" Equally stupid. "You mind if I ask you a few questions?" Too FBI. "You guys students at Michigan State?" Too, um, pedophile. As I ponder this I lock eyes with the guy with the green hair, and it just pops out: "Between you and me, I think the green sweats are a little over the top."

He laughs a bit. "They're kinda hot," he says.

"You should watch that," I say. "If you sweat, your face will run." He laughs again, then falls silent. He's not going to make it easy, but I'm on a roll. "So let me guess," I say. "Louisville fan?"

He opens his mouth to speak, but before he does his buddy with the sleeveless shirt leans forward and looks over at me. He throws me a crab flex with both arms curled in front of his body and yells, "STATE!" The entire place stops and turns to look. He faces the room, thrusts a fist in the air, and once again yells, "STATE!" Other MSU fans in the place start to cheer and whoop, which of course leads the Illinois fans and Louisville fans to start sounding off, too. When the dust settles, we fall into an earnest debate about MSU's chances.

"You guys can't consistently hit the three," I argue.

"You're crazy," sleeveless guy spits. "Neitzel can shoot it. Ager can shoot it. Ager's a great shooter. How many times have you seen Michigan State play?"

"Inconsistent and streaky," I counter. "You can play off those guys to stop the penetration, and Paul Davis just isn't strong enough to make it happen inside without those treys falling."

Sleeveless is apoplectic. Others are drawn in, mostly MSU

fans, although a few Illinois followers pipe up as well. Meanwhile the rounds keep coming. Sleeveless's friends have caught on that I'm baiting him with my anti-Spartans arguments and are now finding the heights of outrage and disbelief my criticisms inspire in him to be funny.

And so it goes, until more than an hour later we've reached only one conclusion: It's time to leave for the arena. My new friends don't have tickets - they're planning to stay and watch from the bar — so they won't be coming with me or become my posse for the entire weekend, but as we clink and share one last good-luck toast, I realize that we had fun while it lasted.

★ A buzz of pregame excitement fills the streets outside the Edward Jones Dome. School colors permeate the crowd. Face paint abounds. On every corner, people yell into cell phones, trying to arrange last-minute ticket deals. Those not lucky enough to score some jam into makeshift sports bars that have popped up on the streets surrounding the arena — tents or trailers that serve beer and have a phalanx of TVs hung from the framework.

Inside, the building pulses with even greater excitement. People hustle to find their seats. TV commentators and their bright lights ring the court for their pregame lead-ins. The teams in the first game — Illinois and Louisville - run through their drills, the familiar squeak of sneakers and the thud of basketballs set off a warm thrill of expectation, and every dunk in the lay-up line brings a cheer. Each school's fans have been allotted a corner, effectively color-coding the stadium, so it's easy to figure out who is where. The sections in between are corporate ticket-holders, but even among them are little strongholds of orange or green or blue or red.

The alumni-watching is fascinating. Older folks in their sixties and seventies amble around wearing T-shirts of their alma maters so new I can still see the creases where they were folded on the shelf. Then there are the Carolina swells, who all seem finely turned out in high-end baby blue sweaters, or better yet, blue and white argyle sweater vests accented with tasseled loafers and no socks. Most prominent are the packs of middle-age white guys squeezing into tattered old school sweatshirts or sporting button-down shirts tucked into jeans and secured with a thin dress belt. They're trying to make their casual Friday wardrobes look like college Friday cool, and the mismatch serves as a visual reminder — a virtual billboard — of exactly how large a gulf exists between who they are now and the former version of themselves they are trying to recapture. I realize that this is exactly what I would look like if I were here with my old college friends (although, I know enough to dress age-appropriately) reliving our glory days, but I feel that my status as a solo flier on a vision quest allows me to point fingers at my own kind as if I weren't one of them.

The pep bands crank out happy, pulse-raising tunes. I talk to one kid in the Illinois band, a trombone player with orange and blue stripes on his face and a huge orange afro wig. "This is fantastic," he says. "I still don't realize how big it is. I probably won't realize until I look back on it in twenty years. And Bill Murray's here. He was great. He came down and shook hands with all of us."

Murray, an Illinois native, is there in the Illini section in a bright orange tie and brown vest. A few sections over sits the actor Vince Vaughn, raised in Lake Forest, Illinois, and presumably an Illini fan, although if that's true it's hard to tell, since he wears not a shred of orange but all black. Besides these sprinklings of Hollywood, though, the place is notable for its lack of theatrics. Unlike an NBA game, the lights aren't dimmed and the players aren't brought out with fireworks and lasers and WWE-like introductions. And unlike the Super Bowl, there are no pregame concerts and celebrity-studded on-court presentations.

Instead, the Illinois band plays the anthem under a bank of game lights so bright and clear they're like a sunny afternoon on the Alaskan tundra. Actual cheerleaders — not strippers dancing with their clothes on — exude actual enthusiasm, and men run on the court with those big flags you don't see anywhere but college sports. The pointlessness of a guy running around a court with a huge flag is somehow emblematic of what college ball is all about. Whatever the NCAA gets wrong — and that's quite a bit — it at least gets one thing right: The games are about the contest between the two teams and the sheer unbounded passion that allows people to go nuts over what is largely a pointless enterprise.

My seat is in the third row, and as play begins I'm immediately reminded of the particular intensity of seeing a basketball game up close. The thud of the ball and the rumble of the two teams sprinting down the floor together are physical sensations — you see, hear, and feel them. When you peek up at the Jumbotron and see a picture of Rick Pitino yelling at his team, you can also hear Pitino's voice reaching across the floor. The court looks tiny, crammed with massive players who don't seem like they can all fit out there at once, and they are so fast that what little space there is gets eaten up in an instant.

The fans are incredible. The Louisville faithful don't embarrass themselves in the noise and enthusiasm departments, but they can't match the Illinois crowd, who seem to be here in the largest numbers. And not only are they extremely loud, but they do those cool, old-school Big Ten call-and-response cheers. "I-L-L!" one section shouts — there's a pause — "I-N-I!" the other half finishes. It's like a scene from *Hoosiers*.

The players don't notice any of it. Watching their faces, you can see they're caught up in the intensity of the moment. Illinois's Deron Williams goes up for a three-pointer and Otis George comes charging out at him, a look of frenzied insanity on his face as he yells, "AYYYYY, ah, ah, ah, ah." Louisville's Taquan Dean fights through some physical defense, hits his shot, and yells, "Take that, motherfucker," as he runs back down the court. Later, George and teammate Ellis Myles exchange heated words after a defensive breakdown. It's a good game. The score is tight, right up until Illinois pulls away with less than ten minutes left.

The Louisville fans are bummed, but they don't leave the building. That's how captivating these games are. Even if your team is out of it and you're a little depressed, there's no way you would consider skipping the second showdown. There's just too much on the line.

Almost immediately, the energy starts building for the next game. The Carolina fans are suspiciously quiet, and I turn to ask the two guys behind me what's up. We'd talked for a while earlier, so I know they are both Carolina supporters who live in the Raleigh-Durham area, and one of them even grew up in Louisville. "Forget them," says John, the younger of the two. "It's a total wine-and-cheese crowd. It's worse at a football game. If you ever want to have a good time, don't go to a Carolina football game. A basketball game on campus is pretty good, but anywhere else, I don't know . . ."

Michigan State fills up any void. The faithful are not as numerous as the Illini, but because they have that Big Ten connection, the Illinois fans take up their cause. Together they rock the building with an echoing "GO WHITE!" — pause — "GO GREEN!" chant. I decide that I have to get a closer look at what it's like up there among the possessed, so during a stop in play I make my way up into the State section. There are no recognizable seating assignments at this point, as everyone is standing. I slip into the end of a row. The sound is deafening. Carolina point guard Raymond Felton is bringing the ball upcourt and the State faithful are hopping up and down and yelling "ohhhhhhh" to try to unnerve him. The arena itself seems to be shaking, and as I'm taking in the scene the guy next to me glances over, a questioning look on his face as he observes my nonbouncing, nonshouting state. Suddenly self-conscious, I start hopping and screaming.

Carolina scores, but when they next come down the court I don't hesitate: I'm hopping and yelling again. I'm rewarded for my effort, too. This time Carolina turns the ball over, and my bleacher mates explode in applause. As the team settles in on offense the section goes still with anticipation. State makes a shot and we go wild — clapping, screaming, letting loose with ear-piercing whistles. The guy next to me turns and thrusts a hand in the air; instinctively I slap him a high-five. I'm one of them now. My mere presence has announced me as an assumed comrade, and as long as I don't do anything to indicate otherwise, I'm accepted as part of the crew, no questions asked.

As the half proceeds, we continue to shout, bounce, chant, and generally go nuts. Every possession is a cause for face-contorting tension. When critical junctures come we pound on the seatbacks in front of us, which makes a sound like a hard rain falling on the roof of a tent. We lock arms and sway. Adrenaline flows. Sweat beads on my forehead. Our unofficial and unquestioned leader is a hairy guy with no shirt and a big green S painted on his chest. He runs up and down the aisles, whipping us into a frenzy. It's a total blast.

When the second half starts, I'm back in my real seat. My stint among the foam-finger set lasted all of thirteen minutes on the game clock, and I'm exhausted and I feel like I need a shower. From the relative calm and quiet of a third-row seat at a Final Four game, I continue to look up at the section where I'd joined the crazy brigade. On the one hand, I don't miss it — it's comfortable and I can see a lot better from here — but on the other hand, it sure was fun to lose myself in the action for a while. That is, after all, what we're all doing here: stepping outside ourselves. Not just those of us in the arena with tickets. Sure, our proximity allows us to feel less foolish about colored wigs and shows of emotion, but the same thing is happening to lesser degrees in the bars outside, back on the campuses of the schools involved, in the cities they are near, and everywhere anyone has a rooting interest. Maybe that's the joy of these sporting events? That they allow us to jostle on a sea of frivolity that we don't normally get to?

It's possible, but it doesn't make me feel any better when MSU, which I've sort of adopted, loses.

I shuffle out among the masses, and to my surprise there isn't really any sense of loss and dejection in the air. In fact, there's a sort of afterglow, an energy pulsing through the crowd not unlike the sugar high a four-year-old rides for an hour or so after eating a piece of birthday cake. We're all still floating on the game's leftover energy. That couldn't be clearer than when we emerge out the main doors.

There, hundreds of people crowd onto the sidewalk in a frenzy of activity and excitement. It looks like a scene from the Chicago Mercantile Exchange, with people flashing fingers and shouting numbers as they frantically negotiate with one another. It takes me a minute to realize what's going on: The fans of the two losing teams are selling off their tickets to the final game. I wade into the crowd. "Need one, need one," a guy yells at me, holding up a single finger, a pleading look on his face. Around the periphery, men offer wordless come-ons, standing silently with fingers in the air, four, two, one, representing how many tickets they're hoping to buy. "Upper tier, for $300? I paid $250 to get eighth row this afternoon," one guy protests. Wads of cash flash everywhere.

I make my way back to the Study Hall to see if my friends are still around. I can't find them, but I wish I could. I want to tell them about my antics rooting for their team. I want to tell them how, for a little while, I became one of them.

★ Sunday is a day of rest for the basketball players and recovery for their followers. By noon I'm back at Laclede's Landing, cruising the scene for the greasiest pulled-pork sandwich I can find. I buy a sandwich at an outdoor stand and decide to eat at a table in an adjacent courtyard. First, though, I step into a bar to get myself an iced tea. The place reeks of stale beer, BO, and smoke. Three guys at the counter talk to the sole bartender. "Budweiser," one says.

"Nope," says the bartender, checking his inventory.

"Bud Light?"

"Nope."

"Heineken?"

"Nope."

"Rolling Rock?"

"Hold on," the bartender says. He walks to the far end of the bar and slides open a cooler. "I've got two Miller Lites. You wanna split 'em?"

The guys look at each other and discuss going elsewhere. "Same thing everywhere," the bartender says. "Until the delivery trucks come, everyone is tapped out."

Oh my God! They've drunk St. Louis out of beer!

With my tea and sandwich, I head for the courtyard, since it's an even more perfect day than yesterday. The people who've emerged by this time are a little more subdued than they had been last night. Small klatches sit sipping coffee and sharing quiet conversations. A mother and her son work a crossword puzzle over eggs and muffins.

I'm halfway through my lunch when three ghosts of parties past appear. They are weary and bedraggled, pale, with dark circles under their eyes and unshaven mugs. They hide behind orange Illinois caps pulled down low over their eyes. As the woman selling the sandwiches fumbles to make change, she says to them, "Sorry, I'm a little slow today."

"That's okay," one of them replies, "I'm not moving too fast myself." To my great delight they gather their stuff and sit at the table next to me. I immediately begin eavesdropping, but there isn't much to hear. Mostly chewing and grunting interrupted by occasional mumbles and a bit of low snickering or bewildered head-shaking. The brief bursts of conversation seem to be recounting last night's adventures, and one of them definitely seems to be taking the brunt of the abuse. With each assault, he stops, lifts his chin, and repeats some sort of mantra, which I can't quite make out but for the words "bitch slapping."

Still, it seems vaguely familiar, and I spend a good part of my lunch trying first to hear it clearly and then to place it. Finally, he says it again and with the casualness of someone asking the time, I say, "Where's that from?"

"What?" he says, looking down at his shirt.

"That line," I say. "You keep saying that line. Where's it from?"

"Oh," he says. "Um, have you seen *Deuce Bigalow*?"

I can't believe my luck. I tell them about seeing Rob Schneider at the Super Bowl and that's it, I'm in. The Schneider story leads to the larger Super Bowl story, which leads to the story about my yearlong quest to hit the ten greatest sports events. It also takes me into my Villanova story and that in turn leads to *Sports Illustrated,* which leads to the Swimsuit Issue and Rick Reilly — of course. It seems to go over well.

In return I get their stories. All three are juniors, from various parts of Illinois. The tallest one introduces himself as CD. He has light brown hair and wears flip-flops, faded jeans, and a T-shirt with a caricature of college hoops analyst Dick Vitale on the front under the words, "I'm a moron, baby!" The second guy is Leo, who's shorter but also thin and athletic-looking, with darker hair, and sideburns that reach down the sides of his face. His orange Illinois T-shirt proclaims "We love Head" across the back, referring presumably to Illini guard Luther Head. The third guy is squatter and even more disheveled. He wears shorts and a standard Illinois shirt that's faded and threadbare. His wavy hair sits atop a round face that's punctuated with a patch of brown hair on his chin. His name is Steve Muccero, which has been wonderfully smushed together to form the nickname Smooch.

By the time we've covered all that ground, it's after 1:00 P.M. We've definitely bonded, but we're at a natural breaking point, and I like these guys, so I make a bold move. "I'm thinking about heading to one of those places down the street that's already gotten its beer delivery. You boys interested?" They are, and just around the corner we find a place with tables, free pretzels, and beer to spare. Score!

We settle into our afternoon, talking sports — not just college hoops, but college football, NFL, baseball. We solve most of the big problems, everything from the Bowl Championship Series (we opt for a limited playoff using existing bowl games) to steroids (zero tolerance) and come up with an exhaustive list of the ways in which Donald Fehr, head of baseball's players association, should be tortured. Most important, I teach them to throw, a practice of making decisions through binding rounds of rock, paper, scissors that my friends and I used in college.

Eventually, Smooch wants to move to another bar, but Leo is resisting. I suggest we throw for it. Being only college students themselves, they agree that this seems like a sane and reasonable way to settle disputes. By the third throw, Smooch eliminates everyone else, so we give up our now coveted seats and step out into the late-afternoon sun.

The roadway and sidewalks have grown considerably more crowded and a few doors down a DJ works outside one of the bars, blasting music that fills the street. In front of the DJ, women —

coaxed out of the crowd — dance provocatively on top of large round planters that have not yet sprouted any flowers. This is enough to stop our crew, who take up a position on the edge of the curb and buy beer from one of the several outdoor bars that have been set up along the street. If it doesn't quite qualify as a carnival atmosphere, that changes when a guy shows up with a monkey on his shoulder. The primate, Elvis, wears a diaper and occasionally races down his handler's arm to take a sip of the man's brew. The DJ eventually busts out the bane of wedding goers everywhere, the Electric Slide, and as if we've suddenly been transformed into a scene from *Ferris Bueller's Day Off,* an entire section of the street breaks into unified, choreographed dance.

There is an unhurried air to the day. We are basically spending time wasting time, and it is that more than the T-shirts and the marching bands and the rah-rah of school spirit that evoke the feeling of college. When else does a person have such a radical oversupply of these three particular things: time, friends, alcohol?

Maybe that's the appeal of these big events — they allow us to revisit a life where we had fewer responsibilities and more fun. When it was not only okay but virtually expected that we would spend a Sunday afternoon pursuing a whole list of activities that wouldn't be acceptable in our other, more corporate, politically correct lives. If there is a defining ethic to the week thus far, it would be youthful exuberance.

There certainly seems to be evidence of such a phenomenon afoot. Leo points out a woman in her mid-fifties walking past wearing a shirt that says: "Live Long, Love Well, Shag Often." The incongruity of this seemingly dignified, silver-tinged woman wearing a shirt you might expect to see at a frat party strikes a chord and we adopt the slogan. Whenever we get a fresh round of beer, we touch glasses: "Live long, love well, shag often." At one point a girl standing on a porch reaches down, flips up her skirt, and reveals the two perfect, well-tanned globes of her ass, separated only by a thin piece of fabric. "Hoooo," yells CD, the only one of my newfound buddies who has a steady girlfriend, as he lifts his beer: "Live long, love well, shag often."

At one point we stand on a corner, throwing to decide our next move, when the crowd parts and bouncing down the road comes none other than recently defeated vice-presidential candidate John Edwards. His hair is perfect and he wears a blue oxford with the sleeves rolled up and a pair of chinos. As he goes by, yells of "Hey, John!" and "You should have won!" rise around him. Although he looks like he could be, he's not campaigning today, and if there is any joy behind the big smile plastered across his John Boy face you get the sense it's because he doesn't have to stop and talk to anyone. After he's gone, everyone sort of looks at one another as if to ask, "Did you see what I just saw?"

"Live long, love well, shag often," CD announces in the afterglow. So we raise our plastic cups and drink one to the former senator from North Carolina.

★ As it grows later, my crew becomes more and more focused on the night's romantic opportunities. This is fine enough at first, although it forces me into a role in which I become less one of the boys and more avuncular consultant. Still, I've got some worthy advice, which I dispense willingly, and the guys seem happy to have it or at least polite enough to act happy.

By 10:00 P.M. we've come to rest along a chainlink fence that borders a parking lot. A huge tent covers the lot and there's a concert going on inside, which is so loud that even from this distance my chest rattles. The guys have run into another group of friends from school, two dudes and five women, and they are chatting it up, which has pushed me even further to the periphery.

From there I watch the crowds of students and alumni and general fans stagger up and down the streets, which by now are filled with bottle caps, smashed plastic cups, empty cans, and broken glass. They sing and yell to each other and occasionally break into a chant. The flow of it all is suddenly interrupted when a scrum bursts out of the side of the tent in a mass of yelling and scuffling. A few bouncers are ejecting two guys from the concert, and those guys are followed by some of their friends. The bouncers, huge, beefy guys, manhandle the offenders, seeming to be rougher than necessary, and one woman screams at them to take it easy, arguing that it wasn't their fault (whatever "it" is).

The entire disturbance doesn't last more than three minutes and it takes all of ten seconds afterward for the crowd of gawkers to resume their pursuits. Dumb college kids getting beat on by bouncers shouldn't surprise me, but this scene stays with me. Perhaps it's because such ugliness was not part of my vision, my expectation. I struggle to get back the carefree feeling that had seen me through an afternoon of drinking and shooting the shit with my new friends.

But no sooner have I pushed out the memory of the fight when another couple comes stumbling down the street. They're so drunk or stoned or whatever that they literally can't walk. They're arm in arm, leaning on each other while a third friend holds them up. But when she lets go for a moment, they tumble hard to the ground.

They are incapable of getting off the ground, and their friends must help them to the curb. The guy sits and stares, as if he's just woken up and he can't figure out what all these people are doing in his bedroom. The girl begins to cry. It doesn't seem as if she's hurt, although it wouldn't be surprising if she was, but for whatever reason, or maybe none at all, she sobs, and great tears that glint in the streetlights roll down her face.

My guys, unperturbed, have returned to their affairs. Earlier in the day Leo had spoken with passion about the big game. "It would be great if we won," he said. "Our players weren't the best players coming out of high school, but they worked really hard to get good, and they play as a team, which makes them better, so I feel like we deserve it." And all three of the guys seem to know a lot about the team and the players and its explosive three-guard offense, but we've never once raised our glasses and said, "Go Illini."

Maybe I'm reading too much into it, but on the heels of the fight and the fall-down incoherent drunks something starts to feel wrong about the whole scene. I want to call that girl's parents, so they can come pick her up. I want to tell those bouncers to leave that kid alone, he's drunk and probably in the wrong, but he's just a kid. If they want to beat on someone why not go up the street and get after the forty-five-year-old pillars of society who are sliding their wedding rings in their pockets and buying Mardi Gras beads by the handful.

I take a minute to note the similarities between my first three big sporting events: beer, women being encouraged — and happily complying with requests — to disrobe, beer, street parties, games, beer, and ESPN and Fox Sports sound stages, which seem to attach themselves to these things like ticks on an elephant's ass. Perhaps it's a cumulative effect but it's suddenly too much, the drinking, the carrying on, the desperate attempts to get in the background of a *College GameDay* broadcast.

I had ridden the wave of frivolity all day, rolled with the good times and the easy conversation. But everyone has his limit, and it seems like I am hitting mine. What had been an afternoon — admittedly a long afternoon — of harmless fun is threatening to reveal itself as something more sinister and untoward. I'm not prepared to let that happen, not to one of my ten events.

I tell the guys I've got to go. We exchange phone numbers and make vague plans to hook up tomorrow for the big game. I'm trying to shake the bad feelings, but they are pressing in around me. Walking back through the crowd, past the thumping nightclubs, the packs drinking in the streets, the masses crowded into beer tents, talking on cell phones, trying to scalp tickets, I realize that while I'm not wearing an old sweatshirt or a thin belt, I might as well be, and a sense of self-loathing rises in my gut like so much pulled pork and beer.

I reach the hotel, cross the lobby, and lean against a rail overlooking a restaurant and lounge. As I look across the space I see Jim Gray, the ESPN reporter. Gray made a name for himself in 1999 when, after a ceremony for baseball's greatest players at the World Series, he ambushed Pete Rose with tough questions about his history of betting. It was a celebratory night and a baseball high point for Rose since his banishment from the game. Afterward, a lot of people criticized Gray, saying he'd been overly aggressive and it wasn't the right time or place for those questions. To me the timing of the questions was awkward, but Rose has always struck me as a liar and a bit of an ass, so I didn't much care. Moreover, I have a lot of respect for Gray. He's well-prepared, he thinks on his feet, and he's fearless.

I lean on the rail. Gray leans on the rail directly across from me. A steady trickle of fans approaches, asking for autographs, taking photos with him. He handles it very well, friendly and accommodating, but something about it bothers me. Who does Gray think he is? Where does he get off signing autographs? Just because he's on TV? Slowly the feeling of self-hatred raging within me transfers to Gray. He becomes the new target of my anger and disillusionment. After fifteen minutes, I can't take it anymore. Someone has to set Gray straight, not just about his seeming sense of self-importance but about his role in the Rose fiasco, and since none of the fans seem to do anything but suck up, the job falls to me.

I wait until there's no one else around, then approach him. "Hi, Jim," I say. "Hi," he says, offering a smile. In the next moment I notice all those things that don't show up on camera: He's better-looking although a bit older than he appears on TV, and he's smaller, too. The phenomenon passes. I'm unmoved. I launch. "I need to tell you that of all the preposterous, ill-timed, self-aggrandizing assaults that the media have inflicted on itself in the previous half-decade, your stunt with Rose is among the most egregious, unnecessary, and disheartening."

Clearly startled, Gray leans back a bit. I can see him formulating a response, but I can't sense if he will be apologetic or defensive. Finally, he squints, shakes his head from side to side, and says, "Whaaa?"

My words play back in my head: "I nee t-tell you tha ovv all the preposperous . . ." I'm suddenly aware that it is after eleven and I have been drinking since one. I use the back of my sleeve to wipe away the spittle that has accumulated on my lips, turn around, stumble to my room, flop down on top of the covers fully dressed, and go immediately to sleep.

★ Monday afternoon is bright and sunny even if my head remains a little foggy with beer and disillusionment. As I stand on the corner, a small white car speeds up to the Edward Jones Dome. The door swings open and like clowns from a Yugo, out climb the Kansas Jayhawk, the Duke Blue Devil, the Syracuse Orange, the Missouri Tiger, and the Kentucky Wildcat. On the sidewalk in the afternoon sun, their bright colors and oversize features seem even louder and more cartoonish than they do inside an arena. They stand and talk for a minute, then gather themselves and bound off toward the arena like puppies let off a leash. This helps. I realize that an event that allows a grown man to put a giant orange on his head and run around like an extra in a Richard Simmons video can't be that bad.

Upon reflection, it was not so much the night's drinking and mayhem, the March Madness, if you will, that got to me. After all, unruly behavior has long gone hand in hand with bigtime sports. I may not be a frat boy anymore, but I was once. No, sports as a chance to escape is okay with me. What's bothering me is something else, though I can't say exactly what it is.

My cell phone rings and I recognize Smooch's number. I don't answer. The stuff that brought me down last night wasn't his or anyone's fault. They were typical things that happen when large gatherings of people get together and step outside the strictures and concerns of everyday life. It's definitely part of the culture at these big sport events but not the sum total of what they're about, as it might be in, say, Vegas or Key West. Beer, sex, gambling, the proverbial stuffed underbelly of sports. I don't want to pretend that it doesn't exist — or that I didn't have a good time visiting it for most of yesterday — but I have no desire to go back there today. Especially now that the mascots have perked up my mood. At this point I just want to see the final and get out of town. The game has become a formality.

Except that the game is a joy.

The Illini fans are so plentiful, an entire third of the arena is solid orange, with large pockets of the same color spread throughout. When they all join in on one of those "ILL-INI" chants, it hurts my ears to the point that I actually wince. I'm making that face universally understood to signal that something is too loud —

eyes squinted, corners of mouth pulled out, head scrunched between shoulders like a turtle — but this is no pantomime. Armed with a fresh load of blue and white pompons, the Carolina fans have taken it up a notch for the big night as well. They're louder and they answer with a "TAR-HEEL!"

While the game is under way, a steady beat of clapping and drums raise the pulse, adding a tribal bloodlust to the air. Except for in the corporate sections, which stick out because they're neither blue nor orange, no one sits. Although Carolina seems to control the game, it's tight, and the fans rise and fall on every play. With every pass, every missed shot, every contested dribble, the roar ebbs and flows. When Illinois scores, the fans behind me stampede in place so that the whole floor shakes.

By the second half, Carolina is up by fifteen, but as Illinois makes a run, the impossible happens: The intensity increases by another order of magnitude. When the Illini tie the score with five minutes left, I'm sure the Illinois fans are actually going to start pulling the seats out of the floor and hanging them together. The players are never more incredible: It's so loud that cogent thought is barely possible, but the players are unaffected inside the bubble of their own intensity.

In the end, though, Illinois has spent too much energy catching up, and Carolina makes too many plays coming down the stretch. As the clock runs out, the ceiling explodes and streamers fall from the sky and cover the court. The air fills with the scent of a lit match. The Carolina players run and jump and throw their arms in the air. They drape themselves in 2005 National Champion hats and T-shirts. Carolina fans stream down and press in around the court. A few of the players rush into the crowd to give hugs and high-fives to friends and family. Then they begin the ritual cutting down of the nets.

I wander out onto the court. Rashad McCants hops by, barechested, holding up his Carolina jersey for all to see. I look up to the Illinois section, where rivers of orange flow out of the gates like rusty water through a drain. Roy Williams gives one of his patented "Aw, shucks" speeches (which seems totally insincere), and on the large monitors over the court plays the CBS recap video, a montage of shots and moments from the entire tournament spliced together and played over a cheesy song — "One Shining Moment" — meant to evoke the greatest degree of emotion and nostalgia. No one seems more enraptured by this maudlin production than the players themselves. And as I stand there, watching them watch us watch them do what they've just done, I get a shock of nearly perfect postmodern glee.

Of course the players love seeing themselves up there on the screen. They've probably been watching these sentimental recaps since they were kids. Picturing themselves receiving the heroic glaze of elegiac slow motion is probably at least part of what drove them to excel at the game in the first place. Part of what makes these ten events so special, I realize, is the sheer ritual of them: the traditions, the matchups, the memories of people and places.

When we watch the Super Bowl or the Final Four or whatever, we're in some way rewatching all the Super Bowls that have come before, and we're reconnecting with the people we were with and the places we were when we watched them. And while that bittersweet experience is one of the things that keeps us coming back, we can never actually return to those people or that time. My mistake was that I didn't attend the Final Four for its own sake and let part of the experience be the way it reminded me of 1985. Instead I tried to actually re-create 1985, and that — an impossibility — led to my problems. I'll never watch another Final Four without thinking of CD, Leo, and Smooch, but I'll never try to go back and recapture that afternoon with them either.

As I walk off the court, I pass a Carolina fan standing along the edge of the bleachers, talking into a cell phone. "I'm done," he says. "Been there. Done that. That's it."

He's right.

4 ★ The Masters

April 7–10, 2005

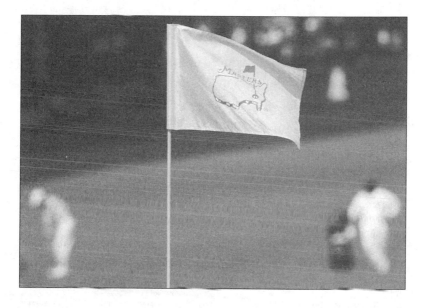

Augusta, Georgia

L ESS THAN EIGHTEEN HOURS after arriving home from the Final Four, I find myself on a strip of grass bordering a traffic-clogged four-lane road in Augusta, Georgia, sizing up John Daly's merchandise trailer. Some afternoons, Daly sits out here signing autographs while people line up to buy something from his emporium of golf trinkets — everything from John Daly shot glasses ($6) and ball buckets ($10) to one of his signed replica golf bags ($400). Augusta National Golf Club, home of the Masters, sits about a mile up the road.

The tournament comes at a perfect time in this quest. The first three events, by coincidence, were all beer and testosterone celebrations with a sort of lowest-common-denominator appeal to the grunting, monosyllabic Neanderthal in all of us, whether that's our usual state or just a persona we slip on for the big game. The Masters promises to be different — less cluttered, more pure. In my head I revisit an image of the club, tucked away on some pristine, pastoral swath of land, a little oasis of golf among the rolling hills and swaying Georgia pines. To put it in Freudian terms, if the Super Bowl and the Final Four are a projection of the sports world's id (its inner child run amok), the Masters will be all super-ego — control, repression, plaid outerwear.

There's one catch. I have to get inside the gates first, a feat that requires scalping a ticket while traversing the blight of Washington Road, a chain-store-and-strip-mall-pocked street that runs right past the National. Although one could probably find a similar strip in almost every medium-size community in the country, the contrast between this one and the famous club it runs past is jarring. During tournament week, it has the additional burden of playing host to dozens of scalpers, roadside merchants selling everything

from cars to cannabis, and various preachers, punks, and repro-
bates who tread its concrete sidewalks.

Already I've passed T-Bonz, a middling steakhouse and bar that
passes for fine dining in the area — not much of a feat, considering that the competition includes a drive-through fast-food Italian
place and a chicken joint with a marquee that reads: "Two can dine
for $7.99." Otherwise, it's chain city: TGI Friday's, Lone Star, Ol-
ive Garden, and SONIC Burger. Parked next to a Hooters, Daly's
trailer, in one way, blends in perfectly among the jumble of signs
and lights and prefab ugliness.

Yet it stands out, so that I feel compelled to stop along the way
and admire it. I can't help but marvel at the results of thinking
small. Among pro golfers, Daly's popularity is rivaled only by that
of Tiger Woods, but while Woods has a staff of MBAs maximizing
his leverage as a global brand, Daly has an RV with a cash register.
Of course, the difference between Daly's down-home approach to
business and Tiger's (or even Augusta's) style of cold corporate cal-
culation is part of what makes him so popular to begin with. At the
same time, it's emblematic of the wasted talent and lost opportunity that have marked his career.

Daly burst onto the golf scene by getting into the 1991 PGA
Championship as an alternate. After driving all night to make his
tee time, the chubby, mullet-wearing twenty-five-year-old from Arkansas went on to win the event. Four years later he triumphed at
the British Open, played that year on the Old Course at St. An-
drews. The self-proclaimed redneck had won his second major at
the home of golf. But his enormous skills came with an aircraft
carrierful of personal baggage: alcohol abuse, gambling problems,
wild behavior, a lack of responsibility. He leavened these short-
comings with his soft personal touch. He may not show up for a
tournament he'd committed to, but there was also a chance he
would arrive, hear a sob story from a fan, pull out a wad of bills,
and hand over a few hundred bucks on the spot.

Fifteen years later, a guy who had the talent to provide Tiger
Woods everything he could've handled in a rival has won five times
on the PGA Tour. He's just filed for divorce from his fourth wife,

who recently served five months in federal prison on a money-laundering conviction, and written his second autobiography, *My Life In and Out of the Rough,* which includes further revelations about his ongoing issues with booze, betting, and sex addiction.

And yet, Daly is beloved by fans. On another level he represents something unique to sports, a connection between the fans and the games. Sports — like everything else in a media world filled not just with newspapers and network TV coverage but with hundreds of cable channels, Web sites, and blogs — is subject to unprecedented scrutiny, leading to a seemingly never-ending parade of controversy, analysis, and scandal. In the last months, stories about NBA players brawling with fans, steroids in baseball, college players hiring escort services and committing acts from assault to rape, to sundry other offenses including weapons charges, domestic violence incidents, and a string of DWI busts have all made headlines.

Fans don't seem to care. They're acutely aware of these infractions and can discuss them at length — everybody's ready for his ESPN close-up — but it doesn't stop them from going to or enjoying the games. The controversy and scandal live somewhere else, on some other plane. They're good for debating in the bar or for berating the opposition, but they've got little to do with the game.

Most fans, in fact, will tell you that the media focuses too much on the negative (although I can tell you that articles about scandals or controversial players are often the best read). What most fans seem to want is affirmation. They want to see their favorite team or player recognized, analyzed, or praised. People don't hate Dick Vitale just because he heaps so much praise on Duke. That's a big part of it, but they also hate him because the Duke love comes at their team's expense — by the time he's done slurping up Coach K, there is no time or superlative left for anyone else. Fans seek that validation. It's all about reflected glory, baby.

I know, because I've needed it, too. I used to watch Giants games on TV, and if they won I'd watch the highlights on ESPN *PrimeTime* because I wanted to hear Chris Berman do his shtick about the mighty G-men, as he calls them. Not only was the praise satisfying in itself, but so was the idea that such love was being broadcast to the larger sports-watching public. That's why TV is such a large part of these bigtime events. TV validates the experience. If it's important, it must be on TV, and if it's on TV, it must be important.

Augusta National is no stranger to any of this. In the last few years it's been embroiled, to varying degrees, in a controversy about its lack of female members. After the initial protest was railroaded out of town, the club hasn't met much resistance to its policy, except for a few dozen pieces written each year, but the issue continues to hang over the place and the tournament. Fans haven't cared at all. It has not hurt the TV ratings or the attendance.

Maybe I'm part of the problem. Personally I feel that the club should admit women, and not just one token. Private clubs have the right to restrict their membership, and there are certainly plenty of women-only organizations around the country. But, as others before me have pointed out, Augusta is not a truly private club. It holds a seat on the World Golf Foundation alongside the PGA Tour, PGA of America, the USGA, and the LPGA, giving it an equal footing with the game's other organizing bodies in an industry oversight group. Incidentally, all of those other groups have antidiscrimination clauses that prevent them from playing at clubs that don't have open memberships. So none but Augusta could sanction an event at Augusta.

Several Augusta members sit on the executive board of the USGA, the governing body of golf in the United States, including the last two presidents. I understand that it's possible to do the mental gymnastics necessary to belong to a club that discriminates against women and yet still run an organization that oversees the U.S. Women's Open and the U.S. Women's Amateur and is responsible for selling the game to young girls. But the mixed message it sends, the "Do as I say and not as I do" paternalism, is indefensible.

In addition, the club has repeatedly raised the possibility of using a special tournament ball that doesn't fly as far as current golf balls in order to protect the course's design values. Such a switch could literally change the sport. That's a very powerful position for a private club to be in. The members would like to have it both ways, claiming the club and the tournament are two separate things, but they are not. The tournament is run by the club, and together they give Augusta National a very influential place in the game, which is why I don't think the "We're a private club" defense holds up.

At the same time, I would never skip the Masters. As with the controversies surrounding other sports, the stuff that happens away from the game itself is different. The controversy adds a layer of corrosion to the exterior, but at its core the Masters and its mission remain unsullied, pure: the greatest players in the world competing on one of the sport's best courses.

★ I have a ticket for Thursday's opening round, but it's only Wednesday and I'd like to get in to see the practice rounds, which are more relaxed and less crowded. So I leave John Daly and his trailer behind and head toward the club, following a bare path that has been trampled into the grass in lieu of a sidewalk. Along the path, groups of men in shorts and polo shirts stand holding big pieces of cardboard that say "I need tickets — practice rounds," which in the upside-down world of scalping often means "Tickets for Sale." Above them, a huge yellow billboard with red letters dominates the airspace: "Golf Badges wanted. Top $ paid. Strictly confidential."

I've chatted up a few of them but haven't struck a deal yet. I'm wary. Every year the police bust a few out-of-town scalpers the week before the tournament and make sure it gets plenty of coverage on the local news to try to discourage the practice, and I don't want to become a poster boy. Still, I know most scalping goes unchecked. In fact, many of the locals who receive tickets every year sell them off for big money, and the club allegedly turns a blind eye, allowing their neighbors to profit on the tournament as a way to build goodwill in the community.

I stop to buy water from a woman and her twelve-year-old

daughter, who sit on a large blue cooler along the curb across from a Roman-themed hair salon. The white brick building has columns and faux-marble statues out front, and it's windowless, which makes me think it must have once been a massage parlor or go-go bar. It's an anachronism among a string of anachronisms. Here, too, sit the Masters 7 Cinema (a triplex) and the Caddy Shack lounge, and every restaurant, store, and motel has some sort of sign or banner offering glad tidings: "Welcome Golfers." Hundreds of lawn signs planted along the way look like bread crumbs left by some disgraced marketing executive hoping to one day find his way back to the course. They not only offer up tickets, but shill for every little store, lay out the drink specials at the local sports bars, or advertise places to park (most of which come with a "free ride to the course," because we all know how much golfers hate to walk).

The water lady, it turns out, has lived in Augusta most of her life. I ask if she's been to the tournament. "Oh, plenty of times," she says.

"How do you get tickets?" I ask.

"It's easy," she says, explaining that people with daily passes often show up at 7:00 or 8:00 A.M. and leave by three or four in the afternoon, when there's still four hours of golf left to be played. Usually, she assures me, it's simple and relatively cheap to buy those day passes from people as they come out of the gates. I check my watch. It's almost two thirty, and I'm only about halfway to the club. I thank her for the information and get moving.

As I get closer to the entrance, the intensity of the roadside capitalism increases. Instead of coolers and folding tables, here sprout tents and the sort of professional displays one might see at a trade show. The wares range from sunglasses and hats to customized street signs and cigars. A jewelry store has two Nextel Cup racecars (Jeff Gordon's 24 and Tony Stewart's 20, I now recognize) parked out front as part of its effort to sell high-end watches right there on what has now morphed into an actual concrete sidewalk. Pushing luxury goods on the street seems odd, but they may have the right idea. I step into a tent where a man sells fine prints and lithographs of famous golfers and golf scenes. "Pretty pricey stuff," I say, poking around. "This week," he confides, "the more-expensive stuff sells better."

Even the local churches are in on the act. Like good Calvinists, they're both doing good works and seeking financial gain as a way of proving the Lord's love. At the National Hills Baptist Church, a sign out front lets the world know that Sunday mass will be followed by a "Free breakfast" at 9:45. At the massive Whole Life Ministries, they're offering "Welcome Services, Mon–Thurs 7:30 P.M.; Come as you are." As a sign of goodwill, church members stand out front handing out little cups of lemonade with stickers on them that say "A Smile for You." All the better to get people to pull into their gigantic parking lot, where they charge $25 a car. (The meek shall inherit tax-free real estate in a very advantageous location.) And just in case anyone forgot, they also sell film. The nice lady at the table will take your $5.95 for a roll of ASA 400 and then jingle her WWJD bracelet without a hint of irony.

The intersection where the church sits may, in fact, be my favorite spot at the Masters, the ministry on one side, a gas station next to it, and the walk-in entrance to the course — an opening in the long row of tall hedges that line the grounds — across the street. It is the nexus of the Masters hustle, with the ministry selling film, the gas station hawking photos, Pepsi, and "Special this week: A Carton of Marlboros $24.95," and the club itself pushing licensed gear at a small gift shop next to the entrance. Evangelicals preach and street merchants call their wares to the hundreds of people waiting to cross the street. One guy stands on a pallet of water bottles, yelling, "Ice-cold water, one dollar." Five feet away, another guy holds up a life-size crucifix and shouts, "The blood of Jesus washes away your sins." It is an intermingling of the secular and the religious, of bald commercialism and red-state values, an intersection of the American class system — the superrich, the rich, and the struggling to get by — that can't help but be fascinating and yet another reason to love sports: Where else can you go in this country to see our social condition laid so bare?

Outside the hedges I give a kindly gray-haired man forty bucks for his day pass. It's just after three thirty in the afternoon.

★ I'm walking through a grotto of trees, filled with the smell of newly fallen pine needles, past a cluster of low green buildings that include a massive gift shop with an impressive switchbacking walkway that seems like something out of Disney World. Ahead, the darkness created by the overhanging branches is broken by an opening in the tree line where the sun bursts through, sending long shafts of yellow spreading across the ground. This light brings forth a rush of anticipation, because I know that the sun-drenched clearing is the golf course. I find myself walking up on my toes a bit and lifting my chin to get a glimpse. Finally, I clear the forest and I'm here. I'm on the golf course at Augusta National.

The thing that hits me from this spot along the first fairway are the greens. Not the things the players putt on, but the array of green shades. It's green on green. The electric kelly green of an Irishman's underwear on Saint Patty's Day, the dark shadowy green of a still pond, the depth of a Coke bottle, the brightness of a watermelon. Green on green on green. It's like the Eskimos and their fabled vocabulary for variations of snow; I didn't realize there could be so many shades of green until I stood at this spot.

Once I drink in this sea of greens, I notice that the course is more open than I imagined. From here, I can see across six or seven fairways. Sure, there are trees, the famous Georgia pines, but the groves are not as thick, and more strategically spread out than I pictured. Next come the hills. The two-dimensional space of TV flattens out the slopes that the holes climb up and around. It's steeper than I imagined.

It's an odd feeling to be here, staring out at everything I expected combined with so much I could never have dreamed of. I walk out to the rope along the fairway. The grass is incredibly short and cut so that it leans toward the hole. It's yet another shade of green, Granny Smith green, and shiny, so that it looks waxed. Forget about how fast the putting surfaces are, it's hard to fathom how fast these fairways must be. Or as one guy standing nearby says to his wife and buddy, "These are fairways? Look at these fairways! Murph, she doesn't know, would you explain to her what a fairway looks like?"

I head out across the course. I'm sensitive to the things one never sees on TV. The marshals, who open and close the ropes along the fairway so that no one crosses when they're not supposed to, wear white jumpsuits and yellow hardhats with green numbers that correspond to the fairway they guard. On the one hand it's a practical and reasonable outfit — safe, cool, organized — but there's something about it that's also so self-serious as to be laughable. I mean, they're glorified hall monitors, crossing guards protecting pedestrians not from oncoming cars but from golf balls.

I'm also sensitive to the history. To walk the course at Augusta National is to be confronted by a steady barrage of memories and images. As I make my way around the back of the first tee, I can see Snead and Nelson hitting all those ceremonial first shots. Heading down the hill brings me face to face with the ninth green, where Jack Nicklaus made birdie in 1986 to kick off a streak in which he completed the last ten holes in thirty-three strokes for a final-round sixty-five and a historic four-stroke come-from-behind victory. His sixth Green Jacket, won at the age of forty-six.

Then I come to seventeen, the long par four that bends back up the hill to set up the final hole. In the fairway stands the Eisenhower Tree, named after the former president and Augusta National member because he hit his ball into it so many times that for years he campaigned to have it cut down. Beyond seventeen lies the fifteenth, a treacherous par five where make-or-break moments are piled up like so many pine needles, starting with Gene Sarazen's double eagle in 1935 (he holed a four-wood from 235 yards), which propelled him into a playoff. He won the next day in a thirty-six-hole head-to-head showdown.

At last appears Amen Corner, holes eleven, twelve, and thirteen, a par four, par three, and par five that zigzag back and forth over the treacherous Rae's Creek. Here again the moments are overwhelming, popping up in my mind's eye like a highlight reel from The Golf Channel: Mize's chip-in; Couples on the sidehill; Strange hitting into the creek. The physicality of it is striking, too. TV never shows how close the twelfth tee is to the eleventh fairway. It never captures the banked curve of the thirteenth fairway.

I find a terrific spot where I can see the eleventh green, all of twelve, and all of thirteen. For most people, Augusta National exists solely as an image on a TV screen, so upon arriving at the actual place there is a sort of backward recognition. Look at the azaleas and the Hogan Bridge and listen to the water tumbling along Rae's Creek, and I can almost hear Pat Summerall's voice and the tinkling strains of classical music. Instead of the broadcast bringing the place to life, the place animates the broadcast.

I move on toward the sixteenth hole, a perfect place to hang out during a practice round. The short par three requires players to hit the ball over a large pond to a narrow, sloping green. During practice, the huge galleries that sit in the stands around the hole chant "Skip, skip, skip" as players walk off the tee. Depending on how rushed they are and how well their practice is going, maybe half of them drop a ball on the downslope in front of the tee box and hit a low burner that skips across the water and, every now and then, hops up onto the green. Success isn't really the point; players get a huge cheer just for trying.

If the words "carefree" and "raucous" can ever be used in the same sentence as "the Masters," then it's in reference to this spot. Little pockets of betting pop up. When a player stops to hit a skipper, you hear the bettors calling to each other "Wet," or "Dry," to indicate on which result they're placing their money. Betting or not, the people here run the range of types. There are straw boaters, yacht belts, and calico pants beside jeans and T-shirts beside golf chic. The woman next to me wears a white shirt, pink sweater vest, tan shorts, golf shoes, and visor. Does she believe there might be an open tee time for her later in the day?

Perhaps due to the influence of Tiger Woods, there are some brown faces mixed into the crowd, but as with all the other events so far, with the possible exception of the Super Bowl, the crowd is overwhelmingly white. I suspect that has something to do with the price of entry and that the back halls of corporate America, where so many of the tickets are distributed, are still thin on minorities.

This being golf, it is a favorite of the business world, a plum perk. In fact, after leaving the course I meet up with a friend of a friend who works for a large corporation that treats the Masters as a giant networking party. Each year it rents out a number of homes in an upscale gated community not far from the golf course. There, the company's top brass host customers, employees who've performed particularly well that year, and prospects they're trying to woo.

Their guests get passes and shuttle service to the tournament, free rooming in one of the houses, and unlimited golf on one of the courses that sits inside the compound. They also get to come to dinner in the main house each night, which has been cleared of furniture and outfitted with a bar and tables. A celebrity chef prepares incredible meals, and everyone stands around chatting about the food, and the golf, and how fond they are of the host company. Among the people I talk to are hard-core golfers, casual fans who can't identify anyone beyond Tiger Woods and Phil Mickelson, and some folks who don't know the first thing about the game. I meet one guy who keeps checking his cell phone. When I ask why, he tells me that his wife is due the following week and he's nervous the baby will come early. "Why didn't you stay home?" I ask.

"Are you kidding?" he says. "It's the Masters."

"What is it about the Masters that would make you risk missing the birth of your child?"

"It's awesome. It's pure. It's pure golf. Just to see these guys hit these incredible shots, and to be out on the course. It's so beautiful out there. It's not like anything else."

This comment leads me to think more about how the Masters is different. The first three events had their share of corporate fire-sniffers, those who were just there for the experience, to get close to the flame. But they also had their share of die-hard fans, people with a sort of tribal loyalty to a team or individual, people there for the game, specifically to root for a certain outcome. Golf doesn't foster such allegiances. People may have their favorite player — they may really want Tiger to win — but they're mostly there to see a good show. They'd just as soon see their player go by the wayside in exchange for a tense and exciting finale. This may be because so few people are there for the conclusion. I might follow Tiger around on Thursday and Friday, but unless I show up for four straight days — which most attendees don't — I'm not going to see him win or lose. So while I'm there, the investment is not so much in the tournament's outcome as in the progress along the way.

That's why the Masters is so different from other sports. People don't necessarily come here expecting to see the outcome decided. They come to see the course, walk the grounds, stand near their favorites, maybe witness an incredible shot or two. They come to hear the Masters roar.

It's been said that there's nothing like a Masters roar and it's true. At the other events, the crowds were just as loud, but the bursts came amid a steady stream of ambient noise. When a great moment occurs at the Masters, the crowd goes from complete silence to an instant, unified burst of cheering, the aural equivalent of 0 to 100 in one second, which makes it seem louder. Then there's the geography. The clubhouse, as well as the first tee and eighteenth green, sit at the highest point. The rest of the course falls off downhill, with many of the most dramatic holes — eleven, twelve, thirteen, fifteen, and sixteen — lying in the hollows at the far side of the track. When massive galleries let loose with a huge roar down there, the sound ignites out of the trees like a rocket blast, hits the flat upper part of the course, and expands out across the plateau. It's a two-part effect, the initial explosion and then a mushroom cloud of sound bursting outward.

★ When I arrive at the course on Thursday morning it's raining, which has a weird effect at Augusta, not so much for the players as for the patrons. Like everything else, the lords of Augusta have figured out a way to control the rain. They have a SubAir system under the greens, some fairways, and some crossings, which, without getting too technical, allows them to suck water out of the ground and blow air up through it, thus drying things up quickly and keeping the playing surfaces fast and hard. Alas, there is no such system in most of the areas where the galleries walk and stand.

Instead, the rich Georgia clay — now I know what Scarlett was talking about — turns into a sort of maroon slop that creates a slight sucking sound when I try to lift my foot, and it permanently stains my shoes the color of a rusty pipe. To combat those problems, the grounds crew is throwing down something akin to that stuff grade-school janitors use to clean up vomit. The result is that over large portions of the course lingers a horrible smell that combines something earthen with a chemical undercurrent. Like detergent poured over rotting leaves and left in a sun-baked aluminum shed.

Despite the rain, I've come early because I want to be here when play starts. Jack Nicklaus is teeing off at 10:11 A.M., for what he says will be his final Masters. I'm not usually the type for hero worship, but for some reason I can't yet explain, I want to witness this. I want to see Jack called out on the tee for his last Augusta appearance. I want to see him hit his opening drive down the first fairway and then wave goodbye.

I'm not alone in this either. When the rain stops and Jack's time comes, I'm among a throng heading for the first tee. At one point we all crowd together as we wait for play to clear so we can cross a fairway. I overhear an older man talking to a guy standing next to him. "Two hours ago I didn't even know I was gonna be here," the old-timer says. "My son sent me a plane ticket and said, 'Why don't you come down to Atlanta for the weekend and see your grandkids.' Then he picks me up at the airport and we start driving out I-85. I said, 'Where are we going?' And he hands me these passes for Augusta. I couldn't believe it."

"You must be a good son," the guy says, looking at the boy, who's probably in his mid-thirties, and stands beaming beside his father, who's silver-haired, well-tanned, and probably half a head shorter.

Both of them have rough features that make it look like they work outdoors. "Well," the son responds, "he's a good dad."

"If you were gonna take him someplace, you sure picked a great one," says another guy, who'd been listening.

"Oh, yeah," says the son. "This is it. Everyone should come here at least once. You should have to. It should be a federal law that everyone go to the Masters at least once."

The sentiment is met with nods of approval. Why do people feel this way? I must agree with them. I did, after all, put the Masters on my list. As I search my own feelings I think about the guy from the party last night and the word he used keeps coming back to me: pure. Somehow, the tournament has maintained its essence without compromise. The focus always has been and always will be on the golf and the golf course and the players.

It goes back to the legend of Bobby Jones. A phenom, Jones played in his first U.S. Open at eighteen, finishing tied for eighth before going on to win thirteen major tournaments, including what was then considered the Grand Slam in 1930. Along the way, he picked up degrees in English lit from Harvard and mechanical engineering from Georgia Tech and went to law school. He was, in his day, more popular than Tiger Woods is today, but what makes Jones a legend, a virtual saint in the eyes of golfers, is that he never turned pro. He played for the love of the game, remaining an amateur his entire career and retiring at the age of twenty-eight.

The same year he won the Slam, he decided to build Augusta National, and enlisted the renowned golf designer Alister MacKenzie to help him convert a former plant nursery into a parkland course with European, links-style shot values. There was no rough, but fast, sloped greens to provide the challenge. It makes sense that the club he envisioned, the course he helped design, and the tournament he created would carry with them the same high-minded principles by which he played.

Through the years, the club members have done whatever they could to maintain the purist ideal attached to Jones's name. They've clung to their traditions and exclusivity. They don't have any visible advertising on the site. They don't interrupt play to stage a rock concert. They don't bring in Hollywood stars to call out the names on the opening tee box. It is rare and refreshing.

The problem with purity, though, especially as it relates to sports, is that some fans come to revere a place or event so much that they fall into sanctimony. For a sports fan, Augusta is a unique venue and the Masters an awesome event, but no one should be so cowed setting foot on the grounds that they feel the need to kiss the ring of some green-jacketed knucklehead.

Purity, after all, doesn't have to be pristine or holy. The bazaar on Washington Road is a sort of pure, unfettered market, which is why it's possible for me to find as much joy walking the streets outside the club as the grounds within. John Daly is pure, in that he is consistently, unapologetically true to himself. Flawed, yes, but pure in a way, too. Perhaps that's why he remains so popular despite all his failings.

Among the people who have fallen prey to the sanctimony and self-seriousness that sometimes surrounds the Masters are the members of Augusta National themselves. Consider the broadcast, which started in 1956. For fifty years Augusta has stuck with CBS. Not because the club was getting the best deal it could, but because the "Tiffany Network" gets the sort of classy image Augusta is trying to project through the screen and consistently accedes to the club's demands. The classical music leading in and out of commercials, the reverent tones, the length of the broadcast. (Not until 2002 did the club allow the entire eighteen holes of the final round to appear on TV.) Although the club denies this, it also places restrictions on how the TV announcers speak. There are no "customers" or "viewers" and no "rough" at Augusta. Instead, "patrons" stand along the "first cut," where they watch play not on the "front nine" or "back nine," but on the "first nine" and "second nine." And in 1994, when irreverent CBS analyst Gary McCord said that the greens were so fast they must have been bikini-waxed, he'd officially covered his last Masters.

On the course, the caddies must wear white jumpsuits, and everything else that conceivably can be is green. The TV towers, the bleachers, the concession stands, the garbage cans, even the little plastic bags the sandwiches come in. This way, when the cameras pan across the grounds, nothing disrupts the impression of pure woodlands bliss that the members would have you believe their club owns a monopoly on. This urge to control and manipulate its image is so strong that even the coffee cups come with directions instructing patrons on how to dispose of them. Printed in white letters on the green exterior: "Please crush the cup and throw it in a trash receptacle."

Not that this is all bad. The club allows only three sponsors, which get a total of four minutes of commercial time an hour during the broadcast, a financial loss for the tournament but a pleasure for anyone tuning in. And the price of on-course concessions are kept low. A sandwich for $1.50 and a beer for $2.00 is unheard of at a major sporting event, where a cup of brew usually starts at around six bucks and goes up from there. Of course, there's a creepy undercurrent to such measures. I can't help but wonder if the white-haired men who run Augusta National are trying to not just remember their old friend Dwight Eisenhower but to re-create the purity of the Eisenhower era.

★ Nick Faldo, Tom Lehman, and Peter Lonard are teeing off as I arrive at the first tee, which is ringed by a crowd stacked about four deep. At the back of the tee, an ancient green-jacketed member sits on a bench made out of a halved log. As the players prepare to hit, this creaking man stands and announces them in the sort of classic deep-Georgia accent that turns four-letter names into two-syllable words, so that, for example, Mike Weir becomes "Muh-ike Wi-ear."

Finally, it's time for Jack to tee off. There's a buzz in the air and, glancing back, I see that the gallery has swelled to twelve or fifteen deep. When Jay Haas and Shingo Katayama walk onto the tee, a guy near me jokes, "That's what they're wearing? I thought you had to wear a tuxedo to play in the Masters."

Then Jack appears and a roar goes up. He acknowledges it with a quick wave and a sheepish grin. The three players shake hands and mingle amiably for a few minutes. Jack tees his ball and quips something to the crowd. I can't hear what he says, but everyone laughs. He takes a few practice swings. The gallery goes quiet. There is in his motion a certain familiarity, an instant glimmer of recognition. Perhaps it's not as long or as fluid as it once was, but what I'm watching is unmistakably Jack's swing. He addresses the ball. Pulls the club back, and with the sweet *tink* of impact the ball sails off down the fairway. Jack leans a little left to will it away from the bunker, and it works, the ball bounding up the fairway. The applause jumps again. Jack tosses his club to son and caddie Jackie, and they head off down the fairway as people call out, "Get 'em, Jack," "You can do it, Jack," and "Thank you."

And then there he is, marching past as I've seen him march down so many fairways before. And I realize that that is why I've made sure to be here for this moment. Unlike other athletes who can last for maybe twenty years, professional golfers can go forever. Jack has been on the scene for almost fifty years. His career traces the rise of sports as a cultural touchstone in our society. From the chubby, crew-cut twenty-two-year-old who won the U.S. Open in 1962, to the long-haired thirty-something of the early '70s, to the plump, middle-age master of the satisfied '80s, to the injury-plagued, nostalgic star of the '90s, Jack has been a mirror we've held up to ourselves. He is a stick against which we measure not only how golf and the world have changed over the last half century but also our own ability to master them. If we pull for him to succeed, it's because the idea that he can still do so reinforces the notion that we can, too.

The same can be said for Augusta. It is the history of the place that gives it weight. The course may not be holy ground and the tournament something less than a sacrament, but it is special and distinct. All the great shots, worthy champions, and back-nine Sundays are why those of us who love sports have always turned our attention to northeast Georgia on the second weekend in April. It has been a constant through time. It's a means by which we can test ourselves against those who came before us, like a little kid trying on his father's shoes.

That is at least in part because of the way the men who run it have protected and nourished it. It's rumored that the club makes enough money off TV rights to finance everything else it does, but if the tournament were only about making money, the club could make much more. In an age when everything has a price tag, the members of Augusta have refused to sell out. Perhaps it's good that change comes slowly here (though, in some ways, too slowly).

On my first trip to Augusta, I had the pleasure of lunch on the veranda of the Augusta National clubhouse, a stately white building with large columns. The second-floor veranda is a legendary gathering place during Masters week, a hot spot of see-and-be-seen glad-handing and venomous gossip for the game's power brokers and insiders. A colleague and I sat at a side table and had excessively polite southern boys in white tuxedos serve us tall sweaty glasses of iced tea and the club's deservedly famous chicken sandwiches (the pimento cheese sandwich is a Masters tradition, but an acquired taste).

From my perch I could see the giant oak that stands behind the clubhouse and functions as a hub of activity. The roped-off area around it is the main passage for players on their way to and from the locker room and the course. Regular day-pass holders are not allowed inside this roped-off area, so spectators often crowd around to get a peek at who's coming and going, which on that day included everyone from Arnold Palmer to Jim Caviezel, the actor who played Bobby Jones in a recent movie (as well as Jesus in *The Passion of the Christ*).

I could also look out over the course and see the first tee and the practice green, where players bend over putts, looking like penitents bowing before the large leaderboard that rises in the distance. The people around me leaned back in their chairs, telling loud stories and laughing, completely comfortable in what is for them an everyday milieu. Briny Baird, a Tour player, sat two tables over, discussing his round. I thought too about all the conversations that have taken place here. Beyond Eisenhower, the membership has always included men of power, cabinet members, senators, CEOs from the largest companies in America, and lawyers from the most powerful firms. When William Clay Ford Sr. and former U.S. Steel chairman Thomas Usher bump into each other in the Grill Room, what do they talk about? What policies have been sounded out at these tables, what deals cut?

I've also been at the course early in the morning and stood under that veranda next to the tree looking out over the trees and hills. In the cool morning, little dollops of fog hung in the low spots. A train line passes near the course and in the relative quiet a mournful whistle echoed in the air. From that vantage point there was not one visible sign of modern life: no wires, no high-rises, no traffic lights. Just trees and fields and, in the distance, a few water towers. Even the hand-operated scoreboard next to the eighteenth green appeared timeless, and it struck me that it could have been 1935 or 1965 as easily as 2005. I understood how the men who sequestered themselves here could fall a bit out of step with the times.

★ As Jack disappears down the fairway, I have the choice to follow him or go off and find a spot on the course to settle in. I decide to follow Jack for a while and begin the haul, first down and then up the hill that comprises the first fairway. There is a different feeling now than there had been yesterday. Everything seems a bit sharper, the colors brighter, the pace of the walking a little faster, the between-shot buzz a tad more intense. Far more people have crowded onto the course and they seemed to be dressed a little better, more tucked in and buttoned up. Those who plan to camp out in one spot for the whole day haul fold-out chairs, and when I stop behind some of them to see Jack hit his second shot, a little whiff of sunscreen rises off them.

By the green, the grandstands are packed, and most of the spots from which I might see the entire putting surface are stacked five or six deep, making it hard to get a look. Over the next few holes I stick with the jostling masses who've chosen to give Jack a sendoff. It's fun to be a part of, but eventually I decide to check out what's happening at my spot down at Amen Corner.

When I get to the area, it's packed with about three times as many people as had been there yesterday. I guess I'm not the only one who thinks it's cool to perch there and watch all three holes. I'm certainly not the earliest riser of them. The folks with the prime real estate are entrenched in a way that says they got there early and won't be leaving until late.

I wander over to eleven and spend some time marveling at how difficult the second shot is, hitting the ball over the knob in front of the green without carrying it so far that it runs into the water. The mental exercise is as interesting as watching the different players march through. I spend most of the day like this, nomadically wandering from spot to spot, catching a variety of golfers, both famous and obscure, contemplating strategies, striking up little conversations and minirelationships with people, and enjoying a good walk.

Finally, I settle into a place on the ropes along the thirteenth fairway. A par five, the thirteenth bends around a sharp corner, leaving a long shot into a shallow green with the creek running right in front of it. Among the denizens of the thirteenth fairway gallery, a good deal of the chatter revolves around analyzing players' drives and deciding if that guy should or shouldn't go for the green on his second shot.

I don't say much, but I enjoy the banter. It adds a sort of running commentary that's far more interesting and entertaining than anything I've heard on TV. "No shot from there," a tall guy in a striped polo says when Vijay Singh's ball runs through the fairway and settles on some pine straw. "Well, he's got a good lie," retorts some unseen observer a few rows back. "Ball's above his feet, and he's 230 to the hole," says polo guy, with the slightest bit of admonishment in his voice. "It's sittin' up, though," says a third observer. "He could get driver on that. I'd hit driver from there."

As the debate rages, Singh and his playing partners make their way up from the tee. It's late in the afternoon and the sunlight is slanting through the trees. Along the far side of the fairway the azaleas and dogwoods glow in early spring bloom. Singh pulls an iron from his bag and makes a few practice swings, the sound of the club cutting the air with a whir. A breeze moves the grass.

Okay, maybe not a federal law, but certainly everyone should really try to do this at least once.

★ On Sunday afternoon, I'm on the phone in my office as the tournament rises to its climax. On my computer, the last three days are being reconstructed in words and pictures that bring back everything that has led to the drama unfolding on the screen. Woods and Chris DiMarco are locked in a dramatic duel, one in which Woods will prevail on the first playoff hole but that will be best remembered for his circus-like chip-in on the par-three sixteenth hole. The shot, which he played off a bank fifteen feet left of the cup and struck perfectly so that it stopped and in slow motion rolled back down the slope and in, was one of the Masters' and Woods's finest moments.

The writer I'm on the phone with is standing about thirty yards from the eighteenth green. Thanks to the mass of people surrounding the putting surface, he can't see a thing, so I'm telling him what's happening. At the same time, the experience of watching it on TV is different and better for my having been there. I can picture how steep the sidehill is when someone hits from the slope of the tenth fairway. I have felt with my own feet the punishing slope of the ninth green. When Woods makes his final putt to seal the victory and a roar goes up around the eighteenth green, I can translate the shadow of it that comes through the tinny speakers into the sound that rumbles across the fairways.

In that roar there hide no questions about female members, or John Daly, or Dick Vitale, or green wrappers on the sandwiches. There is only the caw of triumph; the patrons' man has won. In that roar can be heard the voice of joy, sweet and pure.

5 ★ The Kentucky Derby

May 6–7, 2005

Louisville, Kentucky

I DON'T EVEN KNOW what's in a mint julep. What does it look like, taste like, will I like it? No idea. And yet I'm prone to these visions of myself sipping a mint julep, one hand holding the glass, the other stuffed into the pocket of my seersucker suit. Women with large feathery hats and parasols stroll past. At the passing of a droll comment I don't produce my usual wry snicker, but throw my head back and unleash a full-throated guffaw.

Like Augusta National, Churchill Downs is one of those places that people view with mythological regard, and the Kentucky Derby, like the Masters, is an event that's celebrated for its rich history. The race is somehow connected, at least in my mind, to the genteel manners of the Old South. I think of Jefferson Davis. I think of William Faulkner. I think of Colonel Sanders.

The historical echoes are well-founded; the track was built in 1875, and ever since, the world's best three-year-olds have arrived on the first Saturday in May to run for the roses. The problem is that I have my own three-year-old, and like the rest of the kids in America, he's supposed to spend the second Sunday in May paying tribute to his mother, and as freak coincidence would have it, this year the first Saturday and the second Sunday fall on the same weekend. Since neither my boy nor his five-year-old sister are able to celebrate Mom on their own, my participation is mandatory. How, though, do I go to the Kentucky Derby and still pull off a satisfying Mother's Day celebration?

It's not like this particular mother doesn't deserve the day of pampering and thanks. The Derby will be my fifth trip in the last thirteen weeks. And while in my mind working through my list has become necessary for my life and mental health, I understand how my wife, Karin, could see the process as a self-indulgent pain in her ass. Lucky for me, she usually supports my crazy flights of curiosity and my sports jones. She's not thrilled by them, but she endures. It makes sense, since it was sports that brought us together — sort of.

Shortly after we met, I moved out of an apartment I shared with two friends and into a studio. I didn't own a TV but decided I didn't need one because I was going to live for one year without watching the tube. It would be an adventure in self-discovery and a social experiment (I tend to throw myself into these sorts of things). But baseball season began to heat up and the resurgent Yanks of Buck Showalter were, shockingly, in a pennant race. I followed them in the newspaper, but before long that wasn't enough. As the race heated up, I began appearing at Karin's apartment, only three blocks away, to hang out and catch the games. By August I was letting myself in before she even got home from work, and once football season started, it was all over. Not that we wouldn't have ended up married anyway, but the draw of sports caused us to spend a lot more time together early in our relationship than we might have otherwise.

Still, while I've been on the road searching, partying, and absorbing the atmosphere, she has been back home with two tykes who have just entered the "he's touching me" phase of their budding sibling rivalry. They typically begin their first argument within minutes of waking in the morning and don't stop until they're asleep, and even then my son has been known to yell at his sister in his dreams. They can play wonderfully together for hours, but they can also drive you into a stupefying rage in about sixteen seconds.

Like me, Karin has a full-time job, running her own company, no less, which means hers is even more hands-on and stressful than mine. My excursions have been cutting into the little time she has to keep our collective lives organized, run errands, and maintain her own sanity. Anyone who's part of a family with young kids and two working parents knows the never-ending succession of planning and running and chasing that's necessary. My kids are in different schools that start and end at different times, and each has its own schedule of conferences, meetings, concerts, and plays. They go to gymnastics classes. My daughter plays soccer and takes dance. They each have their own friends, which means a steady diet of birthday parties and postschool get-togethers (I refuse to say "play dates"). The grind can be soul-deadening.

It doesn't help that at *Sports Illustrated* we work on Sunday, which means that on one of Karin's two days off, I'm not usually around, leaving her to fend for herself with the two little monsters from ten in the morning to ten at night. Despite all this she has been a trouper through the first four legs of my little experiment in sports tourism — she understands better than anyone my compulsive need to get this out of my system. That's not to say things have been all sunshine and lilies. I've received phone calls — four of them, to be exact — in which my bride's voice was filled not so much with anger or resentment, but with a sort of hopeless desperation. I don't mean to overstate the case, it's in many ways an interesting, comfortable, and rewarding life, but it can wear you down. And not taking the time to acknowledge the effort on the one preordained day for just such tributes, well, that is no way to treat a lady. I need a plan.

Then something so simple but so spot-on occurs to me, it's a wonder I hadn't dreamed it up sooner. She'll come with me.

We'll get someone to stay with the kids, and the two of us will zip down to Louisville for a few days of racing and relaxation. We'll fly home either late Saturday or early Sunday so she can see her babies on Mother's Day, and by then she'll be relaxed and mentally refreshed. She's not much of a sports fan — she'll watch the Olympics and an occasional baseball game — but she loves a happening. The Derby is the least sportsy event on my list. It's a fashion show and a party and an extravaganza. It's perfect.

So perfect that a week later when we're out to dinner with our dear friends, Kevin and Tara, we tell them about the plan, and they're so taken with it, they decide to join us. The women are talking hats. Kevin is planning his cigar selection. It's all so much fun we can hardly stand it.

The aura of joy and frivolity lasts exactly two weeks, until we start to actually plan the trip. I want to go down a day ahead of everyone to attend the Kentucky Oaks, a slate of races that takes place the day before the Derby — or, as I was informed rather dismissively when I admitted I'd never heard of the Oaks, "the second biggest day in horse racing." The plan calls for me to fly down alone, with the three of them joining me later. But Kevin and Tara want to leave from a different airport than Karin. And there's the problem with hotels: There are none. Proposals and counterproposals fly back and forth. For every solution there's an additional complication. Kevin and Tara call to say they're having trouble finding a babysitter, which is funny because we are, too.

Finally Karin gives up. "You should just go," she says. "The stress of trying to set it up is worse than being here without you for the weekend. We should just call the whole thing off." I hate to admit it, but I know she's right. I send an e-mail to Kevin and Tara putting a knife in the whole idea, hoping they, too, will be relieved and not mad.

The next day an e-mail arrives from Kevin. He's got one last suggestion. It turns out to be the idea that saves our trip.

★ In the terminal of the Louisville airport stands a woman in a sky blue hoop-skirt gown with white trim, and a white straw hat with little ribbons and streamers tumbling off it. "Welcome to Looahvul," she drawls as passengers deplane and stream past. A violinist plays softly. We're a long way from the Super Bowl.

Her presence conjures the antebellum charm and high-roller ethos most of us associate with the Derby, setting the stage for a bucolic day of racing and rubbing elbows with the rich and fabulous. But when I pull off the highway and arrive at the neighborhood that surrounds Churchill Downs, I experience something akin to the cultural whiplash I got outside Augusta National. The neighborhood is filled with tall leafy trees and small but mostly well-kept houses, and there is a mix of average suburban existence and lower-middle-class edge. Just blocks away from the Lord of Our Savior Seventh-day Adventist Church and the Larchmont Church of God stands a giant strip club with a giant banner out front: "Welcome Race Fans, XXX Derby Special, All Nude." Farther along is the Derby Dollar Store and the Derby Diner, where you can get "Good home cookin' at down-home prices."

The one unifying element is that this week, everybody's in for the big sell. Lord of Our Savior is getting ten bucks a car, while a block closer to the track, Larchmont gets twenty a pop. I opt for Lord of Our Savior, and notice a sign on the table where I pay: "Free water for a $.75 donation."

Weaving through the tight gridlike streets as I make my way the five or so blocks over to the track, I see someone in every yard. Dads, bikers with tattooed arms, teenagers with signs and nasty mullet haircuts standing in yards, waving cars into driveways. Everyone's selling parking, ranging from eight bucks about ten blocks from the track to $40 in prime territory. Beside them, old ladies in lawn chairs sell everything from bottles of water to sunscreen and Derby trinkets. One guy has converted his garage to a concession stand with two grills, a bunch of coolers, and two signs mounted on the wall. The first is a bill of fare offering burgers, dogs, potatoes, and various beverages. The second reads: "Show us your tits."

I flush at my own naiveté. It's all a little unseemly compared with my preconceived notions, and the sign, in particular, is a surprise. I don't think this is how Jeff Davis or Billy Faulkner or even the finger-lickin' Colonel, a man who certainly appreciated a good breast, would have phrased it.

As I navigate out of this bizarre bazaar, large, open parking lots unravel before me and the track itself shoots up out of the landscape. Its central section is instantly recognizable, a classic old white clapboard building with tall steeples, called the Twin Spires, and black roofs. The spires, constructed in 1895, are an emblem of the Derby, and seeing them compensates for the disconnect of the roadside grill man and his sign.

Of course, it doesn't prepare me for what I see on either end of the long, low central structure. There sit two frightening monstrosities: sweeping wings that must be five stories tall and molded of sand-colored concrete, totally incompatible with the rest of the building and the surrounding neighborhood. If I didn't know where I was, I might imagine I'd just arrived at the Dubai Radisson. Not all of the parking lot is paved, so I see them through a screen of windblown dust that adds to the sense of desert chic.

Inside, the mood and the architecture are similar in that there are two distinct worlds — an old one and a new one. The older parts of the grandstand show their age; as I walk along the bare concrete beneath them they look like the underside of my high-school football bleachers. So much so that I half-expect to see a few kids tucked under there smoking pot and making out. Exposed pipes hang from the rafters, and here and there water drips (at least I think it's water). Outside in the stands, metal folding chairs stand on bare wooden floors, and the back wall is built of unpainted cinder blocks.

Within the newer pavilions, it's a much different scene. They're painted and cool. Parts are even carpeted. There are levels upon levels of lounges and clubs that get more and more exclusive the higher you go. Many of these seating areas are glassed in and therefore air-conditioned. Up on the second level (as high as I'm allowed to go) little TVs mounted along the rail of each box show odds for the upcoming races and broadcasts of the races themselves. The padded seats are filled with swells in blue blazers and ladies in party dresses and extravagant headgear.

Along one of the concourses I spot a wonderful-looking restaurant, which reminds me that it's time for lunch. I walk up to the maitre d'. A delicious buffet spreads along the wall behind her and I can see that the place is about half full with people leaning far back in their chairs, signaling peace and satisfaction. "Table for one," I say.

"Can I see your ticket?" she asks. I show her what I've got. "I'm sorry," she says, "this restaurant has been rented out for a private party."

"Oh," I say. "Is there somewhere else up here I can get some lunch?"

"I'm sorry," she replies, "all the restaurants on this level and above have been reserved for the weekend. There is a food court a little farther along." She's right about that, but it's so packed that I continue hunting elsewhere. Eventually I follow signs to a small room on the ground level that sells sandwiches over a counter. I buy one, a decent pulled-pork number, find a table, and sit. This looks a lot more like my past track experiences. A windowless room, rickety tables, scuffed linoleum floor, closed-circuit TVs mounted on the walls, and the stench of desperation. At the tables around me, low rollers spit out numbers. "In her last start the 7 finished the last quarter in the same time as her first."

When a race starts they all stop what they're doing and stare up at the TVs. The action builds to a crescendo. One or two people stand up. A few shouts of "Go, go!" rise. Then the race ends. No winners as far as I can tell. Everyone goes back to their sandwiches and their conversations and their racing forms.

It's a far cry from the tony restaurant upstairs, and it takes me back to the Super Bowl. Daytona had a wide diversity between haves and have-nots, but there were not many of either — most of the people were comfortably in between. The Final Four was largely homogenous and there was little difference between the facilities available to everyone. The Masters had the most consistent crowd, made up of haves and have-mores. It was the Super Bowl where there was a distinct caste system split between the street partiers and the hospitality-tent people. As I walk past the lines of bettors after lunch, one image drives home the point: woman with perfect makeup, sparkling jewelry, a long black dress, and a black-and-white-striped hat with large white feathers stands directly behind a guy, skinny to the point of emaciation, who wears ripped, dirty jeans and a sleeveless white Budweiser T-shirt.

★ As much as I've heard about and seen pictures of the grand Derby tradition, the headwear and the haute couture and the high-rolling crowds, I've also been informed about the other side of the Derby. The infield at Churchill Downs is known as a giant, raucous party. There are stories about drinking and mayhem and, on rainy days, massive clothing-optional mudslides. It's purported to be a cross between a college football game and Woodstock.

While the ladies with the hats and the jewelry seem to get all the seats in the grandstand — and the media attention — I want to follow the guys in the ripped Bud T-shirts into the tunnel that leads under the track and into the center oval. I do, and when I come out the other side, I find bunches of people milling about among equipment trucks, temporary bars, and picnic sites.

As I stand surveying the scene and taking a few pictures, someone approaches me. "Man," he yells as he walks up. "Man, man, man," he continues after I look up and realize he's talking to me. "Get a shot of me, dude?" He's wearing a shiny green top hat, shiny green tuxedo tails, and no shirt. He's sort of a cross between the Notre Dame mascot and the guy behind the counter at some independent music store who sneers at whatever lame disk you're buying.

I tell the little leprechaun my story — that I work for *Sports Illustrated* and I'm on a journey to see the ultimate sports events. "Man," he says when I'm done. "I've got to show you some shit." And so, just like that I'm on a tour of the infield with the guy from the Lucky Charms box.

Our first stop is a small area where four guys dressed like Austin Powers — purple velour suits, white ruffled shirts, thick black glasses — are decorating the female population. That is to say they're giving temporary tattoos. The process is undoubtedly an interesting one. While families, couples, and older folks stretch out around the area on blankets and in folding chairs, chatting, enjoying little picnics, and watching the races, the four Austins crank their theme music from a boom box. When they get a volunteer, she sits on one of their laps while two dance on either side of her. The fourth applies the tattoo. At a kids' party such things are affixed by first wetting them with a washcloth and then pressing them against the skin. The Austins have reduced that two-step process to one: They simply lick the tattoos on.

As I look around at some of the young women dancing and partying with the Austins I see that they have tattoos on their necks, shoulders, lower backs, and just above their cleavage. The Austins are having themselves a good day, and it's only just past noon. This isn't as crazy as I'd been told it would be, but it's certainly creative.

"Man," the leprechaun says, "these mothers got it figured out." Then, like a horribly underdressed Sherpa, he leads me off to greater heights. When I ask his name he makes a face that calls to mind someone who's just been offered a plate of bad-smelling cheese. I decide to call him the only thing he seems interested in calling me, "Man." So we go, two men wandering across a virtual beach party. Shirtless dudes throw Frisbees and footballs, a beach ball pops up in the air repeatedly. Women in shorts and bikini tops lie out on towels, lolling in the sun.

Man needs to reload, and so he leads me to one of the many outdoor bars, where on his recommendation — "It's a must" — we buy black-eyed Susans. The ugly stepsister of the renowned mint julep, the Susan is a vodka-and-rum-based libation of the Old South. It's sweet and citrusy and nearly undrinkable, but when Man flashes me a look over the rim of his cup, I smile and nod as if I'm loving every ounce of it, because for some reason I feel the need to protect his feelings. Maybe it's his complete passion, his unwavering conviction about the drink's greatness that makes me not want to let him down, but there's also something about how out of nowhere he's adopted me and dedicated himself to making me happy. I feel obligated.

Anyway, we stand there for a few minutes sipping and staring, soaking up the increasingly hot Kentucky sun. A few feet away stands a large tractor-trailer, and I notice that a line of people have set up their chairs in the sliver of a shadow it has begun to cast as the sun moves past the center of the sky. I take maybe my fourth tentative sip of the black-eyed Susan, then look over at Man, who's draining the last drops from his cup. With the theatrical flourish of a symphony conductor, he slams the empty into a trash can and says, "We must see the band." He looks at me, flips his head toward the far end of the track, and begins to walk. Without thinking, I fall in next to him.

As we walk I ask if he's bet on any of the races, but he has not.

He doesn't know anything about them, doesn't care. As far as he's concerned the races are secondary. As if to prove the point, a few minutes later, horses rumble around the far end of the track, and I look to watch them go by. Even from this distance, I can see their muscles working beneath their deep brown coats, which seem to shine when the sun catches them at just the right angle. With each step their heads thrust forward, and the black bristles of their tails extend out behind them like the point of a paintbrush. I'm captivated, even if for only a moment. Man does not look at all. Nor do many of the people around us. Some do, no doubt, because there are betting booths set up under the temporary bleachers, and between races long lines snake out of them, so there are folks out here with a moneyed interest in the outcome. But there are just as many who couldn't care less.

Man instead leads me to the center of the track, where a cover band cranks tunes from a large stage. The sound system is horrible, scratchy and blaring, so it's hard to decipher a single note or lyric. Yet a few hundred people stand up close, rocking their heads and bobbing up and down. Out around the edges, others sit on blankets, drinking, and in spots people dance. After watching for a minute, Man slowly bops and sways his way over toward two college-age women in jeans and half shirts who are dancing together. A few minutes later he's dancing with them, which in his case means a disjointed alternation between spasmodic full-body twitching, jumping straight up and down, and brief interludes of air guitar.

It's fun to watch for a few minutes, but soon I wander over to the next clearing at the end of the track. It is more bucolic here. A group of boys plays tackle football. Families recline, some playing cards or checkers. I'm lost in a reverie when I hear a familiar voice shouting from close behind. "Hey," Man says, "emergency mission." I turn to look and he is pointing to a row of portable toilets. I nod and wave to him. "When I get back we go there," he says, gesturing over my shoulder. "There is *sick,* man."

I follow his finger to a red, orange, and black trailer with a gate at one end. The outside says "Copenhagen Saloon" in big letters, and a smaller sign says "Adult smokers welcome." I have no idea what goes on in there, but I'm not terribly intrigued. I didn't come to the infield to party like a trust-fund kid. I wanted to check out the scene, and see what the other side of the Derby looked like, but I'm now getting dangerously close to crossing over. One more black-eyed Susan and I may wake up tomorrow morning with a green top hat, no shirt, and a day-ruining headache. What's more, being here alone fills me with a feeling of isolation. Man, while nice enough, is a random, nameless stranger, which only makes plain my lack of any true companionship.

It's too early to leave for the day, but in the grandstands across the track I can see well-dressed men and women moving back and forth. That's what I came for. I decide it's time for Man and me to part ways. I take a peek back over my shoulder. He's nowhere to be seen. As quickly as I can, I make my way back to the tunnel and disappear from the infield forever.

★ Kevin's last-minute suggestion was a deal-saver. He was able to secure the use of a corporate jet, which meant he, his wife, and Karin could fly down on Saturday and we could all return that night, eliminating the need for overnight childcare, hotel rooms, coordinating flights, and pickups. We would be back in time for Mother's Day celebrations. Suddenly everything clicked into place. They would arrive around noon. The races start at eleven but the Derby itself is the twelfth race and not scheduled to start until 6:04. (It's a little-known fact that there are actually two more races after the Derby on Derby Day, although few stick around to watch them.)

That's tomorrow, though. Today, there are still five races to be run, including the Kentucky Oaks, so I figure I'll go scout our seats. Three ushers and a lot of walking later I come to four metal folding chairs hard against the cinder-block wall in the back row of the first-level grandstand. It is not the lap of luxury, but it's a spot with charisma. Located just across from the start of turn one, it provides a good view of the start/finish line and the turn, but it's split with white-painted girders, low-hanging pipes and beams, and the extravagant foliage of fashionable hats, all of which give it the rustic, Old World feeling of a period movie.

Right now the area is sparsely populated, a pleasant change from the infield, and I take a moment to sit and relax. There seems to be a lot of smoking throughout the complex and a drift of cigar in the air adds to the mood. Vendors yell: beer, ice cream, roses. One, like some lovesick songbird, repeats again and again: "Bip ju bip. Bip ju bip." It's maybe ten minutes of hearing this over and over before I realize he's actually saying "mint julep."

This is already far different from my past experiences at the racetrack. I'd only seen trotters before and only at night. But more than the type of race or amount of sunlight, what makes this different is the sense of history. Horseracing has been taking place in Louisville since 1783, when there are reports of racing in the streets and on various tracks around town. It was one hundred years later when horse enthusiast Col. Meriwether Lewis Clark (grandson of the explorer William Clark) decided to build a track on eighty acres leased from his uncles, John and Henry Churchill.

Clark announced three premier stakes races for the new track: the Clark Handicap, the Kentucky Oaks, and the Kentucky Derby. All three were run for the first time in 1875, and despite a variety of renovations, the founder's suicide in 1899, and a number of ownership changes, they have taken place every year since. Two developments in the early years of the twentieth century allowed the Derby to become *the* horserace in the country. First, Matt Winn, who took over the track in 1902, convinced horse owners from around the country to send their colts to Kentucky in early May. Second, the idea of the Triple Crown — a single horse winning the Derby, the Preakness, and the Belmont Stakes in one year — captured the public imagination. In the aftermath, the Derby became the kind of event that attracted the attention of people who normally didn't pay attention to horseracing.

That certainly applies to me. My ten or twelve previous visits to the races were notable for their sense of decay and the sort of polyester ethic of the crowd. Still, that wouldn't stop me from attending the Derby. From what I've seen and heard of it, the race is just one small part of a week full of activities. And unlike some other events, such as the Super Bowl, that sense of outside distraction doesn't diminish the actual event, but seems to add to it. Rather than making a football game seem smaller, all the hoopla converts a two-minute horserace into something bigger.

As I think about all this, I notice a little pocket of activity off to my left: a kid with a racing form talking to two or three groups of guys in front of him. With his soft brown hair, round cheeks, and freckled nose, he looks to be about eighteen, but he's taking long pulls from a can of beer. "Don't like the favorite here," the kid's saying. "Last two times out haven't been as fast as her best times." This sets off a flurry of nods and assents as everyone dives back into the agate type of the sheets before them. "What about the 2 horse?" someone shouts. The kid makes to respond, but just then his cell phone rings and he pauses to answer. "Yeah," he says. "No, don't like it. You like the 2?" he says, his voice rising at the end as he looks up and points at the guy who asked the question. "Yeah," he says. "I don't think I'm going that way, but I'll put it in for you."

After he hangs up, he makes a few last notes on his sheet, then heads off for the betting window. The rest of the guys continue to doodle and discuss things before splintering off in twos and threes. During the race I watch the kid, who's calm the whole way around, giving a little fist pump at the end that tells me he didn't break the bank, but he did win something. When things settles down, I strike up a conversation with him. He's Drew, a twenty-two-year-old soon-to-be graduate of St. Louis University. When one of Drew's cronies hears that, he says, "What are you majoring in kid, ponies?" Actually it's math. Drew learned about horses from his father, who likes to bet on them, and his uncle, who owns them. He's here at the races with his parents and a few cousins. He's been coming to the Derby since he was ten, and can't imagine a year without a weekend in Louisville.

I don't know why everyone seems to put so much faith in what he says, but my guess is that he's been winning all afternoon. I've never been much of a gambler. When I was a sophomore in high school, I bet some kid in my class twenty bucks on the NCAA

Championship. It was Houston's famous Phi Slamma Jamma team, with future NBA all-stars Clyde Drexler and Hakeem Olajuwon against a bunch of NC State role players with a charismatic but not yet famous coach. It was an even-money bet — no points, no conditions, nothing — and I assumed it would be the easiest twenty I'd ever make in my life. Moreover, it would be twenty of the sweetest, because the kid I bet with was one of my least favorite people in the world. He was loud and obnoxious and dumb, generally a pain in the ass. Like the prom or puking your guts out the morning after someone steals a bottle of schnapps from his dad's liquor cabinet, seeing him humbled as he handed over the money promised to be a cherished high school memory.

Of course, I turned out wrong. NC State won on a freak last-second play. As I paid up I took his off-the-chart gloating and incessant braying as a sign from the heavens that I was not meant to gamble on sports. I haven't since.

Sure, I'll fill out my brackets every year for March Madness, and I've been in my share of football pools, but as far as laying money on a game, I won't do it. I know that betting is a huge part of following sports for a lot of people. For some guys, it's the only reason to root. And I understand that appeal, that sense that a game with a little jack riding on it suddenly has more at stake. That sense of competition against the odds. It's just not my thing. Unless I'm at the track.

I know I'm going to be laying down some money tomorrow, so I try to ask Drew a few questions about picking horses. It should be easy for me to learn something, since I know almost nothing, but we keep getting interrupted by his cell phone and questions from the other eager students sitting nearby. "Who you like in the Oaks?" one asks. "Don't know," he answers. "Haven't looked yet. If I look too soon, I second-guess myself."

"Oh, I'm the same way," the guy shoots back.

This segues into a detailed discussion of online betting, which holds little interest for me, but when it finally winds down, I get back to picking his brain about picking horses, which leads to a tutorial about how to analyze the myriad numbers in the racing form that makes my eyes glaze. I cut him off and ask about that thing you always see in movies, where guys check the horse's teeth. What does that tell you? I want to know. "Well," he says, perhaps sensing his chance to ditch me, "you can view the horses right before the race down by the paddock. Sometimes you can really get a feel for a horse that way. A lot of people pick based on what they see down there."

Okay, so I'm off to the paddock. As I walk I think about Drew and Man. I could not draw a more perfect distinction between the grandstands and the infield. They're both young guys here to enjoy the day, but one sits in the stands in black dress pants, a light pink oxford, and wraparound shades studying numbers and juggling phone calls from tipsters and wayward bettors, while the other prances around like a deranged elf with only the faintest idea that the races are taking place. I don't know that one approach is any better than the other — drinking vs. gambling, it's a Christian Coalition nightmare — although I know which I prefer. More than anything, though, the pair captures the two sides of the Derby. People come to enjoy one or the other, but seldom both.

The paddock features a stable that opens onto a courtyard where a brick path encircles a section of hedges and brilliant flowers. Along the eaves of the main building, the names of all the past derby winners ring the outer wall. Most of the names are printed in white letters. Except the Triple Crown winners — those names appear in gold, making them stand out even more. They are the names a sports fan knows even if he doesn't follow the ponies. War Admiral. Citation. Secretariat. Seattle Slew. Affirmed. Then there are the other ones that jump out, especially from recent years. Funny Cide. Smarty Jones. Their stories engaged people as much as their speed, and the presence of their names here in the paddock reminds everyone of their achievements and the glory at stake.

As the horses for the next race are brought out, they're paraded around the path and led to a stable, where they're saddled by handlers dressed in blue blazers, pleated khakis, and, oddly, beat-up shoes. As the thoroughbreds prance by, their coats glint and the muscles in their necks flex as they pull their heads up and shake them from side to side. Jockeys emerge from another building and walk by. With their colorful outfits and bouncy strides, they look like little boys with men's heads.

I know that, for many people, part of the appeal is the horses themselves. They revere them. Talk about their personalities and character. I can appreciate the sentiment, but I've never really felt that way. They're fantastic creatures to look at, but I don't connect with them the way some people seem to. I imagine the devotees who press up against the iron fence that surrounds the entire scene, craning and stretching to get a view of the animals, are the horse lovers. The true fanatics have camped out in the best spots along the edge of the fence. Two guys next to me sit on a cooler drinking Coors Lite from the can. I know they've been there for a while because when one of them raises his hand to drink, pink sunburn lines appear on his arm where his sleeve rides up. Beside them a blonde in a rhinestone-encrusted blue dress and horseshoe-shaped earrings studded with diamonds shouts into a cell phone: "Tell him he better rate that horse. If he doesn't rate that horse he'll never ride it again." Not only does she own horses, she wants everyone to know it.

A Kentucky state trooper stands inside the gate where the jockeys enter. "Hey, how can I get seats like that?" someone asks him, referring to the officer's prime position for horse watching.

The officer smiles. "Join the police force."

"No, thanks," the guy yells back. "You got an easier way?"

"Yeah," the officer says. "Become a millionaire."

That might be the most valuable insight I get while visiting the paddock, although there is one other. All the horses look huge and powerful and ready to go, so I get no additional information about where to place my money by watching them bray and stomp while standing in a stable. But one of them, I notice, relieves himself on the ground, and I wonder if that means it will run faster. As his handlers saddle him, they continually step in the steaming pile with a casualness that indicates just how common an event it must be. Now, at least, I understand the bad shoes.

★ Derby Day. The early afternoon has been an incredible success. Karin, Kevin, and Tara met up this morning and easily jetted down to Louisville, stepped into a waiting rental car, and parked at the church where I'd prepaid and reserved a spot for them. No lines, no waiting, no hassles.

The day is grand, sunny and beautiful, about eighty-three degrees, with big puffy clouds floating by. The atmosphere is something like going to a football game in your best church clothes. There's a sense of sophistication and formality, and yet we're outside, we're drinking, and the air is filled with excitement. Thus far we've lunched, seen notables — Richard Branson, Minnesota Vikings coach Mike Tice — and people-watched.

The best perch for this proves to be a small balcony overlooking the paddock area, which is three times as jam-packed today as it was yesterday. This is the Derby as advertised. The brave men who've strayed from the blue blazer and khakis dazzle with red sport jackets, green trousers, linen suits, and plenty of seersucker, occasionally even accompanied by a bow tie and a straw boater. The women are a kaleidoscope of colors and shapes and hats, from tame wide-brimmed straw ones to outsize, crazy things that force other people to duck every time the wearer turns around.

One woman goes by sporting a number with a long line of black feathers attached. "Oh, my," Tara says, "someone got a hot glue gun for Christmas." Karin, to her dismay, spots a woman wearing the same dress as she. "Well," offers another lady standing near us. "As long as she's down there and you're up here, it's not a problem." On our other side I listen in as one woman tells another conspiratorially, "She bought a six-hundred-dollar hat from Neiman and her husband told her no way. So she took it back and traded it in for one that cost four hundred."

Back in our seats, we sip ceremonial mint juleps and place bets on the next race. I'd say the flavor of the drink is not what I expected, but I didn't really have any expectation of what it would taste like. I just assumed it would be good. Why else would it be such a hallowed tradition? Truth is, the mint julep is a bit of an acquired taste, neither sweet nor smooth nor necessarily tasty. I persist, though, because it's the Derby and I'm going to drink a mint julep, dammit, which I suspect is exactly how the tradition has survived.

Having grown bored of the hat watching, the women strike out to find a gift shop. As the race starts, Kevin and I are standing casually. Through turn one we start to yell for the 5 horse, on whom we've plunked our dough. Down the backstretch we start to stretch and crane and rise up onto our toes. Finally we jump onto our chairs to get a better view of the horses rumbling out of the last turn and into the homestretch. The 5 horse is running third. The entire crowd has risen and the level of noise ratchets up in a mishmash of contradictory wishes, prayers, and enthusiasms. I'm yelling "Go 5, go 5," while Kevin has opted for something a little less cliché but that makes up for its unorthodoxy with an admirable simplicity and straightforwardness: "Run faster," he screams. "Run faster!"

Perhaps Kevin should have been more specific, because it is the 7 horse that runs faster, leaving us outside the winner's circle. In the denouement of the race, a ripple of chatter runs through the stands as winners share the news of their good fortune and everyone else recounts their near misses. There are no lingering hard feelings, though, because there are still races left to be run, including the big one, which lends a feeling of anticipation.

And there are still plenty of icy beverages and the whole grand, flamboyant sweep of Churchill Downs on Derby Day. Kevin and I sit back down. I take a long bitter sip of my julep. Kevin goes for his beer (he ditched the julep) and looks around for someone with a lighter for his cigar. Karin and Tara return and we all delve into our racing forms so we can get our money down for the next race. After spending the day alone yesterday, it's great to have them all here. None of us knows much about horseracing, but we have fun figuring it out together.

The pace is a pleasant one, with leisurely thirty- or forty-minute intervals between races, during which we can chew over the last run, talk about our kids, make dinner plans for the following month, scan the racing form for the next race, and place our bets. As post time approaches, there's a gradual buildup of tension, people run off to get their bets in, hustle back to their seats, begin to rise and stretch to get a peak at the horses as they are paraded out to the starting gate. Then the bell rings, the gate bursts open, and there follows a minute of pure excitement. Thus the afternoon passes in a combination of pomp and circumstance intertwined with laughter and beer and loud yelling at distant thoroughbreds. We win some, we lose some. We make friends with the people around us. It is, I think, one of the most pleasant afternoons I've enjoyed in many years.

But there's also an odd undercurrent that reminds me of being a kid on December 24. No matter what I do and how much fun I have, there is always the specter of a bigger moment waiting. The anticipation of the Derby hovers over everything. And like Christmas Eve, it makes things more exciting and delicious but it also produces the sense that everything else is just prologue. Everything builds toward the moment that has brought us here to start with.

Finally, it's Derby time. The horses are walked out from the barns on the far side of the track, then paraded before the grandstand and into the paddock area. This, I'm told, is one of the Derby's three great moments, along with the singing of "My Old Kentucky Home" and the race itself. I must say that as the horses go by they appear even more majestic than usual, like gladiators. Maybe it's the sudden weight of the actual event, in which fortunes and glory and, for the creatures themselves, limb and life are on the line, but whatever it is, it makes me feel for the horses in a way I never have before. The conversation percolates. Around me people strain to look, pointing, studying, discussing how the animals look and move. Notes are made. A few minutes later, the post call trumpets through the sound system (*bump, bump, bump, bump ba-da-dump, ba-da-dump ba-da-dum*) and there is a final surge toward the betting windows.

The voice on the PA asks everyone to rise for the singing of "My Old Kentucky Home." What follows is a bit of surreal comedy. There is a band set up across the track and the lyrics to the song come up on a large screen opposite the grandstand. A pixilated ball bounces over the words, but there's no music. Everyone's standing and waiting for the song to start; they have no idea it already has. Some distant strains of music from the band finally make their way back over the crowd noise. A few people catch on and try to jump in with the lyrics, but they can't hear the melody, so the result is some disjointed chanting spread through the crowd. There's a swell on the final lyric and the words "my old Kentucky home" approach something like audible level, and then the song is over. Everyone is sort of looking at one another and laughing a little bit. What is supposed to be a stirring tradition has been a complete farce. I guess once upon a time everyone who came to the race knew the words to this song, but now it seems almost no one does.

The moment passes, though, and they begin to load the horses into the gates, and a roar goes up from the crowd. I glance to the infield, which is packed in a way I couldn't have dreamed of yesterday. All day long people have been filling in the vast open spaces, laying blankets, pitching tents, hauling coolers and even little step stools and platforms to stand on. Thousands of them push forward to find a spot at the chainlink fence that surrounds the oval, looking like prisoners pining for their emancipation.

The horses are in and set, everyone is on their feet, and many, including us, stand on their chairs — a tricky proposition because you have to hold yourself high enough to see over everyone else, but low enough to see around the various poles and beams and under the pipes hanging down from the ceiling. I have the sense that everyone is leaning just the slightest bit forward. On my past visits to the track, the races themselves have provided jolts of excitement, mostly when my horse had a shot at finishing in the money, but I've never experienced anything like this. I can feel the anticipation of 156,435 people who've been waiting all day for this moment; it presses down like hundreds of millions of dollars stacked on the roof.

At last the gate clicks, the crowd surges, and the horses charge down the frontstretch in a burst of swerving and flying dirt and jellybean-bright colors catching the light. They career into the clubhouse turn and around into the backstretch.

I'm all in on Flower Alley, a strong finisher who went off at 41–1, so I'm happy to see that he's not burning himself out early at the front of the pack. As the horses head down the backstretch we shift our focus to the Jumbotrons across from the grandstand. In what seems like a heartbeat the horses are going into the stretch turn, and the pack is tight. It's anyone's race, and into the final stretch, Flower Alley is there in a pack just behind the leaders. He's in the perfect position to kick on the jets and go. "Hit it!" I yell. "Go!"

At that moment we are no longer a crowd. We are a collection of individuals, isolated in our respective dramas, fully concentrating on our singular dreams, represented by a twelve-hundred-pound animal charging over a four-hundred-yard stretch of dirt that hasn't been anything but a place for horses to run for 130 years. Nobody cares who's next to him or in front of him or beside him. I am the guy who bet on Flower Alley. Kevin is the one pulling for Afleet Alex. Even Karin, standing right next to me, has laid her money on a separate horse and is enveloped in her own sphere of hopeful urging. There is a tunnel-vision focus on the track and the sounds of people yearning. "Flower Alley!" I yell. "Flower Alley, Flower Alley, Floweralleyfloweralleyfloweralley," and then finally, "Aaaahhhhhhhhhhhhhhhhhhhhhhhhhhhhhhhhhhhhhhh," as he fades down the stretch.

In the end it is the mottled colt, Giacomo, a 50–1 longshot who rallies to jump ahead in the final yards. As he does, people throw up their hands, toss their stubs into the air, fall back into their seats. They turn to one another, suddenly remembering they're not alone, to relive some moment of "if only" conjecture. There are gestures of despair and disappointment everywhere and isolated scenes of celebration, and yet the atmosphere remains buoyant. The residual electricity pulses through the crowd. We are again united. We are the people who have come to the Kentucky Derby.

The struggle is individual, the experience collective, although stratified.

As we make our way to the exits, I look out at the infield denizens, who have started packing up all their belongings before the long, jostling walk out through the two small tunnels. In the exodus, the mood begins to wane. That feeling of unity and bonhomie that pervaded the place in the aftermath of the race is now as much a part of history as the result. Out in the concourse, the people descending from the club levels above us — including ones with names like the Jockey Club and Millionaires Row — have their choice of elevators and escalators, all of which lead directly to the limo pickup area.

Outside, we find ourselves walking behind the actors Jerry O'Connell and Rebecca Romijn. I played golf with O'Connell and actor/comedian Bill Bellamy twice, and I consider calling out to him but decide not to. I'm sure he'd remember me — it's probably the only two times in his life he's played golf with a black comedian and a magazine writer — but something doesn't feel right about it. These two tabloid regulars are walking among us, she striding tall and proud and he bouncing along carrying her hatbox, but they are not of us and something in the context makes that clear.

Instead we reach our rental cars and make the quick drive to the airport. Lucky for us, we're among the first to arrive. There are so many private planes in town — more than four hundred — that the two biggest makers, Gulfstream and Bombardier, have new product displays and salespeople on hand. If we aren't at the front of the line for takeoff, it could be hours before we get out of here. Kevin, thankfully, has called ahead, and when we arrive at our Lear 35, the pilot has the engine running and is ready to go.

The Derby ended at about 6:25; at 7:09 we're airborne. We pop another round of fresh drinks and nosh on a platter of gourmet sandwiches — sans crusts — as we jet above the clouds. By 9:20, barely three hours after the race, I'm in my driveway. My children, asleep in their beds, will wake up in the morning to find their mother waiting for them. A happy Mother's Day will follow.

On the downside, I'm officially ruined for commercial travel. But not all of my Derby brethren are. I began this journey believing that sports brought people together, especially men. It was a secret language we could speak. Stuck at a party where you don't know anyone? Talk sports. Time to kill before a business meeting? At a bar? In line at the Home Depot? Sports, sports, sports. In the outside world it is a unifying phenomenon. The week after the Derby, I'm in the grocery store and in the produce aisle is a stock boy, maybe twenty, African American, jeans hanging low on his hips. He's talking to a shopper, a white guy, maybe fifty, with white hair, jangling the keys to a luxury car. They're trading theories about what is wrong with Derek Jeter specifically and the Yankees in general. It was a debate among equals, and it's hard to imagine another topic that would bring these two together.

At these bigtime events, though, there is a weird effect in which people move apart rather than together. In some very obvious ways, yes — Patriots fans versus Eagles fans — but in more subtle ways as well. In almost every case there are clearly drawn lines of privilege and access based largely on money. In the stands, on the infield, and at the ticket booths we were not all one sportsloving nation, but a swarm of dollar signs, separated by chainlink fences and security checkpoints as much as by our taste in sparkling carbonated beverages.

This is a reality that I've now lived with quite easily from both sides of the equation, but the recognition of it is a surprise. It will not be the last.

6 ★ Wimbledon

June 20–24, 2005

London, England

WIMBLEDON IS LIKE A DREAM. Not just because of the quaint little town where the All England Lawn Tennis Club sits, with its brick-lined streets that curve away like cart paths in a Euclidean landscape, and its old stone houses and tiny shops, with slate roofs that tile on top of each other like picturesque dominoes that have yet to be toppled. Not because of the cottages and stately Tudors that line the neighborhood, complete with ivied walls and trim sun-dappled gardens, like something out of Jane Austen. And not because the complex itself sits up on a hill behind wrought-iron gates and brick walls, greenery climbing the exteriors and purple and white flowers filling in the architecture. Yes, Wimbledon, both the complex where the games are played and the area surrounding it, fulfills my preconceived notions beyond any other venue I've visited so far. But the particular dreaminess I'm experiencing is born from more than just a fantasy-like atmosphere. In truth, I'm half-asleep.

The last few weeks have been a blur. Golf season is at its peak, with the U.S. Open just finished and the British Open closing in quickly. I've worked straight through two of the last three weekends. After the last all-weekend shift, I went straight from the office to the airport and caught an overnight flight to London. British Airways has a rep for good service, but they take it too far. They woke me up to serve me food I didn't want — twice. Then there was a minor commotion when a fifteen-year-old boy who was seated in my row turned whitish blue on his way back from the lavatory and passed out in the aisle. I managed about three hours of sleep on the seven-hour flight.

The plane touched down at 9:10 A.M. local time on Tuesday, and my first step was to check in at my hotel. I resisted the two freshly made beds in my room and headed out to the club. When I booked the room I had asked if the location was convenient to Wimbledon. "Yes," the excessively polite travel agent had said. "I believe you can take the train right out there." In a technical way, she was correct — the train does stop in the village of Wimbledon. What she failed to mention was that the trip required a cab ride and two different trains. If in the confused high that comes from too many caffeinated beverages, not enough food, and no sleep the place takes on the hallucinogenic trappings of an oasis, I don't think I can be blamed.

The most surreal part is that when I finally arrive, after a full workday, a seven-hour flight, and ninety minutes on public transportation, I don't even have a way to get onto the grounds, although it's not for lack of trying. For the last three months, I'd been e-mailing and phoning in requests for media credentials, and at every turn I'd been given assurances that things were in the works. The problem was, I'd been given no assurances that I'd actually be granted one. With ten days left before the tournament, I forced the issue and at last got an answer: "Sorry, no."

I'm not giving up that easily. I have a few tricks up my sleeve, which is why I've rushed out here today. At one of the gates, I approach a steward. I might have called him a guard or an usher, but his nametag and armband clearly identify him as a steward. "Where is the media center?" I ask. He directs me to a gate on the far side of the complex, which consumes an entire three-block triangle of land. As I make my way around, I pass Gate 3, where about three hundred people are lined up. A man offers me a coupon and directs me toward the line, assuming I am part of the ticket-holding public, but I wave him off and carry on.

At the media center entrance I boldly announce that I am here to pick up my credential. A woman leads me down a passage, through a building, down a few sets of stairs, and along a matrix of corridors before finally depositing me at a desk in the media center. Another young woman rolls her chair up and says hello.

"Hi," I say. "Jim Gorant from *Sports Illustrated*. I'm here to pick up my credential."

"Okay," she says, and begins searching through a small file box in front of her for a credential I know she'll never find. Finally, she shakes her head. "I've got one here for *Sports Illustrated*, but it's in someone else's name."

"Right," I say. "He's coming, but there should be one for me also. It was all arranged."

She's now randomly searching through other files. "No, I don't see anything."

"I'm certain it's been taken care of," I say, staying polite but keeping the pressure on.

She glances over her shoulder but does not see whomever she is looking for, because she turns back to the file. "Betty's just in a meeting," she says. This is good. Betty, I know, is Betty Sommes, the woman who'd turned me down. Her unavailability is just what I was hoping for. This is a key moment. The girl behind the desk is a little harried, confused, and lacking any authority figure to guide her. This is the point where she might jump off the script and take the initiative to issue me a credential to make the problem go away. All she needs is a little push in the right direction.

"Well, we don't need to waste Betty's time, anyway," I offer. "I'm sure she's got a ton of stuff to deal with this week."

The young woman pauses. She looks over her shoulder again. She's on the cusp. I can feel it. Come on, I think. She glances up. I give her my most pathetic look. She hesitates, but, alas, "One minute," she says, and goes off to consult someone. "Betty will be out in just a moment if you'll wait," she tells me upon returning.

Okay, that didn't work, but not all hope is lost. Yes, Betty has denied me once, but it's easy to say no via e-mail. It's much harder to do it to someone's face, especially when that someone has hauled his ass across the ocean to be there. I'll play it polite and a little innocent.

Meanwhile, I wait. And as I do more people come to the desk. Slowly I get pushed into the corner near the door. Streams of people flow in and out. The girl who'd helped me now sits flirting with some guy. Maria Sharapova's match has just started and everyone who isn't otherwise engaged watches it on the TV mounted on the opposite wall. It would be easy, ridiculously easy, for me to walk out the door and disappear into the complex.

But I've given my name and used the magazine's as well. If I were to disappear now they'd figure it out. Perhaps they would refuse to give our writer who was actually covering the event his credential. That wouldn't go over too well with the folks back in New York. So I resist the temptation.

Finally, someone calls my name, and I turn to see a frazzled-looking woman coming across the room toward me. She extends her hand. "Betty Sommes."

"Hi," I say as we shake.

"I thought we'd discussed this matter?" she says, her tone flat.

"Well," I say, "I was here anyway, so I thought I'd stop by to see if there was any way you might be able to squeeze me in." I search her face for any hint of sympathy and softness but see none. Her eyes are cool and gray. Her bristly hair arches back from her face, giving her the appearance of an overused toothbrush. She does not smile. She does not flinch. She does not break eye contact. She just opens her mouth and says, "No."

I'm still not ready to accept that answer, and offer a few lame pleas. She brushes them off with equal dispassion. As I struggle to come up with something, some magic words that will break her icy exterior, I catch her eye. We connect. Our pupils linger on each other. I can feel something happening. I hold the gaze longer than I normally might, longer than is comfortable. Something's going on behind those eyes, and I realize that my best bet right now is to keep my mouth shut and wait for her to speak.

It doesn't take long. A moment — dare I say two heartbeats — pass, and then she opens her mouth. "I'm going," she says, "to have to have you escorted from the grounds."

"Actually," I tell her, "in an odd way, I consider that a compliment."

I never would've imagined it, but this comment seems to soften her. "Just a moment," she says, holding up a finger. She disappears into a back room, and soon reappears tailed by a tall man with a beard. He's a *Sports Illustrated* photographer who lives in London and is very intimate with the club. He'd tried unsuccessfully to help get me a credential the previous week, but I take his presence now as a good sign. "We've just been talking," Betty says, "and I can arrange for you to get a grounds pass for tomorrow for sixteen pounds. It'll allow you onto the grounds on any of the courts except Centre Court and Court 1. Does that sound good to you?"

It sounds great. I pay her my sixteen pounds as fast as I can sort the coins. Moments later, a female steward arrives to walk me out. In her blue skirt, stiff yellow button-down, official armband, and high round hat with a short bill, she looks like a plucky, stiff-upper-lipped ambulance worker in a World War II movie. Chatting about the weather with such a woman as she leads you through the hallowed halls of the All England Lawn Tennis and Croquet Club and deposits you in the street is not an entirely unpleasant experience, especially when you've just scored a grounds pass for the following day. I may not be able to tell a story about the time I snuck into Wimbledon, but you can bet your ass twenty years from now I'll be boring the crap out of someone with the tale of how I got thrown out.

★ Cut loose with a large part of the day still ahead, I decide to explore the town. Although I suspect that it's a tacky tourist pursuit, I'm determined to enjoy some strawberries and cream. Like a lot of other people, I first started watching tennis seriously during the mid-'70s, sucked in by the legendary showdowns at Wimbledon. Connors and Nastase, Evert and King, Evert and Navratilova, Borg and McEnroe — especially Borg and McEnroe. I hated McEnroe. Those rivalries fed the tennis boom of the '70s and early '80s, and they always seemed to peak at Wimbledon, which, like the Masters, exists on a higher plane than other major tournaments. There was a distinct feeling of history and tradition to Wimbledon and a sense that people wanted to see it more and players wanted to win it more. Wimbledon was what made tennis cool, and even as preteens it inspired my friends and me to go find a court for a few weeks each summer and make like the pros.

And of course we watched. We watched for the tennis, but also for the royalty in boxes and the supermodels and actresses in the stands. And just as they inevitably overused the term "fortnight," Bud Collins and Dick Enberg yapped about the strawberries and cream. Well, I'm here now and I can't sit with the royalty or meet the supermodels, but I'm certainly determined to have some strawberries and cream.

I take off around the back of the club, where a path along the fence leads to an open view of the practice courts. A number of players are out hitting balls, and one of them is almost surely Anna Kournikova, the buxom blond Russian who's more famous for her looks than her play. I'd thought she'd retired from tournament competition but I'm fairly certain it's her. Besides the body and the long blond hair, there is one other clue: Three blokes stand a few yards away with their faces pressed to the fence, mumbling fast, low salivations to one another as they watch her.

Two of them wear blue uniforms with name patches on the breast and the third has sweated through a brown uniform shirt with the sleeves torn off. This last fellow pushes his cell phone through the fence to take pictures. After a few minutes I figure out it's not Kournikova but some aspiring knockoff, the inevitable "next Kournikova," and I think the boys have figured out as much, too, but when she stops to shove an extra ball up the thigh of her body-hugging shorts they couldn't care if she was Anna Karenina. They hoot and giggle and high-five one another as if they'd just seen the queen's underwear. That is, until one of them spots a film crew setting up next to the courts to tape some of the action. "Look," he says, "they're filmin' it."

"Ah, shit," says the guy in brown, pushing away from the fence, "they'll see me at work." They scatter up the hill, laughing.

Back out front, a long line snakes down from the main gate over a footbridge that crosses the road, down onto the sidewalk on the opposite side, and trails away past the edge of the grounds, maybe a quarter mile altogether. I walk toward the end of the line to see what's going on. A steward hands me a coupon and points me toward the end of the line, just as the other steward had done this morning. "What happens here?" I said.

"Keep that coupon," she says. "When you get to the front you can buy a day pass for sixteen pound."

"You mean the event isn't sold out?"

Yes, I'm told, months in advance, but each day they sell five hundred tickets for Court 1 and Centre Court and another five hundred general grounds passes on a first come, first served basis.

There's something you have to love about socialism. Unlike the scalpers or the day-pass resellers outside Augusta National, where it was every man for himself and the only criteria for success were money and bargaining skill, the Brits have instituted a scalping welfare program. For them it doesn't matter how much money you have. If you're willing to wait in line and you've got your sixteen pounds, you've got as good a shot as anyone else. With all these people queued up, any self-respecting American would be tempted to take his day pass to the last guy in line and resell it for twenty-five pounds, but that doesn't seem to be happening here. Everyone is treated equally, unless they're royalty.

The steward says I'd probably get in at about five thirty, which isn't a bad deal considering that play goes on until eight thirty or nine. But it's only about three o'clock now, and there's no way I can stand in line for two hours in my current state. I give away my coupon and start the mile-long walk back to the train station.

Along the brick sidewalks I keep an eye on the concessionaires who have set up shop. There are, by my count, six, most of them locals who are trying to cash in on the fortunate location of their driveways. Three sell T-shirts, a couple push ice cream, and there are several burger flippers, which I find surprising, partly because I think of burgers as distinctly American and partly because I think of burgers as distinctly tough to sell in the country most closely identified with mad cow disease. No one offers strawberries and cream. At the same time, I know I'm not at a major sporting event in America because no one sells thunder sticks or ticket holders or Mardi Gras beads.

I stop at a friendly fish-and-chips shop with a blue awning and outdoor seating. Nothing. A 7-Eleven–like convenience store and a little grocery. Nothing. A bakery where fresh loaves of bread sit unsliced on the shelf. Nothing. What does a guy have to do to get some strawberries and cream?

★ Back at the hotel, I drift in and out of a restless and unsatisfying sleep. If Wimbledon is a dream, it is one I can neither completely wake up from nor fully surrender to. A few times I emerge from my slumber realizing I've been dreaming about my mother. I find this notable because in the days after her death from cancer, it seemed like everyone — my father, my sister, my wife — was dreaming about her, but I was not. I'd wondered if there was something wrong with me. I was sad and I missed her, but I did not dream of her. In fact, I had a hard time picturing her at all.

One day shortly after her death, I called my father at one of those rare moments when he was on the phone and also had a call waiting, so the machine kicked over to the seldom-used "we're unavailable right now" message. My mother's voice, which had been replaced on the main message, still delivered this one. The sound was instantly familiar, at once comforting and sad, and it brought back a flood of memories that I could not have conjured if I tried. I attributed her sudden appearance in my London hotel to a similar evocation: My only other trip to London was on one of her crazed sightseeing tours, fifteen years ago.

That my memories should be rooted in such an excursion is not surprising, because she loved to travel. After I started working and began to hit the road more and more, she'd regularly force me to tally how many states I'd been to (forty-two), and try to convince me it was worth my time to find ways to get to the last eight (Hawaii, Indiana, Kansas, Michigan, Nebraska, North Dakota, Oregon, South Dakota). In fact, a year after our London trip, she and my sister drove to Memphis to see a King Tut exhibit that wouldn't get any closer to New York. While there, she drove across the Hernando de Soto Bridge into Arkansas. Went about twenty miles to the information center. Walked around. Got back in the car and left. This way she could say she'd been to Arkansas. That meant something to her.

Her approach to sports was similar. She'd just as soon skip the pesky details and swoop in for the big game. She'd never watch baseball, but she'd come around for the playoffs and the World Series. She'd never watch football, but every year she went to an all-women's Super Bowl party. When the Giants made it to their first Super Bowl after the 1986 season, my dad and his business partner, lifelong fans, got tickets and prepared to go to Pasadena for the game. The wives wanted in. Tickets to the game didn't matter, they just craved a few January days in Southern California. But once she got there, my mom couldn't resist. She was right outside one of the hugest events in the world, and there was no way she wasn't driving across that bridge (metaphorically speaking). Five minutes after kickoff she slipped an usher fifty bucks and she and the other wife sauntered in.

I hadn't thought about these things in a long time. Perhaps it was some combination of being in London again and having too much time alone to think that was bringing it all back to me now. But there was also this: I flew into London on June 21, which would have been my parents' forty-first anniversary. The year before, they'd celebrated their fortieth in a hospital room, and three days afterward my mom was dead.

I didn't resort to bribing a steward, but I realize now that I did my mom proud by weaseling my way into Wimbledon. Suddenly, I feel as if I'm driving into Arkansas.

★ When I disembark at Southfields Station on my second morning in London, I notice things that I hadn't seen on my first pass through town. For one thing, the station is dressed up like a tennis court: green carpet with court lines drawn on it covers the ground, green wallpaper clings to the walls, and a large-screen TV mounted in a kiosk shows the matches — it's all a giant American Express ad, of course, but how did I miss it?

The town of Wimbledon, I'm happy to see, hasn't changed much. But today I'm here for more than just the town. Armed with my day pass, I glide past the stewards and onto the club grounds. This is it. I'm inside. The original event — the world's first-ever organized tennis tournament — was played nearby in 1877, but the All England Lawn Tennis Club moved to this location in 1922. So as I make my way up the brick-paved path, I'm striding the very earth where kings and queens and dukes and duchesses have trod. And where an entire list of athletes — Bill Tilden, René Lacoste, Rod Laver, John Newcombe, Maureen Connolly, Steffi Graf, and even Boris Becker — turned into more than tennis players; they became household names. It's where Billie Jean King and Martina Navratilova set incredible records. Where Connors and Borg and McEnroe staged epic battles. Where Althea Gibson and Arthur Ashe went from merely breaking racial barriers to changing the way people think.

I take a moment to get my bearings. The place is a maze of courts cut into the side of a hill, like terraces in a Japanese garden. At the high point, there is actually a little pond with floating lily pads and a waterfall that runs down toward the courts before disappearing underground. Hedgerows line the courts, so I can't really see anything but the players' heads as I walk by, but I know they're playing because there's the distinctive, ever-present *thwop* of a ball being smashed by a racket.

At surprising places there are overhangs and balconies where I can see into the courts. Some are surrounded by one or two rows of benches, while others have ten or fifteen rows of bleachers on each side. Small lines form outside the courts as people wait for a seat to open up. This is true everywhere except the two show courts, Centre Court and Court 1, which require a separate ticket.

As I pass by, Court 1 looks like a typical modern stadium, although it's painted green and purple, Wimbledon's colors, and draped with flowers and ivy. I wonder if that's where they serve the strawberries and cream. As always, I burn to go where I'm not welcome, and I try to size up the possibility of sneaking in. It looks like there's some potential, but probably not a good idea to begin my day breaking the rules. The Court 1 mission will have to wait.

Not certain where I'm going or who's playing, I stumble upon the line for Court 2. This seems like a good place to queue up, since it allows me to watch the action on Court 6 while waiting. It's already seventy-five degrees, but with the sun beating down it feels hotter and there's not a spot of shade. The match features Roberta Vinci and Anne Kremer.

This close up — there are two rows of people between me and the court — I can get a sense of how hard they hit the ball and how fast they move. I can also see the weird skids and low hops the ball takes off the turf, something that they're always talking about on TV but that I couldn't completely appreciate until now. The grass itself is something of a marvel, too. The tight coils, which wear and brown over the course of the tournament, seem too short and thick, too resilient to be actual grass. It reminds me of Ronco's hair-replacement system; it can't really be grass, it's just dirt painted green.

I'm enjoying this match, but the line moves quickly and soon enough, I'm led up the stairs and into Court 2. Most of it is reserved seating, but at the top of the bleachers on either side there are large standing areas, where I push in and find myself a spot. The match features Feliciano López of Spain vs. David Sherwood, a twenty-six-year-old from Scotland and therefore a fan favorite in Great Britain's ongoing quest for a male winner of its most famous sporting event for the first time since 1936. Thanks to Sherwood, the hometown fans are packed into the court and pumped, as are a small but vocal group of Latinos who regularly yell "*Venga* Feli." Even though I'm farther away for this match, it's obvious how much faster the men's game is. Both guys hit serves so incredibly deep and fast, it's impossible to tell if the ball lands in or out of the service box.

All the surfaces up here are dark, and the heat is brutal. Within minutes I've sweat through my shirt, and looking around I can see I'm not the only one. Several people along the back row have popped open umbrellas to give themselves a break from the sun, and several of the women standing around me have sweat beading up on their foreheads. There are leaning posts, but nowhere to sit, and with a steady churn of people coming and going, I'm constantly getting jostled. This is not Wimbledon as I imagined it. This is not sitting primly in a comfortable seat, watching the ball hop back and forth over the net, rewarding winning shots with polite applause.

Still, there is a sense of uprightness and decorum. I hadn't planned it, but I notice that I'm wearing a white shirt. As I think about it, I realize that all I packed were white shirts. Tennis whites for the trip to Wimbledon. It must've felt right in my head when I was packing, and the experience supports the instinct.

From this vantage point I have a good view of the grounds. Thousands of fans meander among the courts, giving the impression that at any given time, half the people in the place are watching tennis and the other half are simply out for a stroll. In the far corner of the complex I spy one court that has a smaller grandstand covered by an awning. Shade will be mine. I make my way over and after a fifteen-minute wait, I have myself a seat out of the sun at Court 13.

A new match is just starting. An all-Russian showdown I surmise from the two names on the scoreboard: Pastikova and Vaidisova. A glance at the program shows that both players are from the Czech Republic. Oh well. It also makes clear that I don't know either of these players. Wrong again. They step out on court and I instantly recognize the latter as the Kournikova lookalike from yesterday's practice session. This should be fun. I settle in and get ready to watch. The molded-plastic chairs aren't the lap of luxury, but they beat standing in the sun. Throughout the complex, they rent out seat cushions, but I've had a hard time bringing myself to get one. In another of those quirky variations between American and English, the locals over here don't use the phrase "for rent." Instead they say "to let," which means whenever I see one of the stands renting seat cushions I think I see a big sign above it that says "Toilet." Needless to say, I don't want any of what they're renting there.

Such petty concerns give way to the steady back-and-forth rhythm of the match. From this position, the experience is more like what I had in mind. Around me, snippets of conversation bubble up between points. People pull homemade sandwiches from portable coolers. It's all very proper and cozy.

Sometimes too cozy. When Vaidisova starts to pull ahead early, someone yells out, "Come on, Pasti, make it int'restin'." There is something more personal about the heckling at Wimbledon, whether it's encouragement or derision. Because the game is so quiet and the fans so close to the action, almost anything yelled is audible to everyone around the court, giving the entire setup an intimacy that is both endearing and alarming. The court itself looks different from up here, too, as if it's been stretched. And there is a three-dimensionality to it that doesn't come across on TV, which doesn't provide an accurate gauge of the size and speed of the players or their relation to the court. At home I never understand the relative distances between the lines and to the shots. There are so many balls that it looks like a player could have gotten to had he or she stretched a little farther, but in person it's easy to see how he or she had no chance.

The players too are so close and never offscreen. It's oddly intimate to watch these women shove the extra ball they keep during service point up the leg of their lycra shorts. With all the advancements in tennis gear over the last decade, they haven't come up with a better place for women to store a ball?

After a while I begin to inspect the crowd as well: mostly white and probably evenly split between men and women, with an unprecedented concentration of women over forty-five. People sitting in the sun have gotten inventive, making hats and protective nose shields out of newspapers. And while cell phones are supposed to be turned off, everywhere I hear the little chirps and beeps of PalmPilots and BlackBerries and phones. People hide their faces behind programs, stage-whispering into their hands.

On the court, the linesmen call out "Fault," or more accurately, "Fawwwt." How I thrill to the sound. Has anyone ever played or watched tennis without imitating the linespeople at Wimbledon? The ball boys (and girls) carry themselves with a martial formality that mocks their actual lowly position. Pasty-skinned ne'er-dowells, they march onto the court and snap to attention with a ball held out in front of them every time a player looks at them. They run everywhere as fast as they can, even if it's a few feet away, which makes them the world's shortest sprinters, all twisted faces and flailing elbows for a twenty-foot race. Their little routines when they change personnel or open a new can of tennis balls defy description; they are beyond parody.

These things alone are worth the price of admission. Of all the events on my list, Wimbledon, because of the distance and the aura of exclusivity, is the most exotic, so to be here absorbing all the little quirks and nuances that I've come to associate with the tournament is a joy. Even better is the experience of Court 13. The outer courts, if positioned properly, carry a certain cachet among hard-core fans. Only tourists and know-nothings crowd into the show courts. Real fans find tense matches between up-and-comers on the outer courts. For movie buffs it would be like comparing the latest alien shoot-'em-up at the 10-plex to seeing Kurosawa at some rundown indie screening room.

By catching the Pastikova-Vaidisova showdown on 13, I'm buying myself some cred and I take a few minutes to play out the imaginary conversations that will follow in my mind: "Oh, Pastikova, give her another year to develop and she'll make some noise out here."

"Vaidisova, I know. Would you believe some people mistake her for Kournikova . . ."

Thus I spend my time between shots, until the match ends with Vaidisova winning 7–6, 6–3. The spot is cool and comfortable, but I decide to move on. I can't help but be distracted by the "oohs" and "ahhs" that rise from other courts. There are so many matches going on in such a small area, it almost always seems like something spectacular is happening somewhere else. It's impossible not to feel like you're missing something.

Back out among the masses, I once again eye up Court 1, but the time still isn't right. Instead, I stop for a few minutes to sit under one of the long, shady rows of flower- and ivy-covered trestles, where people sit and sip cool drinks at small tables. From time to

time players appear out of nowhere. Wearing warm-ups and carrying a bag of rackets, they create little ripples as the stewards clear a
path in the crowd. They walk so close by, you can touch them.

I queue up for a match on Court 18. The line seems short, but
moves very slowly. Seats open up only when someone decides to
leave, and they can only leave when the players switch ends, after
every other game. It can take a while, but for most of the time I'm
in line I can see the match through the opening in the stands. It's
out here, where the atmosphere is a little looser and the noise restrictions not as great, that the most camaraderie springs up. After
a while I find myself openly chatting with my line mates and con-
verted into an instant aficionado. When the guy next to me observes that the one player is afraid of "getting caught in the middle
because he can't pull off the half volley," I hear myself responding:
"I don't know why, he's been killing that guy with the little slice
forehand."

I do eventually make it into the match, and while I enjoy the
tennis, I miss my roundtable partners from the queue. So when it
ends, I leave Court 18 and wander up onto the hill behind Court
1, an area of the complex known as Aorangi Park. It's a large slope
with a few picnic tables where people stretch out on the grass and
watch the action from Court 1 on a Jumbotron. During the semi-
finals and finals, thousands of people sit on the hill and watch the
play from right outside the stadium, creating a cool doubling effect. For those outside, it's like being at the world's largest outdoor
sports bar, complete with live sound effects — the *pong* of the ball
and the players' grunts and exhortations. Inside, the bursts of applause from without add a depth and strength to their own cheering that adds to the excitement.

I buy an ice cream and take a seat at a table where two women
sit applying sunscreen to already bright red skin and drinking some
sort of brown liquid with vegetation sticking out of it. One of them
has curly blond hair and the other auburn hair and full droopy
jowls that make it possible to think she's what Margaret Thatcher
might once have looked like. During a break in their conversation I
ask, "What is that you're drinking?"

"This here?" says Thatcher, holding up her glass. "It's Pimm's."

"What's that?" I say.

"It's a drink, you know," says the blonde, "a Wimbledon thing. It's a traditional thing you drink at Wimbledon."

"Oh, like a mint julep."

"Yeah, I don't know that one, but this is the thing you drink when you come to Wimbledon."

"Is it good?" I ask.

They eye each other for a moment, then the blonde laughs a little and says, "You know, it's the thing you drink at Wimbledon."

Not exactly a ringing endorsement, but I'm sold. I find a concession stand that sells the concoction (no strawberries and cream, I check) and order up a pint. I return to the table and take a sip as the two of them watch. The stuff is not altogether unpleasant, light and lemony with something of a medicinal quality. It's not something you would take a sip of and say, "Mmmm, good," before taking another drag. In fact, it's more reminiscent of the mint julep in that it has a sip-it-slowly-as-you-get-used-to-it kind of taste.

By the end of the second Pimm's I've learned that they both work in the marketing department of a large corporation, which is where they got the tickets, although they don't rank high enough on the company ladder to get passes for week two. Those are for the bigwigs. They've each been five or six times, and usually don't end up watching too much tennis. "Can't be bothered with the queuing and the shushing," says Blondie.

We continue to chat and before long the conversation lulls but the Pimm's begins to work its magic. I decide it's now time for my assault on Court 1. At first glance, it looks like it will be easier than I imagined. I walk up the steps and enter the main building without any resistance. People linger in the hall that circles the court. Sets of steps lead up to the entrances and those are roped off. A steward stands behind each rope. I try sweet-talking a few, but there's no way they're letting me in. I think about my mom at the Super Bowl and consider trying to slip someone a bill, but decide that I wouldn't know where to start.

Finally I come to a gate where the steward has walked to the top of the steps and stands watching the action on the court. This allows me to push against the rope hard enough to climb the first few steps and get a glimpse of the court. The first thing I notice is that the place is nowhere near full. Hundreds of people all over the complex are standing in line to watch some tennis, and here you have the marquee matchups playing in front of a half-empty stadium. The second thing I notice is who's playing. It's women's doubles, and while I don't know all the players I can easily identify one of them, Martina Navratilova.

Navratilova is a Wimbledon legend. She's tied with Billie Jean King for most titles, an astounding twenty. She won nine of them in singles, a record six in a row at one point, and earned the rest in doubles. All this from a woman who'd never played a competitive grass-court match before arriving here for the first time. What's more, she was the dominant figure in women's tennis when I was growing up, synonymous with Wimbledon and winning and veiny biceps. To see her on one of the show courts is a treat.

After a few minutes the steward turns and sees me. I'm sure he's going to shoo me away. He stares. I can see his mind working. No one else has joined me, and I get the sense he doesn't really feel like moving. I must be right because he turns back to the match without saying anything. I take this as an invitation to push it a little farther, slipping under the rope and climbing up one step short of the top. I watch from there for what must be close to ten minutes. Finally he turns and says, "Ticket."

"Don't have one."

"Sorry," he says. "Got to go."

Even if it was short-lived, I consider Martina on Court 1 a success worthy of another Pimm's, so I get one and return to Aorangi Park. Blondie and Thatcher are still there, now mingling with a bunch of rowdy Australians. There has been very little evidence of drunkenness so far, but as the afternoon slips into a sort of dusky gloaming there is a slight change of metabolism. I wouldn't call it rowdy by any means, but the pulse has increased. It's a little louder, a little looser; there are more people laughing; there is, here and there, the whiff of body odor. I fear I'm more part of the problem than the solution. Regardless, it's very easy to lie back on the grass and become part of the crowd. Sipping the Pimm's, "oohing" and "ahhing" at the play on the big screen, and chatting with the Aussies.

I stay until the light starts to dim and my jetlag forces me to think more about my bed than the *pock* of tennis balls. I excuse myself and head for the train station. As I walk I see on the sidewalk ahead of me two young girls sitting at a folding table. It looks like they've set up a lemonade stand. As I get closer, though, I see it's not lemonade they're selling but strawberries and cream. I can't believe it.

I buy a plate and I eat them as I walk through the town. That sort of magic predarkness is settling over the little streets as the Pimm's and the long, dusty day of memories swirl around my head. I want to say the strawberries and cream are delicious. The perfect capper. It's what the story line demands. But the truth is, the berries are a little bitter and the cream, which was probably made some time ago, is watery. Luckily, I'm of the belief that anything with whipped cream can't be that bad, so I eat every last one of them and wipe the paper plate with my finger when I'm done.

★ For the second day in a row I fall asleep as I ride the train, and for the second straight day I wake up thinking of my mother. Somehow she knew I wanted to be a writer before I ever had the temerity to say so out loud. Writing seemed like such an unreasonable thing to pursue. It was impractical. As far as I knew, it was nearly impossible to make a living at. Even more, I had no idea how to go about it. Neither of my parents had finished college. I didn't know any writers. I didn't even know if I could write. I just knew that's what I wanted to do. For the most part, it remained our secret. But from time to time, usually when I was asking for a favor, she'd say, "When you write that first novel, I want the dedication page to say 'For my mother.' Got it? Like the guys on TV say, 'Hi Mom,' I want it to say, 'For my mother.'" At which point I would usually roll my eyes and leave the room.

She'd beaten cancer twice before and been clean for seven

years when she was diagnosed again in March 2004. At first there was a feeling of confidence. What she had this time was much worse than what she'd had before, but we were used to her coming through. We expected it. The chemo and the surgery and whatever else would suck, but at some point it would be over and she would be her old self again.

But this was different. By May it became clear that the treatments weren't working. She continued to get thinner and weaker. Her complexion went gray. When I looked at her, I knew she was dying. I just didn't think it would happen so fast. No one gave us any timelines, but for some reason I thought she'd make it through the summer. So while her death in late June was not a surprise, there was still a sense of the unexpected.

I was despondent in the days afterward. I was upset that she had suffered so much. That she wouldn't see my kids grow up and that they would do so without knowing her. That I hadn't done more for her at the end — I think she wanted to talk about what was happening to her, but whenever the subject came up I brushed it aside because I wanted to stay positive. At the funeral I stumbled through a barely audible eulogy, whatever emotion I had left pouring out of me. Then I was spent. That was it. I had no more to give. For the next few weeks — months, probably — I was numb. I'd find myself thinking about her at odd times, noting things I wanted to tell her, then remembering she wasn't there, coming home from running an errand and sitting in the car for ten minutes, staring at the sky, my mind wandering.

As I sit on a rattling London subway, on my way home from the matches at Wimbledon, it all comes together. I realize it was no coincidence that I came up with the idea for this yearlong journey two weeks after my mother was diagnosed. That the idea came to life in my head even as she wasted away. That two months after she passed, I decided for no reason I could explain to throw excess burden onto my wife, abandon my kids, and take ten trips and cross the Atlantic in search of these experiences. My mother herself couldn't have dreamed up a more perfect travel itinerary (although hers would have been the Ten Department Stores Every Shopper Should See).

Yes, what I'm searching for on some level is some magic key that will help decipher the common denominators between the great events and what lies at the heart of my own sports mania, but I'm doing something else, too. I'm dealing with my mother's death. Running from it, facing it, paying tribute to her, coming to grips with my own imminent demise.

The experience at Wimbledon has been fantastic. As with the Masters and the Kentucky Derby, it is something more to me for having been there. I know that in future years when I see those events they will be enhanced by my firsthand knowledge of the place, by being able to picture in my mind the sights and sounds, the smells, the bustle unique to each. Still, by the time I reach the airport, I'm emotionally drained. And when the plane takes off, I feel as if I'm leaving behind more than another week and a half of championship tennis and a city where I once joined my mother on one of her many adventures.

7 ★ Chicago Cubs
vs. Atlanta Braves

August 24, 2005

Chicago, Illinois

BEING A FAN is romantic. There's no way to root for a team, to pull for a bunch of college kids or distant millionaires, without being at least a little emotional and unreasonable. Without being a bit of a fanatic. Sports, by its nature, involves a search for the heroic and ideal — the greatest game, the best player, whatever.

Within the world of sports, baseball is the most romantic of games. It swims in nostalgia. To listen to the pastime's many poets, there's something about the pastoral ease of it, the lazy pace, the idea of men playing like boys, the annual rite of renewal.

Within the game, Wrigley Field is the most romantic of venues. The cozy little stadium was built in 1914, and although only some of the original structure still exists, it remains very close to the way it looked after a 1937 expansion, with old iron stanchions that block views, oddly shaped outfield walls, and a covered upper deck. The entire field is bordered by a low brick wall, giving it the feeling of a well-kept backyard, and the section that spans the outfield is quite famously covered in ivy, the bright yellow numbers that indicate how far each section is from home plate popping out of the leafy green surrounds.

There's no digital scoreboard or Jumbotron on which to show replays or project animated races to entertain the crowd between innings. Instead there's a large hand-painted, hand-operated scoreboard that resides so high above center field that it's never been hit by a ball. Other than a few small electronic displays, it's a complete, old-school throwback to 1940. In fact, Wrigley didn't even have lights until 1988, which meant that prior to the first Bush administration, there'd never been a night game at Wrigley Field.

The words painted across the top of the visitors' dugout read "Welcome to the Friendly Confines of Wrigley Field." Friendly confines? Who could not be charmed?

I suspect that I can be, and I'm the kind of guy who recoils at the whiff of sanctimony surrounding the Masters, resists any hint of nostalgia, and has to hit the mute button during those sappy, violin-scored features on ESPN. Yet, for as long as I've known about the place, I've wanted to go. Not to just any game either. I want to go to an afternoon game during the dog days of August and sit in the stands and soak up the atmosphere — whatever it is. I've always been told Wrigley contains some sort of seminal sports experience. Something that strikes to the heart of baseball, the heart of America. I've always wondered why. Maybe that's the appeal. Maybe it's that I've heard so much about the place that has piqued my curiosity. I'd like to find out what it's really like. What is it that makes the place so special? The problem for me is that I'm not a member of the church of baseball and Wrigley is a cathedral, so I wonder how that will affect my experience.

I admit this might be a quirky pursuit. The way I see it, the first six events on my list were unimpeachable. Any true sports fan should want to go to the Super Bowl, Daytona 500, Final Four, Masters, Kentucky Derby, and Wimbledon at least once. Even if someone hates NASCAR and doesn't think driving a car qualifies as a sport, he should be curious enough to see what it's all about and why so many other sports fans love it.

Wrigley is different because it's not a singular, marquee event — a championship or a showdown between the best. It's just one snakebitten team playing on their little old field. The desire to go is smaller and more personal. A Cubs-Braves game in the middle of August has little impact, but it is not meaningless.

Even as I settle into my seat on the flight out to Chicago, pull out the sports section, and check the standings, the Braves are 71-55 and are three and a half games up in their quest to win the NL East title for the fourteenth time in fourteen years. The Cubs meanwhile are 61-65 and long out of the race for even a wildcard berth in the playoffs. Such haplessness is part of the Cubs greater cosmic import.

They are the perfect romantic counterpart to quirky old Wrigley. Lovable losers who not only can't push the rock up the hill but often seem to come tantalizingly close before failing. Even before the Red Sox finally won the Series in '04, the Cubs were suffering through the longest championship drought of any team in any major pro sport. They have not won the World Series since 1908. Like any good paperback hero, they're struggling against forces greater than themselves: They're cursed.

As the story goes, a Greek immigrant named William Sianis showed up at Wrigley Field for Game Four of the 1945 World Series between the Cubs and the Detroit Tigers with two tickets: one for him and one for his goat. Whether they were allowed to enter or snuck in is a matter of some debate, but either way the two entered the park and watched some of the game before being unceremoniously tossed — a process during which the goat was apparently verbally assaulted. Angry and hurt, Sianis put a curse on the team as he left the stadium, saying the Cubs would never again win the World Series. In some versions of the story he added that they would never play in one at Wrigley. So far both prognostications have proven true.

The list of times the Cubs have come painstakingly close or been the victim of monumental collapse is long and only adds to the aura of legitimacy. In 1969 the Cubs were up nine and a half games in August, but still lost the pennant. In 1973 they hovered near the division lead for most of the first half of the season before losing forty-nine of their last seventy-seven games. In '84 they took the first two of a five-game NLCS series with the Padres before losing three straight. And in 2003 there was the famous Bartman incident. The Cubs, up three games to two on the Florida Marlins in the NLCS, were only five outs away from going to the World Series. With one out in the eighth, Luis Castillo hit a pop down the left-field line. Cubs left fielder Moises Alou moved over to snag the foul ball as it drifted into the first row of the stands, but longtime Cub fan Steve Bartman interfered with him and Alou dropped the ball. Castillo went on to walk and eventually score as the Marlins poured in eight runs that inning, went on to take Game Seven, and denied the Cubs once again.

If sports ever presented the perfect lost cause for a fan to pour his heart into, this is it.

★ I too am a Greek (the original family name was Goranitis), and I've shown up at Wrigley with two tickets. The second is not for my goat, but for my friend Billy, the same Billy I ran into at the Super Bowl. He of the lost limo and the vagabond group of Eagles fans living in RVs. He is the perfect companion for this trip. A forty-year-old bachelor who's let the pleas of several lovetorn heroines fall on deaf ears, he can afford to get in touch with his romantic side. He's also a great traveling companion because he's got time and money, he's a sports fiend, and he's fun.

I'm happy to have him with me as I head out into downtown Chicago the night before the game looking for a place to eat. After the isolation of London, I'm in no mood to dine alone or sit by myself in a hotel room all night. During the time between events — the longest layoff of the enterprise so far — I've been thinking about the larger questions I set out to answer. The Wimbledon revelations about my mother answered a lot of the personal questions, but I still haven't made a lot of progress on the more general queries about why so many of us are obsessed with sports and what connects the "must-see" events.

I've had some insights, and come closer to understanding what might drive me and others, but six of the ten events have gone by and I feel like I need to focus on the big picture. As I think about Wrigley, I keep coming back to all the people who have gone there before me. Not just the ones who have told me stories and painted pictures, the ones who stoked my desire to see it for myself in the first place, but all of them. All the countless millions who've gone there to see a game over the last ninety years.

These roots in the past connect me to something larger than myself in a way that feels good. And this particular trip also allows me to reconnect with Billy, who I don't see that often. After some aimless rambling we wind up at a local pizza joint where we order a beer and settle in to wait for our deep dish. As the beer, then the pizza, then more beer disappear, it becomes clear just how deeply Billy is into sports. Every year he even organizes a minireunion for guys we went to college with. He rounds up tickets for one of the bigger Villanova games of the season and thirty or forty guys show up, including some from as far away as California. He's part of a group that goes on an annual trip called Baseball Weekend, in which they set off for three days with the singular goal of attending as many games as possible. The initial trip, taken when we were juniors, included the Phillies on Friday, the Yankees on Saturday, and the Red Sox on Sunday, then back in time for class on Monday. Since then the excursions have only gotten bigger and more sophisticated, including RVs, plane trips, minor- and major-league games, and an entire subset of legend and lore that's certain to be relived any time more than two of the regulars get together. (Although often asked to, I've never gone.) "The last few years," he tells me, "we've done it during spring training, which is great."

Besides that he has season tickets for the Eagles, he's at most Villanova home basketball games, a ton of Phillies games, checks in on the minor league Camden Riversharks and Philadelphia Phantoms (hockey), plays on a softball team, and devotes untold hours to Fantasy Football. As he's telling me about all this he gets a call from a friend, a golf pro near Atlanta, who's calling to clarify some arrangements. Seems the Eagles open the season against the Falcons on *Monday Night Football* in a few weeks, and Billy and a few others are flying down for the game.

It's no wonder he's single. While I'm not looking to trade places, it's nice to walk in his shoes for a night. We're in no hurry, have nowhere to be, no one to check in with, and few cares. Still, as the night wears on I can't help but ask about his girlfriend. Back at the Super Bowl one of his friends suggested he was close to settling down with the woman who's been his on-and-off girlfriend for five years, so the question comes out with some bit of hope on my part. "What's happening with your girl?"

"Oh," he says, "that's done."

"Why?"

"I don't want to get married just to get married," he explains. "If or when I get married, I only want to do it once, and in order for it to work, you have to put the marriage first. I've just never felt like I could do that. I like my life, and I don't want to change it, so marrying someone would just be destined to fail."

I want to charge him with harboring some sort of Peter Pan complex, a willful and childish refusal to grow up, but his position is annoyingly mature and well thought out. It's not that he's afraid of commitment or doesn't understand what it is to be married. He understands it perfectly and knows it's not what he wants right now. I have a whole list of unhappy or moderately happy friends who'd have been wise to follow the same path. In the end, marriage just isn't for everyone. As yet another Greek once said, Know Thyself.

At the same time, it's a tragically unromantic position that just won't work for my Chicago fling. Billy is raining on my parade. We drink until we don't feel like drinking anymore. Despite watching sports all night, we go back to the hotel and catch the late *Sports-Center*. We live out of bags. Throw our dirty clothes on the floor. As I lay in bed unwinding, Billy pees with the bathroom door open, the sound a miniature waterfall echoing across the room.

★ Today's Cubs-Braves game doesn't start until 1:20 P.M., so we linger in the hotel room, watching the morning *SportsCenter* and the second half of *Something's Gotta Give,* a romantic comedy in which a lifelong bachelor played by Jack Nicholson eventually gives in to the conventions of the plot to find love and happiness. I'm still a little surprised that Billy and his girlfriend broke up and I realize now it's because on some level I was expecting him to confide that he was going to propose. That his story was going to have a "happy ending." It's what the narrative arc demands. It's what the sports fan can't help but root for. I realize though, too, that disappointment is part of being a fan, especially a Cubs fan and, frankly, on the scale of disappointments it's a small one, maybe not for her, but for me.

By eleven we're on the train to Wrigley. This is more like it. As we ride out, the cars fill with people in Cubs hats and casual clothes. There is an upbeat feeling, and a twitter of excited chatter. I imagine this is what it was like forty or fifty years ago, when another generation of Chicago businessmen took the afternoon off, caught the El from their offices downtown out to the neighborhood field, and arrived in time to catch Ernie Banks or Ron Santo prowling the friendly confines.

When we are finally deposited onto a street with brick tenements and small factories, there is a bristle of activity. We follow the flow of people, past packed bars with outdoor patios, scalpers lounging on stoops waving fans of tickets, and temporary T-shirt stands, where the local favorites seem to be "Cardinals take it up the poo hole" and "Baseball isn't boring, you are." Well, that's sort of romantic.

The stadium itself pops up from the middle of the neighborhood, as unspectacular and unimposing as the surrounding buildings. By almost any objective measure, it's ugly. It's maybe three stories tall, a jumble of little stone-filled concrete slabs and chain-link fence. From the outside I can see people walking up the ramps, and they look disproportionately large, like dogs sleeping in a cat bed. Out front stands a bronze statue of the famed, longtime Cubs announcer Harry Caray singing "Take Me Out to the Ball Game." Problem is that it's not a terribly accurate likeness of the man. In fact, with the Coke-bottle glasses and slicked-back hair it reminds me more of the late power-agent Swifty Lazar, rising from the sidewalk to negotiate one last contract.

The activity on the street makes it clear how little the Cubs' history of losing has hurt their popularity. Wrigley is regularly sold out as fans unite in a citywide — nationwide, really — ritual of suffering. If the Cubs ever won, the team and its fans would lose their identity.

Today plenty of people swarm around the place, although it

doesn't seem like a sellout crowd. I suppose this is to be expected. It is, after all, a weekday at one thirty in the afternoon; people have jobs and this is not the era when an executive could just slip out for an afternoon. With the less-than-capacity crowd, there is a noticeable lack of mayhem that has marked so many of the other events on my list thus far. Everything is a little more relaxed. There's no jostling in the stairwells or lines for the bathroom. That feeling of electric anticipation has been replaced by a sense of the everyday. Like the Billy thing, it's slightly deflating, but I'm here to make the best of it, and if this is Wrigley on an August afternoon, then I'll go with the assumption that this is somehow part of the "magic."

With time to spare, we take advantage of our media access by going on a stroll out on the field, a surprising experience. From the stands or on TV, a baseball field looks like a perfect blanket of green, unspoiled, uninterrupted, thick and cushy enough to lie down and nap on. Up close, though, I can see thin spots, little bumps, and brown-tinged seams where new sod has been laid around the pitcher's mound. And the field is so crowned that from the first-base line it's hardly possible to see the third-base line. The overall effect is less like looking at your finger under a magnifying glass, so that something familiar becomes animated in finer detail, giving you a deeper understanding, and more like looking at your finger under a microscope, which makes it look completely foreign and reveals a side of it you never thought existed.

The Braves are taking batting practice and what's as different as the appearance of the turf is the sound of the bat and ball colliding at field level. Watch a game on TV and inevitably the announcer will say something like "Oh, he just missed the sweet spot on that one, you could hear it" or "You knew that one was gone as soon as you heard it," but at home — or even from the stands — there's not that much difference in the sound of the bat hitting the ball. But one of the things I notice, standing on Wrigley Field on a warm afternoon, is the slight but distinctly different sound the collision of ball and bat makes on every swing. It's sharper, and the *click* of the impact resonates in the air longer. This is especially true when one of the big guys gets a hold of one. The sound is crisp, like that made by snapping a dry twig on a cold day.

Back inside, we pass by the press box to pick up the media packet, which comes complete with lineups, bios, game notes, and reams of stats, then go find somewhere to sit. From up here the field looks so big it's difficult to figure out why it's so hard to get a hit. It should be easy, there's so much open space. From up here I can also see out over the outfield wall and past the buildings that stand behind them. There below the puffy clouds I glimpse the blue of Lake Michigan. Billy begins studying the media packet while I make a few phone calls. At one point he looks up and says, apropos of nothing, "I love reading stats." He then ducks his head back down and continues scanning the page. Reading stats? I'm trying to summon the ghosts of Wrigley and he's reading stats.

Later he gets a phone call from his former roommate. "Hey," he says, "what's going on?" . . . "Who are they playing?" . . . "Oh, tonight?" . . . "Nah, I don't think I'll be home in time." . . . "I'm at Wrigley for the Cubs-Braves game." . . . "It's a long story. I'll call you tomorrow." He didn't need to come with me on these trips, I realize, because he lives on my one-year sports merry-go-round on a full-time basis. For him this is similar to the atmosphere I sensed coming into the park, less special, more everyday.

By the time we get back to our seats, it's almost game time. I look around and notice that somehow 38,033 people have materialized out of the middle of the workweek. I never sensed the place getting crowded, but here they are, all giddy and enthusiastic.

Billy and I get ourselves a few cold beverages and find a pair of empty seats along the first-base line. In an odd way it's more difficult to watch a game live. I can follow the situation — the sacrifices, the steal counts, the bigger strategic moves — but without the benefit of the center-field camera it's impossible to get inside the pitcher-batter battle. Without a seat right behind home plate, I can't tell if the pitcher's throwing an inside fastball to set up the curve. From the stands there's just a flash of white and then whatever result follows.

I wonder if it would help to sit in center field. If the stories I've been told are true, to really get the full Wrigley experience I have to make my way out to the bleachers, which line the outfield. Unlike the box seats, which have backs and arms and in some places waiter service, these sections are nothing but aluminum benches. They're a bargain at $15 and many of them are only sold on game day. To get them you have to show up two hours before the start and wait in line. They're the domain of the everyman fan and the people who sit there relish their no-frills status, taking an odd pride in being a better fan because they're willing to endure long lines and uncomfortable seats to see their team.

Before I came to Wrigley I heard about a University of Chicago anthropology professor who'd spent seven years studying the Wrigley bleacher regulars known as the Bleacher Bums the way one of her colleagues might investigate some lost tribe. Da Bums are known as die-hard eccentrics who come to every game, line up for their tickets, sit in the same spots, and cheer on their team. They and the space they inhabit have been the subject of many stories and much folklore, and they are responsible for whatever cachet bleachers possess. This woman was the first scientist to penetrate their ranks, live among them, and report back on her findings.

Her name is Holly Swyers, and after tracking down an address, I e-mailed her about my adventure. Would she be at the game that day and if so could we spend some time together? No problem. She would and she'd love to talk. How do I find you? I asked. Dashiell Hammett couldn't have dreamed up a better reply:

"Go to section 147 in dead center field. A few rows in front of the concession stand you'll see a big guy with a white beard and white hair chomping on a cigar. If it's hot, he'll probably have his shirt off. That's Marv. Tell him you're looking for Holly in 145, and he'll be able to point me out. If you have a minute you should talk to him. He's far more interesting than I am."

Who could read a note like that and not want to meet Marv?

So with the game tied, Billy and I trudge out to the bleachers. But when we got to the point where you'd pass from the box seats

to the outfield an usher stops us. "Sorry, you can't enter the bleachers from the grandstand during the game." I try my best to per-
suade him, even going so far as to drop a $20 on the ground, but he
does not take the bait. I press hard enough to get a manager called
in, but it stops there. Instead I find myself looking out across the
bleachers, trying to find section 147, my eye falling on every big
shirtless guy with a white beard. There are more than a few, as well
as kids and women and people sitting doing crossword puzzles,
needlepoint, or just holding their faces to the sun, eyes closed.
They are packed in shoulder to shoulder, and the majority of them
spend more time standing than sitting, baking in the hot sun and
yelling their brains out.

I am not willing to concede defeat. "Well," I say, "we'll go outside, go around to the bleacher entrance, buy some tickets, and
enter that way." So we leave, right in the middle of the game, and
take a little walk down Waveland Avenue, where a few dozen peo
ple mill around on the corners or sit in lawn chairs watching the
game on portable TVs and hoping for a ball to be hit clear out of
the stadium — which happens pretty regularly in this small park
from another era. If one of the Cubs hit it, they'll keep it. If a
player from the other team hit it, tradition dictates that they throw
it back over the fence onto the field. Wrigley really wants to fulfill
my dreams — Marv, the bleachers, the hopefuls waiting on Wave
land — but something keeps getting in the way.

At the ticket office more disappointment awaits. The windows
are closed. I ask a guard if I can still buy a bleacher ticket. No, he
says, the game is sold out. Well, can I enter the bleachers with my
regular ticket?

No, no, no, no.

So there I stand, another angry Greek denied access by the
Cubs. I don't have a goat, but I've got Billy. I don't have the heart or
the Greek vocabulary to curse the team's World Series future, but I
do remember some of the choice phrases my grandfather used to
throw at us when we were getting on his nerves. I shout them at
the sky and feel better when I'm done. Although I'm not sure of

everything I've said and how it will affect the team's future, I'm certain they know I want them to stop running and keep their feet off the coffee table.

★ I'm getting all too real a vision of the despair that comes with being a Cubs fan. At least they let us back in the grandstand (I actually checked if they would before leaving). I may never meet Holly or smell the cigar-laced breath of Marv, but I do call her once I return home and she tells me a little bit about her work. She is studying the Bleacher Bums as a community and comparing how their relationships function in contrast to a traditional community. It might be very interesting, but it also reduces the luster of the place by painting it in the drab colors of science.

That will come later, though. Right now, Billy and I have to find ourselves new seats — our old ones have been taken. As I look over the stadium I catch sight of the rows of buildings that line the blocks behind Wrigley. Over time, these too have become one of Wrigley's many charms. As the buildings grew around the stadium, people took to watching the games from the neighboring rooftops, which provided a view of the field over the walls in left and right. It started out small and simple. A fun quirk and a few shots of people lining the top of the buildings outside the field became a must for any Cubs broadcast.

But like so much else, this too became commoditized. Most of the buildings now have a precarious-looking set of bleachers perched on top and people spend more for the privilege of sitting in them than they would for a ticket inside the stadium. On several of them, plumes of smoke rise from large barbecue grills and the sound of loud music trickles down. Tour packages are being sold, money being made. So much so that the Cubs eventually sued and settled out of court with the businesses. From what I'm told, games are a lot of fun to watch from up there — it's the place to go for people who consider a baseball game nothing more than a good chance to drink — but no one spends much time focusing on the field.

I must admit, my own focus has been a bit scattered. I've spent so much time running around trying to get the quintessential Wrigley experience that I haven't seen much of the action. When Billy and I finally find seats farther out along the right-field line, I'm again distracted, this time by a cotton candy vendor. I've never eaten it in my life, but the previous summer I took my daughter to a WNBA basketball game. She spotted the cotton candy as soon as we walked in. It took until the third quarter for me to give in, but I finally bought her some. She took two bites, got that icky sticky stuff all over her face and hands, and promptly handed it back to me. It was the best $6.50 I've ever spent.

It was the third game I'd taken her to, two Nets games and then this one Liberty game at Madison Square Garden, because as soon as she saw the men play she asked if girls play basketball, too. I wanted her to see that they did, and it was on as grand a scale as the men.

But remembering how formative my early interactions with sports were, I worry about the message I'm sending her by taking her to these events. Sure, there's nothing wrong with her being a sports fan (research shows girls who play sports are better off in many ways), but I don't want sports to be the extent of our relationship. I want her to know that I value things like art and literature and that she can talk to me about anything. I don't want her to think that the only way she can get my attention is through sports (a task made that much more difficult when you work at a sports magazine). Lately she's been asking about hockey games, and I'm sure I'll take her to one, but I'll do it with misgivings.

If anything makes it easier, it's that we have a good time when we go, and watching her at a game relieves any sense that the experience is having the same impact on her that it did on me. She'll fire off the five or six hundred questions you have to expect from a six-year-old, but she spends most of the time evaluating the cheerleaders and dancers, reading the signs around the arena, and watching the Jumbotron.

Maybe I've been a little too childlike in my approach to Wrigley. I've spent too much time noticing the lack of signs and not watching the Jumbotron. Maybe I need to outgrow my romantic notions.

★ Unlike my little girl, the people here are serious fans. They are excited and energetic and they know the game. With no outs in the sixth, José Macias bunts a runner from second to third, and he gets a spirited round of applause. At the same time, when someone hits a ground ball too short in the fifth, with the Cubs still up by one, a woman near me screams, "Run it out, run it out!" Likewise, when the shortstop bobbles a grounder, but still throws out the runner, people seem to get disproportionately worried. "You've got to get that," one guy says. It seems as if these fans have endured so much bad fortune, they're a little scarred and oversensitive. They almost expect the worst to happen at any given moment.

This, I think, must be at the heart of the Cubs and all sports' romantic appeal. That search for the ideal, the hopefulness, the possibility of redemption. No matter how many times we've failed at things in our own life — sports, piano lessons, getting a new job — we can lose ourselves in the struggles of our team or a given player. The possibility of his success gives us the feeling that we've succeeded, too. If he fails, well, it can hurt, hence the sulking, but ultimately it's also meaningless, because he and we can come back tomorrow or next week and try again. That is part of what makes the big events big, a connecting thread between all the contests I've visited so far. The sense that there is no tomorrow. They carry a finality to them, even if it's only until next season.

The Cubs are different. There's no high-stakes finality to their games, but the ongoing tradition of raised hopes resulting in failure raises the stakes in another way. It requires a greater leap of faith to keep believing, a greater well of hope, a hint of desperation that puts any step in the Cubs' long journey at the level of a mini–Super Bowl.

In the top of the seventh the Cubs give up their 1–0 lead in the most painful of ways — the key plays are a wild pitch and a throwing error — to go down 3–1. The fans are apoplectic. People bury their faces in their hands. One guy in the row behind me throws his rolled-up program on the ground. Almost everyone executes a sigh and a "Here we go again" weight shift.

Yet all is forgiven quickly. For it's time for the seventh-inning stretch and the singing of "Take Me Out to the Ball Game." In yet another of Wrigley's famed idiosyncrasies, Harry Caray put a special twist on the Cubs games by leading the crowd in song, belting the words through the PA system in his grumbly baritone. The practice has survived the man, although it's now the task of guest singers to lead the chorus, including everyone from Roseanne Barr to Ozzy Osbourne to Bill Murray. It's such an honor that sometimes celebrities who don't even have something to promote do it. Today, though, it's strictly C-list: a local weatherman.

Still, the fans are psyched and they belt it out with greater verve and volume than they did the national anthem, Billy and I do our part, standing and singing as if we were *American Idol* contestants. It is, I have to admit, fun, and part of that fun is knowing that you are taking part in a tradition greater than yourself. One that has been taking place since before you were born.

When it's all over, we sink back into our seats. I finally spot a hot dog vendor and Billy gets us fresh beers. For the first time all day I settle into the rhythm of the game. Within minutes I can almost tap my foot to the beat.

With the snap of hide on leather the pitcher catches the ball and paces behind the mound. He removes his glove, squeezes it under his arm, and massages the ball with both hands, once, twice, three times he rubs. He slides the glove back on and ascends the mound. He shrugs a bit, shimmies, removes his hat, wipes his brow on his sleeve, and looks in for the sign.

Clang, clang, clang. The hot dog vendor slams the top of his metal container. "Ha do-ogs. Get 'em fresh, get 'em hot do-ogs." The blonde in front of me leans in closer to the guy she's sitting with and whispers something soft into his ear. He turns and kisses her on the forehead. A breeze stirs through the aisle, moving old popcorn boxes and near-empty beer cups, which roll on their sides so that the last ungulped drops slide out and spill onto the concrete. The papery brown wisps of crushed peanut shells tumble over and over until they accumulate around my feet.

A woman behind me laughs — a staccato pitch — eh, eh, eh. The catcher sidles into position and drops his fingers between his legs. The pitcher nods and sets. The umpire leans in. The batter takes one last swipe at the windmills before him, then steadies. Infielders move forward in little stutter steps, their feet getting wider as their bodies lower, puffs of dust rising around their shoes. The pitcher lurches to life, rocks, twists. A stream of white cuts the infield. Whiff, pop, roar.

The catcher is standing, throwing, the ball smacks the pitcher's mitt, he removes his glove, squeezes it under his arm, and begins circling behind the mound. A thousand conversations bubble to life. A steady murmur. "Beer here. Bea hea."

Streaky white clouds break an otherwise perfect sky. And it's warm. Not the same warm as being huddled under a blanket on a cold night, but the warm of the sun on your skin. Beach warm, spreading over you like poured oil. "Come on, Prior, come on" rises above the chatter, followed by the report of three sharp claps. The *rugga, rugga* of a passing train provides a momentary back beat. The green of the outfield catches my eye. I follow the white lines toward home. The pitcher rocks, twists.

I look over at Billy. I can see the muscles of his face working as if he's about to speak, but he keeps whatever he's thinking to himself, smiling a little closed-mouth smile. It's better that way, I think. I have an idea of what's going through his mind, but to say it, to speak aloud, would destroy the moment.

Billy raises his beer to his lips. I sip mine, too. It's a Wednesday afternoon, and it's possible to see how this could be all the romance a man needs.

November 19, 2005

Ann Arbor, Michigan

O F ALL THE SPORTS on my list, college football was the one I found the hardest to narrow down to a single game. Some of the choices were slam dunks. Golf: Masters. Tennis: Wimbledon. Football: Super Bowl. NASCAR: Daytona. Even what might seem like glaring omissions were easier decisions. Without much handwringing I passed on the World Series, NHL Finals, and NBA Finals, all of which on some level might seem like obvious choices for inclusion. But to me, those seven-game trudges fail to capture the imagination. The Series depends too much on matchups. Does anyone want to see the Mariners and the Padres, to pick one of many uninspiring possibilities? The NHL, while intense and intriguing, has taken 2005 off to fight about money and new rules, so it's out of the question. And the NBA is unwatchable, no matter what's at stake. I was interested in a few other possibilities — the Olympics, World Cup soccer, and the America's Cup, but the Olympics were just too big and the other two didn't command enough stature among U.S. sports fans.

College ball, though, offered a virtual menu of delicious choices. As with every other sport, I was looking for a few things: rivalry, tradition, history, impact, mass appeal, and some other intangible, an aura that can't be explained, only felt. After applying those criteria, and without a doubt my personal biases, I was left with four choices. Alabama-Auburn, Oklahoma-Texas, Ohio State–Michigan, and the Rose Bowl.

Ten years ago I would have picked the Rose Bowl. With its pageantry and tradition and historical matchups it would have made the perfect event, but since the advent of the BCS — the Bowl Championship Series, a sort of matchup system in which the top teams from the top conferences are slotted into certain bowls in an attempt to pit the number one team against the number two team — the appeal of all the bowls has been diluted. Based on the rotating BCS system, the Rose Bowl would host the 2005 national championship (which turned out to be a classic) but even that would have forced me to somehow make peace with the BCS system, and I'd rather watch an NBA game than do that.

That left me with the three grudge matches. As a guy from the Northeast, where bigtime college football is only one of many choices of what to do on a Saturday afternoon (and traditionally not terribly well-played), I didn't have the deep connection to some of the subtle rivalries. But I'd watched the games many times since I was a kid and these blood feuds had penetrated my consciousness. Alabama–Auburn, known as the Iron Bowl, would allow me to get a taste of the storied SEC tradition. Maybe these two schools no longer supported the kind of fan base where debutantes in ball gowns and southern gentlemen in blazers and bow ties picnicked on the grotto before the game, like they do at some other schools in the conference, but they were connected to that, and it had an appeal. In the end I decided it was better to go with two teams that weren't in the same state.

Texas–Oklahoma fits that description, and the rivalry certainly has the history and intensity, and both teams have been good in recent years. The annual game even has its own name, the Red River Rivalry, as it's called, and it's even played each year at a neutral site, the Cotton Bowl in Dallas. For some reason, though, I couldn't get excited about it. Not the way I could for the Michigan–Ohio State game.

For whatever reason, this is the matchup that stands out for me. My memories of watching it are sharper and more vibrant. The scarlet and gray of OSU, their helmets covered with battle stickers. The Wolverines in what must be one of the most distinctive uniform designs in all sports, maize and blue with a helmet striped so that it looks like wrestling headgear. More so than not, I remember the games at Michigan, in its stadium, known as the Big House, where bundled masses breathed condensation into the cold northern air, sang what might be the most infectious college fight song, and thundered support down on their star-studded squads. The stadium held upward of one hundred thousand people, which I found incredible. I'd been to packed games at Giants Stadium, which held about seventy-eight thousand people, and I just couldn't imagine adding another thirty thousand rabid college fans to that. Moreover, those games seemed to embody college sports to me. That whole notion of massive corn-fed farmboys of the Midwest banging heads together for greater Big Ten glory. The brassy sound of the bands. The voice of Keith Jackson coming from the TV.

The matchup certainly meets all of the other criteria. The teams played for the first time in 1897, and this will be their 102nd game. Long before that first game, the two fledgling states nearly fought a border war over a strip of land containing Toledo, a dispute that included a few thousand armed troops massed along the border and a lot of animosity. In other words, the emotion and meaning behind this one is about more than just bragging rights: it's connected to a 170-year-old squabble that no one seems to want to let go of. Come on, we're talking about Toledo!

And there's one more thing, although I don't realize it until I'm in the airport waiting for my plane. Michigan is one of the eight states I've never been to, so the game will also move me one step closer to completing my mom's dream list.

★ I park my rental car in the lot next to a frat house. As I roll to a stop, my front bumper just about nudges a sign that says "Resident parking only. All others will be towed at owner's expense." Just below the painted lettering reads an additional warning, scribbled in black marker: "And have its fucking windows smashed." The warning disturbs me because I don't want the car damaged but also because it should be "*their* fucking windows." I thought Michigan was supposed to be the Harvard of the Midwest.

I look at the fraternity house, a huge brick building with white columns. It's just before ten o'clock on a Saturday morning, and there are absolutely no signs of life. I figure I have at least two hours before anyone in there can even see straight, never mind recognize a foreign car in the parking lot. It helps that my destination is a small building just up the street, from which I'll be able to watch the car and therefore (I hope) rescue it before any potential defilement can take place.

As I sit in the car now, cranking the heat to stave off the sub-forty-degree temperatures, I watch the building, where I'm supposed to meet Ian Davis, a Michigan senior I tracked down through a message board, who's planning to party this morning with his older brother, Charlie, an Ohio State alum, and Charlie's wife, Sarah, a Michigan graduate. On hand to oversee the family feud will be the boys' mom, Barbara. What better intro to the UM-OSU rivalry could there be than a family divided by it?

Ian told me he'd be with his mother and wearing a Michigan Bicycling shirt, but all I've seen so far are a few people scurrying in and out in the process of setting up a barbecue grill, a table, and a few chairs on the front porch. One of them wears a plain blue shirt and the other a jacket, and I wonder if that's Ian but his shirt is covered. I begin to dig in my pockets for Ian's cell number when I see a kid walking toward the building with such a shirt and a motherly figure at his side. That's got to be him.

By the time I reach the porch Ian has already popped a can of Miller Lite. I introduce myself and we shake hands. He's a small kid with terrifically white skin and pink, rose-shaped lips. He is, though, a serious bike rider and I can see the way his jeans pull tight on his thighs. He introduces me to his mother, an attractive woman with a ruddier complexion and long curly hair. She seems too young to have kids out of college. Like me, she's the only one on the porch wearing a jacket, which I notice is distinctly nonpartisan in color (white). "This is it," she tells me. "This is our big weekend."

Ian introduces me around. First there's Dan, a friend from home. Dan lives in the house and is in effect the host, although the majority of the work seems to fall to his parents, Dan Sr. and Sheri, UM alums both. Behind them are three scraggly-looking guys, one another hometown bud who's now in the Air Force and two of Ian's roommates. Dan's younger sister, a UM sophomore, has just arrived with two friends. They've been out drinking since 6:00 A.M. (the Blue Luau opened at five), which explains their perkiness. There is a brief lull as we stand around trying not to look cold, although the majority of the party assumes a posture that gives lie to the pretense: hunched over with one hand stuffed deep into the front pocket of their jeans and the other cupping a can of beer.

It's late November in Michigan and no one wears a jacket, just a hat and a sweatshirt or two under a T-shirt or jersey. Jackets, I'm getting the sense, are a sign of weakness. I'm weak, but I'm warm. At least that's what I want to believe, because I've also noticed that the only people wearing jackets are me, Barbara, and Sheri, and I'm afraid jackets are a virtual flare signal that I'm too old to put style before comfort.

Of course it could be a marker of commitment. When someone is a full-fledged member of this rivalry they wear the school colors on the outside and forgo the jacket if need be, weather and Ohio State be damned. It's certainly not the only sign that I've entered a world where normal customs and rules do not apply.

Consider breakfast. I'm more than a little hungry, so I'm happy when Dan Sr., a fit, big-chested guy who's been tending the grill, says, "Grab something to eat, we got plenty." I shuffle toward the food with the others, waiting for the scent of bacon and sausage to hit me. When I get up front, Ian lifts the grill cover and there lie burgers, dogs, and chicken wings. I glance at my watch. It's now 10:08 A.M. Okay, make it lunch.

I get myself a burger and outfit it with ketchup and — since I'm doing it I might as well go all out — I also grab some pickles and chips. I turn away from the table and almost smack into Dan Jr. who's right behind me. He pops a beer and thrusts the can at me without saying anything. I look at it for a second, and I can feel everyone staring at me. I look up at Dan, who's working about three days of beard growth and has floppy black hair emerging from under a tight wool cap, reminding me more than anything of Mike Nesmith of the Monkees. "Sure," I finally say, "I'd love one." Everyone snickers a little.

The ice is broken, but the whole thing feels a little like high school. I assume that I'm now allowed to sit at the cool kids' lunch table and even talk to the homecoming queen, so I settle in to get to know everyone. As I make the rounds, chitchatting with everyone, the morning is broken by high-pitched screams. Three girls are heading up the walk toward the porch. Two wear Ohio State jerseys, and they have thrust their hands in the air and begun whooping and hollering. I'm not sure if these girls are dumb or brave, but they certainly don't have any fear about showing their allegiances in hostile territory.

They are, it turns out, yet more of Ian's friends from home, though he's neither quick to admit it nor too excited about the fact. Ohio State students, they made the two-hundred-mile drive up from Columbus last night and crashed at his place, and now they're here to join our party, which I assume will only make it more interesting if not somewhat more ear shattering. "I couldn't figure out how to work that hair dryer in your house," says the one who seems to be the leader, when they finally reach the porch and begin communicating in tones that are reminiscent of an air-raid siren.

"Well, it's not mine, but I think you just push the button," Ian says in the wry manner I'm already coming to love about him.

The girls are the kind who give the appearance of being conventionally attractive from a distance, with long blondish hair, lots of makeup, snug jeans, and notable accessories, and they do love to yell. Every time someone in an OSU jersey or shirt ventures by they scream and point or shout "O-H!" which is returned with an "I-O!" There's another thing I've learned about this rivalry so far: OSU fans are loud.

I run this theory by Barbara. "Oh, are they ever," she says. "They're very" — she pauses — "enthusiastic." This is in fact the very subtext of the UM-OSU rivalry. Although the two teams have enjoyed great success on the field — Michigan has the most wins (849) and the highest winning percentage (.7442) in college football, while OSU has 774 wins and a .710 winning percentage — OSU fans pride themselves on being more gung ho, while fans at UM ride on being smarter. Or, as Dan Sr. tells me, "That's the thing about those girls and their jerseys," referring to the woo-hooers. "They can wear those up here and not worry. You try to wear your jersey down there [in Columbus] and forget it, it's not worth it. OSU fans are passionate, but they take it too far. They're classless." The offenses he's witnessed or heard about over the years include everything from throwing water balloons and spraying beer to fights and jerseys being ripped off Michigan fans and burned. On the other hand, a favorite chant of the Michigan student section? "Pump my gas," implying that postgraduation the OSU students' career options will be limited to topping off the luxury cars driven by their more successful UM counterparts.

The difference is attributable to several factors. Michigan is a better academic school — incoming freshmen have higher average test scores, grade point averages, class rank, etc. It has a more diverse student body from all over the country, and it's less than an hour from Detroit, a major city. Meanwhile, in Columbus, Ohio, OSU is about the only show in town, so it's covered in the local media like a presidential election and populated by kids who've grown up listening to news programs that lead with stories about recruiting. Their devotion comes from the heart, and possibly even the womb.

A lot is made of these differences, but in the end, the schools are more alike than not. The enthusiasm-academics gap is not as wide as it's sometimes made out to be. The average SAT score of an incoming freshman at OSU is lower, but as of 2002, only about one hundred points lower. And before I go home today, I will see beer dumped on one rather obnoxious OSU fan. In truth, there's no way a good rivalry could exist if the schools weren't on basically the same footing. The sort of fierce hatred these schools share has to extend off the field in order to flourish.

The rest of us should be glad this one has. There's nothing like a good blood feud to spice sports — it's the mustard on the hot dog. When two rivals want to beat each other so badly that it becomes the focus of their entire season, their entire being, it raises the stakes and draws outsiders into the eye of the storm. That may be why this rivalry stood out to me above the others. It only comes once a year — the weekend before Thanksgiving — and it's winner-take-all. The end-of-season timing often means there's a lot on the line for one if not both teams, and one team can salvage a terrible season just by beating the other or it could destroy an otherwise great year by losing. There's a long list of coaches who have lost their jobs and players who've been diminished in stature because they could not lead their team to victory in this one game. The most obvious recent example is John Cooper. From 1988 to 2000 he coached Ohio State to an impressive 111-43-4 record, but during that span he only beat Michigan twice. When he was fired, his failure to defeat public enemy number one was largely believed to be the unstated cause of his demise.

In the best rivalries, like this one, there's something more than just the game at stake. Think Yankees–Red Sox, Steelers-Browns, UCLA-USC. In each case the rivals are not just competing on the field but waging a battle over some larger sense of their self-identity: northeastern intellectual capital, blue-collar Middle American city, Southern California top dog. Or, as the case may be, dominant midwestern university. The length of the struggle and the evenness of the competition add to the mix. A good rivalry can't be dominated by one team for very long. Yet there can be only one winner and the implications carry beyond the field.

In the last fifty years the OSU-UM matchup stands at 24-24-2, and this year's contest promises to be another classic. Coming into the game, OSU is number nine in the national rankings and Michigan is seventeen.

As I talk about some of these ideas with Barbara, I ask her if those larger, off-the-field identities make her lean toward one team over the other. "Oh, no," she says. "I'm right down the middle. I even have a fake license plate that I keep in the back window of my car. Half of it is a Michigan plate and half of it is Ohio and it's got a crack down the middle." I realize that, in a way, I've asked her to choose between her sons, who she explains are as different as the schools. "We actually lived in Ohio when Charlie was born but moved to Michigan by the time Ian came, so they were even born in different states. We should have seen it coming." I look over at

Ian, who's quietly talking with two of his friends, when Barbara adds, "Wait till Charlie gets here. You'll see."

★ If it's possible to dominate a party before actually arriving at it, Ian's brother Charlie manages to do just that. Sometime around eleven, after an hour of speculation about his arrival, a football comes spiraling toward the porch. Dan leans out, snags it from the air, and tosses it back. The bypasser who's flung it is Charlie, and, without ever making it off the sidewalk, he proceeds to have a catch with three of the guys while holding conversations with two other people. His wife, Sarah, stands near him, her arms crossed, waiting for a break in the game so she can ascend the walk without getting plunked in the head.

When Charlie finally bounds up the steps, it's clear why Ian is the family introvert. Charlie is all boisterous hellos and slaps on the back. He steps across the porch to the table and snatches up one of the plastic plates, which happen to be a shade of red not far off from Ohio State's scarlet. "Red plates," he says in a voice loud enough to entertain the entire party. "I can't believe you have red plates. If someone showed up at my party with blue plates, I'd burn them. But here, I'm loving the red plates.

"Where are all the students?" Charlie continues, craning his neck to make an exaggerated sweep of the area. "Must be at the library. Or, no, they're out drinking chai. I bet Starbucks is packed right now." He laughs. "They're playing beer chess." Although they have similar facial features, when you look closely you'd be hard-pressed to recognize Charlie and Ian as brothers. Charlie, who's wearing jeans and a plain gray sweatshirt, is bigger, with dark hair and a darker beard.

Ian knows he has to respond, and he does so in his understated way, in a voice maybe one-third as loud as his brother's. "What's that, a gray sweatshirt? Is that what they wear down there?"

"No," says Charlie, "I'm just getting started. I'm gonna take this off later and burn my whole chest scarlet." Just then a few guys in OSU jerseys cross at the corner. "O-H!" Charlie yells. Their heads swivel. "I-O!" they yell back. The three jersey girls, who'd been busy batting a piece of string, thrust their arms into the air and add a long, high-pitched "wooooohoooooooo."

When the trash talk settles, I ask Charlie and Sarah about their mixed marriage. "I never cared where he went to school, but he had reservations about me being a Michigan grad. I think the only thing that saved us was that we were living in Chicago, which was sort of neutral territory, so it was less intense."

"Yeah, my brother is pretty gung ho," deadpans Ian.

The couple has visited whichever campus is hosting the match-up for every one of the six years they've been together, although they've never had tickets for the game. "We just visit friends and then go to a bar and watch with a bunch of people," Sarah says. "It's just as much fun." That doesn't mean the two aren't intense, because there's a lot at stake. "We have our diplomas hanging in the house," says Charlie. "If Ohio State wins I get to hang mine above hers and vice versa. I've been up there three of the last four years, baby," he says, throwing in a little fist pump for emphasis. Last year, though, the stakes were even higher. Sarah found herself living in Columbus after Charlie, a marketing executive, got a new job that required him to move back to the hometown of his alma mater (she works in IT and could do her job from anywhere).

How, I ask, did he convince you to move there? "It was hard. We had a great apartment right around the corner from Wrigley, but he bribed me. He promised to buy me a dog if we moved." That led to another bet. Whoever's team won the big game would get to name the dog. Charlie threatened Katzenmoyer, after the former OSU linebacker of that name. Sarah countered with Biaka-butuka, after the former Michigan running back Tim Biakabutuka. Ohio State won, but in a move that shows the complexities at the crossroads of love, marriage, and the Ohio State and Michigan rivalry, Charlie compromised on Carter, a name that has appeared across the back of gridiron stars for both teams (receivers Anthony Carter of Michigan and Cris Carter of OSU).

★ The game starts at one, so as the clock inches past eleven thirty our little party begins to break up. Charlie, Sarah, and Barbara have gone off to find friends. Dan Sr. and Sheri have already left for the game. That leaves me, Ian, Dan Jr., Eric (the Air Force friend), and two of the three woohooo girls. As we move toward the stadium, the frat houses on the block shake to life (I had to move my car in a hurry) and the yards out front fill with music and young scruffy guys in T-shirts and flip-flops. They throw footballs, they drink beer, they cheer as a guy in nothing but a dark blue hat appears over the crest of the hill and runs down the street. Seconds later a group spots our friends with the OSU jerseys. "You suck, you suck," they chant before one of them yells to us, "Guys, you can do better than that."

For their part the girls are undaunted, whooping as loud as ever and screaming "O-H" every time they see more red shirts, getting an "I-O" in return. That is until they let out with an "O-H" and a crowd of Michigan fans intercepts with an "F-U" response.

I feel like I'm in one of those movie scenes in which the local townsfolk converge on the main square to witness a beheading. People pour out of every building and every side street, all falling into step toward some distant place that you can't see but can find simply by following the masses and the mayhem and the far-off thump of a marching band.

Suddenly I think of Holly Swyers, the University of Chicago anthropologist who was studying the Bleacher Bums. When I called her she told me a little about her study, which examines the Bleacher Bums as a community, a subset of those who sit in the bleachers, which is a subset of those who go to the game, which is a subset of Cubs fans in general. Her point was that the members of this community, this subset of a subset of a subset, were linked by more than just their love of the team. She referred me to her Web site, where a summary of her upcoming paper reads: "A season ticket to the bleachers of Wrigley Field will not buy a person admission into the community. A Regular becomes a Regular by demonstrating commitment to the community — a commitment that extends to attending weddings and funerals, babysitting children, sharing vacations, buying drinks, contributing to potlucks,

networking job opportunities — in short, doing those things that
are traditionally associated with close neighborhoods."

This, it strikes me, is the Holy Grail. It is, at least in part, exactly what I was looking for when I started out. I'd long ago understood that sports was about connections, both in the tribal appeal
of putting on a jersey, blending into the crowd, and losing oneself
in the screaming, jumping, high-fiving mass of some larger idea or
pursuit, and in the sense that it provides some sort of coded language that allows those who are fluent to speak to each other in a
common tongue, anywhere, anytime. Swyers has taken that idea
and expanded and deepened it. Fandom, for those converts to the
sect, has become a basis for how we relate to one another, define
ourselves, and foster the connections that make it possible to
muddle through the entirety of our existence, not just the second
half of a boring game.

I hadn't picked up on this at Wrigley or immediately after reading Swyers's summary, but the walk from Dan Jr.'s house to the Big
House brings it to life. I begin to see the campus as a large community made up of hundreds of little Bleacher Bum–like communities. When all those microcommunities, linked by their away-
from-the-game connections, come together to cheer on the thing
that unites them all, it's a powerful moment.

And a raucous one. As we hit Main Street, the sights are overwhelming. Kids are not just packed onto the front lawns of every
house, but they're partying on balconies and roofs as well. A banner hanging from one window says simply: "The Game." No further explanation needed. Kids along the road hold up signs reading
"Honk if OSU sucks," and most of the cars oblige. A guy with a
bullhorn shouts, "Go blue," over and over. At another party a DJ
eggs on the passing crowds with calls of "What time is it?"

"Game time!" everyone shouts in return.

But the ultimate scene takes place outside one small apartment
building where a trio of guys on the third-floor balcony pour cans
of beer into a funnel that runs all the way to the first floor. The re-
cipients at the bottom are just about knocked off their feet by the

impact of twelve ounces hitting them at what must feel like 100 mph. A three-story beer bong: It is without question the most impressive and creative display of partying I've seen in all eight events.

As we make our way past the parties, the kids along the edge of the grass have set up a huge line and they're offering an endless string of high-fives to everyone walking past, so you almost feel like a player charging out onto the field. We pass the Michigan band, which stands statue-still in the street awaiting the cue to crank up one of the best-known fight songs in all of sports and march to the stadium. At last we reach the Big House, so called because, although it was built in 1927, it remains the largest football stadium in the country, once hosting 112,118 for the Ohio State game in 2003.

I'm expecting a behemoth to rise before me, a virtual Moby Dick of stadia, but I see nothing as I mount a small hill that leads to the gates. When the stadium finally reveals itself, it is low and unspectacular, maybe three stories tall. How then does this place hold 110,000 people? It's a huge bowl dug into the ground, with the playing surface actually below ground level. Heartland football, it seems, literally rises out of the earth — just like those corn stalks in Iowa that surround a baseball diamond.

Reaching the stadium means that I have to say goodbye to Ian, Dan Jr., and Eric, since their seats are in the student section and mine isn't, but I promise to try to find them once everything settles down. That, I realize as soon as I slide into my seat, may never happen. The field is a maze of movement as the Michigan band works through its formations, late-fall sun glinting off the instruments, brass section blaring and drums vibrating in my sternum.

With the fans packed in, the stadium is a sea of yellow and blue, except for two sections of OSU fans, a large square block in the far corner and a stripe of red behind one end zone. It's the density of people, even more than the number, that impresses. There are only a few small gates through which to enter each section and equally few walkways, which leaves as much room as possible for seating — row upon row of aluminum benches with numbers painted on them in white. This type of seating takes up less room and allows people to really squeeze together, so that they're shoulder to shoulder and fanned out right on top of each other like a deck of cards, maxing out the capacity and creating a physical intimacy that also makes the place feel smaller.

The field, like Wrigley, is surrounded by a low brick wall. Maybe it's just that the wall defines the space while seeming warmer than the typical painted steel, I don't know, but there's something welcoming about it. As the last people find their way to their seats, none of them sitting, the band breaks into the fight song.

> Hail, Hail, to Michigan
> the Champions of the West . . .

The entire place sings along, thrusting their fists into the air on each emphasized beat, so that the whole mass of humanity moves in unison. As the kicker lines up the ball, the crowd begins a slow-building "ahhhhhhhhhhhh" that ends only when the ball is booted into the air. Ohio State gets out to an early 9–0 lead but there's no sign of despair among the faithful. I make my way down to the student section, blending in among the row upon row of rowdy late teens. I may not be a part of any of the microcommunities at work here, but I can feed off the crowd's energy.

I take wild punches at the beach balls that spring by and then disappear across the sea of arms. I sway when the crowd sways and when everyone around me yells "Go blue!" I wait for the people on the other side of the stadium to shout "Go Gold!" before joining in to shout back. Late in the half, Michigan scores to cut the lead to 9–7 and the jubilant turn to celebrate with each other. I notice that these celebrations are not random. Around me are nothing but Michigan students, yet no one just high-fives the first person he sees. They seek out specific people. They perform acts of excitement that are not spontaneous but that have been worked out or done before — elaborate handshakes and such.

Again, I can't help but think of Swyers's concept of communities in the stands. Events like this one make me reevaluate my view of the Super Bowl. Yes, I saw passion and excitement, more than I had expected, but that's only because I'd been led to believe I'd find almost none at all. Then I come to games like this, and the atmosphere blows the Super Bowl out of the water. The truth is, the events that best tap into a sense of community are those that evoke the most passion. The deeper those communities run, the more the team becomes merely an organizing principle, and then the more emotional meaning the games have. Looking back, it was Daytona, where Rod and Jenny had their Daytona family, the Final Four with its roving wolf packs, and the Derby, where I traveled with my own community that I had the best times.

As I'm thinking about this an announcement comes over the PA system. "Ladies and gentlemen, today's attendance is 111,591, the fourth-largest crowd in the history of Michigan Stadium. Thank you for being part of the largest crowd watching college football in America today." The number is mind-boggling and very cool to be a part of, especially when put into such perspective. The announcement drives us forward in our frenzy.

With seven minutes left to play, Michigan is up 21–12. We turn up the volume, waving towels and pompons, shaking plastic bottles filled with coins. Michigan fans take some heat because despite its large crowds, critics say the Big House is not that loud. Like a good Michigan egghead, Dan Jr. explained to me that this is largely a matter of physics. Because the stadium is such a shallow, open dome, the sound isn't funneled toward the field and doesn't rebound off the other side of the structure. Instead, it goes straight up in the air and dissipates, making the place sound quieter than a smaller venue with better acoustics. As the students around me lift some of their fellow scholars into the air and pass them along the rows, I can't say it seems quiet in here at all.

Ohio State continues to fight, but as the clock winds down the real struggle is whether or not to rush the field. Normally, I wouldn't consider it, but before the game I'd asked Dan what one thing someone should do at a Michigan game. Was there some special sight, some place to eat, or some unique, crazy, cool must-see aspect? He thought for a minute, then said, "I would definitely rush the field. When we won two years ago I rushed the field and it was awesome. Ian didn't do it, and I think he's regretted it ever since, so I would rush the field."

I'm more than halfway up the curve of the bowl and it's a long way down many, many steps to the field, and I can't imagine doing that among this mass of people in anything resembling a "rush." It seems like a suicide run, a virtual Pamplona on stairs, with not a dozen but a few thousand bulls chasing behind me. This sense of impending peril only increases the adrenaline, though, and as Michigan moves down for what feels like a predestined last-second win, I and if I'm not mistaken the crowd around me grow even more frenzied.

And then it's no use. OSU gets the ball back one last time and drives eighty-eight yards in the final minutes, scoring the winning touchdown with twenty-four seconds left on the clock. Fate is not on our side — or looked at another way, maybe Fate's insurance agent is on our side. The people around me look like watches in a Dalí landscape. Final score, Ohio State 25, Michigan 21.

In the aftermath, the OSU fans are riotous. Screaming and shouting, taunting and gloating. In front of me, one Michigan student is attempting to claim the moral high ground by rattling off a long list of improprieties that have surfaced in OSU's football and men's basketball programs in the last few years: recruiting scandals, player arrests, firings, etc. An Ohio State guy listens for a few minutes, thinks, then says, "Forget that. That's all bullshit and lies. It doesn't matter. What matters is that WE WON!" He turns to face the crowd filing out, thrusts his hands in the air, and shouts, "O-H!"

For the most part, the Michigan faithful don't take the bait. I hear a few "Pump my gas" chants and see a few one-finger salutes, but otherwise the UM fans go about their own business and let the victors have their spoils. This, to me, is what sets Michigan apart. It's not that the mercenaries who play for their team are better behaved (UM has had its share of scandal), it's the way they approach the game and its denouement.

Don't get me wrong. They are not happy, and I overhear more than one conversation about whether or not coach Lloyd Carr should get the boot, but beneath the surface of disappointment, there is a sense that the entire night lies ahead and they aren't going to let a football game ruin it. As I hear one guy telling his girlfriend as they walk out of the stadium, "No one died here today." This makes me happier than ever that I chose this game. I can relate to the Michigan fans. Obviously they care — 110,000 people wore blue and maize and screamed their lungs out for three hours, so they care — and it hurts, but they're not going to jump off a bridge over the outcome.

This is because it's exactly the way I relate to sports. I love them, I throw myself into them, but afterward I feel a little embarrassed if I find myself too caught up in them. They are supposed to be engaging, but also escapist and trivial, and spending too much time or emotion on them feels wrong. By kickoff I'd spent enough time with my new Michigan buddies and seen enough of the OSU fans to know that I wanted UM to win. I was full-on rooting for them and emotionally invested in the outcome, but in the end, no one did die here. Nothing devastating happened. I'm not feeling or seeing that denial, hurt, or near-violent lashing out that arises in so many fans when their teams lose. *Ich bin ein Michigander.* I wish more people were.

As I wander back to Dan's, I pass a large house. Through the picture window I see a group of students just returning from the game. They're pulling off their hats, tossing gloves onto the table. Some emerge from another room with large platters. A few start putting out a row of red plastic cups. Others set the table. Everyone gathers. They are going to eat and drink and have a party. Not because they won or lost but because they are part of something that's connected by sports but spreads well beyond that.

Back at Dan's place there is a similar calm. His mom and sister are setting up the table in the living room of the small apartment and something is bubbling on the stove. Everyone has gathered around. "Bummer," I say to Ian when we see each other and shake hands. "Yeah," he says, "but not really." Everyone is relaxed and as friendly now as they were before the game, except Eric, the Air Force pilot who's rushing off to Michigan State, where another friend has a ticket for the evening's MSU–Penn State game, thereby allowing him to pull off the rare Big Ten double feature.

We make small talk for a while before I ask Ian if he's heard from his brother. "No," he sighs, "not yet. I'm sure I'll get a message from him tonight. It'll be like eleven and he'll be at some bar screaming so loud I can't make out a word of it."

"What about you," I ask. "You going out tonight?"

"Actually," he says, "I've got a test on Monday, so I'm probably going to stay in and study."

This I cannot relate to. Were I twenty years old and fresh from the thump of the big game, my mind and body would lead me out into the night to work off some of the leftover adrenaline and excess energy. Maybe all hope is not lost for me yet.

9 ★ Lambeau Field

Green Bay Packers vs. Detroit Lions

December 11, 2005

I HAVE COME TO Green Bay for the frozen tundra and the frost-bitten nipples.

"Frozen tundra" refers to more than just the often rock-solid turf of Lambeau Field, where the Packers play their home games. It's a phrase that has come to represent a deeper truth about football. I have no idea where the description originated, but I first heard it while watching the NFL Films highlight reels of old Packer games, spoken in a rich baritone as the Packers, black-and-white heroes of yesteryear, bore down on their foes. There's the 1967 NFL Championship game against the Dallas Cowboys, a game since dubbed the Ice Bowl. Cowboys defensive tackle Bob Lilly is captured on film trying to scrape a foothold into the icy dirt as his team sets up for an unsuccessful, final-seconds goal-line stand.

There are other games, too. Jim Taylor pounding between the tackles and power-sweeping around the side, bits of crystallized grass flying from his shoes. Bart Starr settling behind the center, clouds of breath puffing out of his helmet as he calls the signals. Vince Lombardi pacing the sideline, cajoling his troops. The camera pans to the stands, where hordes of men in fedoras and long black overcoats clap and cheer. The characters who played for the Pack during those years are etched into the collective consciousness as archetypes of the game. Paul Hornung, the irascible running back who succeeded despite his playboy ways. Bart Starr, the cool, cerebral leader. Ray Nitschke, the dominant, maniacal middle linebacker. And Lombardi himself, the do-everything coach: tactical genius, keen talent evaluator, supreme motivator, mother, father, pastor, all wrapped up in one.

To use the words "frozen tundra" is to evoke all the things those teams and players represent: an old-school, hard-core ethic that's defined by toughness, precision, intelligence, and, most of all, excellence. In their history the Pack have won twelve championships, five of them during a seven-year period, including the first two Super Bowls, which is why to this day Super Bowl teams play for the Lombardi Trophy.

It's also why Green Bay is called Title Town. With a population of 100,000, it is by far the smallest city to host an NFL team. Lambeau Field holds about 75,000, which means that three-quarters of the citizens of Green Bay could go to a game. This little-town-that-could act has worked because the people of Green Bay, of the entire state of Wisconsin, really, have shown unprecedented dedication. The citizens own the team: 112,000 people, most of them locals, hold stock in the publicly traded holding company. Whenever the Pack is on TV, the camera flashes to a shot of these diehards, just as the old NFL Films did back in the day, except the men in overcoats have been replaced by a broad range of people in goose down and cheeseheads.

Those aren't the fans I look for. I seek out the maniacs with no shirts on. They're always there. A small group of guys with a crazed look in their eye, an alcohol-tinged scream on their lips, and a touch of frostbite spreading over their pinkening torsos. That, to me, is the epitome of Packer fandom in the modern age, the natural evolution of the old Wisconsin factory workers and fish packers who populated the city when the team was founded in 1921. I admire that dedication. I envy the commitment. I came here to get a piece of it.

★ I'd spent the previous weekend watching sports, too. It was the season finale of my daughter's first-grade soccer team. The team had been fun to watch. The year before, she'd been in a developmental league — in which the kids simply did drills and activities meant to develop the skills needed for the game — dribbling, passing, shooting, and, apparently, eating Dunkin' Munchkins.

This year she's on a real team with uniforms (red) and actual games refereed by junior high students who, while well-meaning, always seem a little embarrassed to blow the whistle loud enough for anyone else to hear it. The first game is something like a cartoon, a cloud of smoke drifting around behind the ball with a jumble of arms and legs jutting out from the fray. Every now and then a foot makes solid contact and the ball scoots down the field with the cloud in hot pursuit.

There is one exception, a girl on my daughter's team who's a head taller and two steps faster than everyone else and unleashes wicked punts that could knock a keg on its side. From time to time she busts out from the pack, chasing the ball down the field and blasting it into the net. Thanks to her, the red team — officially named the Red Rockin' Robins by popular vote after the game — wins its first tilt.

Afterward, I'm happy that my daughter's first true competitive experience was a positive one, but she is a little disappointed. "No one passes the ball," she tells me. "They all just want to get it." This breaks my heart. She has mastered some concept of the sport that goes beyond the sort of primal push-shove-kick-it-at-all-costs motivation of her peers. That, I think, is more important than the fact that she's played an entire game and barely soiled the laces of her brand-new cleats.

As the early weeks go by, the scene becomes eerily familiar. The ball scoots, the kids chase, mini–Mia Hamm breaks from the pack and scores. My girl does all right, getting her kicks in, scoring a couple of goals, and leading the team (possibly the league) in on-field hugs during play, one time even stopping to squeeze a friend on the other team.

Then, about week four, something changes. These girls, led by coaches who actually know what they're doing, start to play the game as it was meant to be played. Not just the Red Rockin' Robins, but the other teams as well. There's a defense, an offense, and little glimpses of strategy. From time to time, there are passes, some of them intentional. Now when mini-Mia gets the ball and heads upfield for a breakaway, there's a wall of defenders waiting to turn her back. Those easy goals no longer exist.

Before we know it, the team arrives at the final game with an unblemished record, but well into the second half the Robins are locked in a 0–0 tie. I note in the voices of the moms and dads of Robinsville the slightest hint of strain. The gentle reminders, the well-meaning directives, have become inflected with a tenor of urgency.

Then the other team scores.

For the first time in their young athletic lives, the Robins are losing. And time is running out. All pretense is lost now. Cries of "Get the ball!" sound from my fellow parents. Dads turn from the field, covering their eyes. Moms do pirouettes of body English, hoping to influence the ball or their offspring. I restrain myself to a few calls of "Pay attention." I don't mind if my daughter plays poorly, but it would be tough to have the other team score while she was pointing out clouds that look like laughing elephants.

This doesn't mean I'm not dying inside. This game has my full attention. I'm emotionally invested. I hang on every bounce of the ball, leaning to keep it from rolling where I don't want it to go. Gritting my teeth, exhaling when our defense turns back one of their assaults. I have not rooted like this in fifteen years. These are six-year-olds, so I can't get loud, but the inner chain reaction and response is no different. I'm out there, it's all on the line. I will rise and fall depending on the outcome.

In the end, the Robins score with just minutes left, saving their undefeated season with a tie. The girls don't seem to grasp the significance or care as they dive into a postgame feast of Gatorade and pretzels, talking excitedly about anything but soccer. The parents are relieved and exuberant. Myself included. And I think: This is how I came to love sports in the first place. That incredible all-or-nothing rush is hard to find anywhere else.

When I started out almost a year ago, I had been struggling with the idea of what kind of fan I'd become. Where I had once been a passionate, committed, near-lunatic who yelled at the TV, went to any game I could get tickets to, and sulked if my team lost, I'd become someone who still watched and still rooted, but from an emotional remove. Doing that allowed me to avoid the highs and lows, and the sense of embarrassment that I could be driven to abnormal joy or gut-twisting misery by a silly game, played by over-fed giants, for that matter, but the price paid for limiting one is limiting the other. And, in the end, who's to say which is better, living and dying by a team at the expense of being seen as an immature ogre or maintaining an intellectual distance but never really getting that thrill of victory? This soccer match between six-year-olds has brought it all back, though. Damn the misery. I want the elation.

I've been getting closer and closer. From Daytona to the Final Four to UM-OSU, my resistance has dwindled and I find myself growing more and more fervent. In the wake of the Rockin' Robins experience, I arrive in Green Bay hoping to pick up on the local love of the Pack and root like I did when I was younger. To transfer that sense of abandon from the Little League fields of New Jersey to the frozen tundra of Lambeau Field.

★ Charlie is bumming on my head. A born-and-bred Wisconsin-ite, he is a writer and editor I met about ten years ago on some random adventure. Since then we've jet skied in near-freezing waters off Nantucket, snowmobiled to the summit of a 12,500-foot peak in Idaho, and raced in rickety outboards to the mosquito-infested Marquesas. I knew I'd become friends with him the first time I read his business card. Below his name and the address for his "global headquarters" (his home in Oshkosh) reads a singular line: "A good man to have along." Over the years, I've continued to find this not only funny but true.

No surprise, then, that I called Charlie as soon as I knew I'd be headed to Green Bay. He not only had a wealth of information to share, but he offered to make the two-hour drive up to keep me company for the day. That sounded great, but he is the bearer of bad news. He's nixing my shirtless-cheesehead plan. Based on our history, I know it's not because he lacks a sense of adventure or be-cause it's a night game in the middle of December. "Three things are generally considered bad form at Packers games," he explains.

"One. Complaining about the weather. Two. Leaving the game early. Three. Taking off your shirt and wearing one of those cheese-heads. Among real fans, it's just not done."

This delivers a serious blow to my fantasy and makes it hard for me to open the trunk of my rental car when Charlie's around, because I don't want him to see that I've already bought a triangular chapeau of faux cheddar. I'm sad, but in the end, I make peace with the idea of wearing a jacket and going cheeseless. I had wanted to do those things because I'd been seeking the quintessential Packer experience, but if they are actually the opposite of what real Packer fans do, I guess I'm going to have to make like a good football team and adjust. In truth it doesn't mean that I can't lose myself in the game, it just means that I won't be wearing my fervor on my goose-pimpled skin. I must admit that this moment of clarity comes after I step out of my car at noon and the twenty-two-degree air takes a bite out of my face, the only exposed skin on my body.

Instead, at Charlie's behest, I take a different path to the heart of Packer mania. He sends me an article by Cliff Christl — a writer for the *Milwaukee Journal Sentinel* who grew up in Green Bay and has covered the Packers on and off for the better part of four decades — in which Christl outlines all the historical Packer sites around the city. I not only read it but e-mailed Cliff, and he agreed to show us around.

So it was that we stepped out of a blustery day and into the old Chicago & North Western train depot. The place has been turned into a bar and restaurant called Titletown Brewing, and there among the green-and-gold banners and black-and-white photos of strapping men in leather helmets and lumpy shoulderpads, Charlie and I find Cliff and his wife and we four sit down for lunch.

Cliff and Charlie trade Wisconsin talk and Packer stories, and Cliff, a jowly guy with a brush of white hair and a diamond stud earring, proves to be a great tale-teller with a ton of knowledge. For instance, this isn't just any old Packer-themed eatery. This was the train station from which the Packers used to depart for games and to which they'd return afterward. Fans would gather for sendoffs

and greetings. When the Packers won the 1929 NFL Championship, Cliff tells us, something like fifteen thousand people swarmed
the station and lined the tracks waiting for the team to return.

This is just the starting point of Cliff's Packer tour, so we load
into his car and hit the streets of Green Bay. The city rides on the
Packers, literally. From the Nitschke Bridge to Lombardi Avenue,
the thoroughfare that runs right by Lambeau Field, the team is
ever present.

We see the remains of City Stadium, where the Packers played
from 1925 to 1956, now a high school field. The school itself sits
on property that includes the sandlot where the team played from
its inception in 1919 until 1925. We drive by the WBAY-TV building, a former community club where fans would gather during
away games to listen to wire reports as they came in. A large grid at
the front of the main room tracked the movement of the ball up
and down the field.

We stop for a minute before the former Northland Hotel, where
visiting teams used to stay. Since City Stadium had no visitors'
locker room, the teams would dress at the hotel and take a bus
over. As a kid, Cliff was once invited onto the bus where the hated
Chicago Bears waited to be ferried to the stadium. They were as
nice to him as could be, shaking his hand and signing autographs.

We see Curly Lambeau's gravesite. Lombardi's houses. We ride
through the deserted downtown, where what was once a typical
American Main Street of shops and storefronts has been plowed
under in favor of anonymous strip malls and banks. It's there, on
Irwin Street, that we stop in front of a small brick house; this is
where Lambeau, the charismatic yet problematic founder, player,
and coach of the Green Bay Packers, grew up. Originally it was
thought that he'd been raised in a different house, but a local kid
working on a high school research project discovered that, as a
young boy, Lambeau resided right here. (Aren't high school research projects supposed to be about the space program? Or the
deeper meaning of the Doors?)

Some of the sites are marked with plaques or small busts, but
just as many give no indication of their place in Packer history.

Marked or not, the places really aren't much to see, especially if Cliff isn't there to provide the narrative. As a sightseeing tour, it makes a pretty good bus route.

As I stare out at these landmarks, I find myself searching for some sort of emotional breakthrough, a moment where I somehow feel connected to the past, but all I see are old high-school fields and aluminum-sided suburban houses. Whatever magic these places once held no longer exists.

Or is it that I'm incapable of conjuring it? During the ride, I sneak little peaks over at Charlie, who looks out the window, mesmerized. He peppers Cliff with questions, and asks for clarification on various points of history. When we get out of the car and wave goodbye to Cliff, Charlie can't stop talking about how cool the tour had been.

What am I missing? Could it be that the heart of the Packer mystique lies not in the bracing cold of Lambeau but in the heated confines of a white Ford Taurus?

★ Eight hours before the 7:30 P.M. kickoff, thousands of fans stream past the giant statues of Vince Lombardi and Curly Lambeau outside the stadium and pile into the atrium connected to Lambeau Field. They browse in the massive gift shop (where you can buy a Green Bay Parka), eat at the Frozen Tundra Café, and pay $10 to walk through the Packer Hall of Fame. Across the street sits Don Hutson Center, where the team holds not only its week-to-week practices but runs its training camp as well. The locker rooms, though, are back in the stadium, a healthy walk anytime and a trudge after a practice in full pads in the heat of summer. So the kids of Green Bay show up on their bicycles, and when practice ends they let the players ride the bikes back to Lambeau, hitching a ride on the back or running behind, often with the player's helmet in hand. The city and the team have embraced each other, all in.

Many of the players hang around the city after their playing days are over. Starr. Forrest Gregg. At least two dozen others. Charlie and I make our way along the grid of streets next to the

practice field, where a patchwork of huge heated tents stands. Inside, music blares, scores of TVs show football games from around
the country, and the Packer faithful sit, stripped down to the first
of the four or five layers they're wearing, drinking beer and smoking cigarettes. We stop at one of these places and bump into Don
Majkowski, the former Packer QB who now does a game-day radio
show, and Johnnie Gray, a former Packer DB who does various odd
jobs around town, including working as a bouncer and going on
cruises where fans pay to spend a week onboard some boat with
former Packer players.

Beyond the shops and restaurants, the entire renovated stadium is a museum. The atrium has an extension of the field inlaid
in the floor. A piece of concrete from the old entrance ramp to the
field has been put down on the new entrance, and the players tap
it before taking the field as a way to touch base with the legends of
the past. And during the game, a constant flow of people step up to
the railing along the south end-zone to take pictures of the most-
revered spot in Packer history: the goal line that Starr surged
across to win the Ice Bowl. The ushers in that section don't even
bother trying to keep people out. When it gets too congested, they
simply call out, "Unless you're taking pictures, you have to keep
moving."

The stadium has become a national attraction, pulling in visitors throughout the year. As a birthday gift one spring, one of
Charlie's daughters brought him up for the full stadium tour. While
they were there, an RV pulled up in the parking lot, and a group
of guys got out and started grilling, drinking beer, and throwing
around a football. When asked what they were doing, they explained that they'd always dreamed of making a pilgrimage to
Lambeau to tailgate and visit the famous stadium. They'd never
been able to make it during a game, so they decided to just come
up, tailgate, and take the tour. A game was almost beside the point.

Earlier in the day, Charlie and I had met at the Hall of Fame.
As I waited for him by the entrance, I watched the faithful ap-
proach. To the side were two giant black-and-white photos, one of
Lombardi standing with George Halas, and another of the '48

Packers at training camp. In between them was a glass case filled with memorabilia of the former Packer Don Hutson, including an old blue-and-gold jersey, game-day programs with him on the cover, and magazine profiles of him. Over the sound system played highlights of past Packer games. It was amazing to see the way people approached this stuff. Many took pictures standing in front of the pictures, as if they could almost infuse themselves into the scene. Two boys, I'd say about thirteen, studied the items in the glass case the way you might expect teenage boys to ogle an issue of *Maxim*.

There was something about this scene that resonated with me. This was not the heart-racing passion of my daughter's soccer game, but there's another kind of passion on display here. The reverence, the adornment of the relics, the sense of sacrament. It has the feeling of religion.

★ As protection against the renowned cold of northern Wisconsin, I'm wearing insulated hunting boots, wool socks, long johns, jeans, a thermal shirt, another thick shirt over that, a fleece sweatshirt, full-length snowmobiling pants, a hunting jacket, snowmobiling gloves, and a hat. But as we set out into the parking lot about three hours before game time, the temperature is fifteen degrees, and it's only going to go one way from there.

I'm no longer much impressed by parking-lot parties, but this particular tailgate at least comes with its own cheap thrills. One guy busies himself behind his truck, setting up miniature goal posts that are strewn with bras, many of them signed by the women who gave them up. I want to believe that this is a totem of good times past, but when the guy opens the truck door I see a box with several pieces of lingerie draped over the top. I get the sense that his is a self-made glory; it's hard to imagine someone removing any bit of clothing in this weather, and even Green Bay doesn't have enough alcohol to convince so many women to root for the Pack while leaving their own team unsupported.

Another new twist here is the animal hats, Daniel Boonesque things made of full animal skins, designed so that the pelt cascades down the wearer's back, complete with little fur archipelagos of former limbs dangling off them. The creature's face, fully intact, stares out from above the wearer's forehead. Talking to someone who sports one causes a confusing moment when I'm not sure if I should be making eye contact with him, or his headwear. After spotting a few I start an informal count. In the end my tally includes coyote, skunk, badger, fox, raccoon, beaver, and one guy who has a stuffed duck strapped to the top of his head. The duck wears a tiny cheesehead.

I'd been told I'd find some serious midwestern hospitality out here. All I'd have to do is say hello to someone and he'd offer me a beer and a brat, went the conventional wisdom, but an hour into our walkabout Charlie and I have yet to be offered anything other than free cell phone minutes if we change carriers. I'm getting hungry, cold, and cranky. That's when Charlie sees a sign that appears like an oasis, or a pair of golden arches suspended above a lonely highway: "OSHKOSH PACKER FANS."

"Oshkosh?" Charlie says. "I wonder if I know them?"

He approaches a man stirring a huge pot with a large aluminum ladle. Street names are exchanged, landmarks, places of business, names of people who might be mutual acquaintances. A stocky woman who's been standing nearby steps up behind the table where the pot sits. "You look familiar. What's your name?" Charlie tells her. "Yeah, that's familiar," she says, putting a finger on her chin. "Well," Charlie offers, "my dad is a doctor in town, has been for years, works at the hospital, so a lot of people recognize my name because of him."

"That must be it," she says, snapping her fingers. "He must have been the doctor on call when we brought Frank in." The synapses have connected. We're made men. I'm pulled over to the table, there are introductions and hellos. She's Deb, short, blond, pleasantly round of feature and chattering away in the notorious Upper Midwest accent that's just short of Canadian and can't help but make me think of the movie *Fargo*. The guy with the ladle is her brother-in-law, Bob. "The trick," he says as he hands me a Styrofoam cup filled with a thick brown bubbling goo, "is to put the noodles on the bottom and the chili on top." I nod. I smile. I take a heaping spoon of the chili. It is hot. And good. Flavorful and just greasy enough to leave my lips feeling a little slick. Charles Plueddeman — A good man to have along.

We make our way around the table and into the tent behind, into the very heart of the Oshkosh Packer club, which, as it turns out, has been in existence for thirty years. Deb points out the essentials: beer, space heaters, a table full of food. Here the club members lounge in folding chairs or stand hopping from foot to foot in the frigid air. "There's about thirty of us," Deb says. "It's great because someone always has tickets. If they're not going they'll give you theirs, or if you can't make it you give them yours, and lots of times we won't even have enough tickets for everyone, but you come to the game anyway and just watch from the parking lot. You can just relax out here and eat and drink and have a good time."

As I finish the chili, I peruse the table. The options include everything from a giant football-shaped sausage to a cake that's an amalgam of crushed Oreos, graham crackers, and peanut butter. It looks and tastes like something out of *Good Housekeeping* circa 1958 or a recipe you'd find on the bottom of a Cool Whip container. None of which prevents it from being delicious. All of it is laid out with care. Placed on the pristine white tablecloth like offerings for a sacrament.

I fall into conversation again with Deb. Only, she turns out not to be Deb but Deb's sister, Jean, who's married to Bob the chili man. I notice that Jean's wearing a pin with a picture in it. "Who's that?" I ask.

"Ohhh, that's Deb's husband, Frank. He died last winter of a heart attack. Very sudden. Shocked everyone. He was a huge fan. So now we wear these pins to remember him."

Just then Deb herself walks up and hands me a cup of hot chocolate. It is the best hot chocolate in the world, thick and creamy, just short of whipped hot fudge. "Mmmm," I say after the first sip.

"Ya, that's from the farm," she says.

"What farm?"

"Ohhhh, we own a dairy farm. My twenty-three-year-old son is there right now, milking the cows. Poor kid, he graduated college last year right after his dad passed, so he got forced into becoming a farmer. I think all he really wants to do is stand on the field at Lambeau and take pictures."

"Well, there are people who do that," I say.

"Ohhh, he'd love that," she says. We talk a little bit about the perils and possibilities of professional photography and about her son and her husband and the approaching holidays. "Of course, we'll be here for Christmas and New Year's," she adds, pointing out that the Packers play home games on both holidays.

"What's the plan for Christmas?" someone asks. "Ohhh, we're going to set up two long tables right here," she says, motioning lengthwise along the spine of the tent, "and we're going to serve lasagna. And we'll set up a separate area for the drinkers because we want it to be nice. But no salad because it'll freeze." Turning from the main part of the tent back to me, she adds, "A few years ago the Packers played on Christmas Eve. That time we made three huge turkeys and had a big sit-down dinner. We served seventy-nine people."

Indeed the Oshkosh Packer club picks up members the way Jim Taylor picked up first downs. As far as I can determine, the prerequisites for joining include being at the game and signing the van. The van turns out to be the central part of the Oshkosh Packer club encampment. It's the sort of minibus they use to shuttle people from the airport to the car rental agency. It's the main mode of transit between Oshkosh and Lambeau for a large part of the club. The inside houses a horseshoe of padded seats complimented by a tangle of spare winter clothing, scarves, mittens, hats, snow pants, and pompons. Packer jerseys are strewn about, dangling from the overhead shelves and stretched across the floor.

One side of the exterior is covered with gold stickers shaped like helmets. People have signed the stickers. Charlie and I are given helmets and a marker and told to sign it and stick it, which we do. The bus is also the support for the banner that flies over the party. It reads "Oshkosh Packer Fans Oshkosh; Borth; Madison; Fond du Lac; Valparaiso, IN; Evansville, IN; Madison, SD."

"Why South Dakota?" I ask Deb. "Ohhh. One year," she explains, "we saw two guys sitting on the curb drinking beer and eating chicken out of a bucket. We said that's no way to tailgate, come with us. So they joined us that day and they've been coming back ever since. They live all the way out in South Dakota, and when they come to a game they arrive a day early and stay at our house overnight. We get people who show up every week from South Dakota. They say, we know the Waysons, and we say, come on in. Here," she says, pointing to two guys in the corner. "We got these two guys from Texas this week."

"Yes, sir," says Joe, a tall, lanky kid of maybe twenty-five who has a long nose and freckled cheeks. "Drove twenty hours, from Dallas. Stopped in Ames, Iowa, to pick up my dad," he adds, nodding to the tall bearded man next to him. "Gave my great-grandma a kiss, then right to here."

"Why the Packers?" I ask.

"Don't know," he says, "just always liked them. Just something about them." His dad nods as if to confirm this. The two have been to a few Packer games in Dallas, including a playoff game in 1994, but this is their first trip to Lambeau. As Joe stands there, earmuffs over hat, one hand holding a beer, the other driven deep into his pocket, I ask him if it's all he imagined it would be. "Oh," he says, "everything and more."

★ In my back pocket is a small bundle of wires. The insulation that covers them is Packer gold and for a good reason: They are pieces of the heating coil that ran under the old field before the stadium was renovated. A brainchild of no less than Vince Lombardi himself, the coil was little more than an underground matrix of wires like the ones in my pocket. The idea was that when the field froze, as it often does, the team could flip a switch and send an electric current through the wires, which would then heat the turf, keeping it soft and playable.

I came across the remnant in a little shop just north of the stadium, adjacent to a gas-station convenience store. The place was filled with Packer memorabilia: posters, programs from as far back as the '30s, bobbleheads, autographed photos of everyone from "Johnny Blood" McNally to James Lofton, Packer lighters, Packer coins, replica jerseys, actual jerseys, Packer flashlights, minihelmets, real helmets, lamps, jackets, belt buckles, shot glasses, and a three-foot-tall Brett Favre statue. It is as much a museum as the Hall of Fame and Charlie and I spent almost an hour browsing. When we came across the little bundles of wire we had to have them.

That they were almost certainly fake actually makes them more appealing. The slim chance of authenticity adds a sense of hopeful magic. It was a leap of faith, not unlike committing to a team in the first place I had to believe, despite the odds and the potential for disappointment. If I put myself out I stood the chance for a great reward.

And while I remain open to the possibility that the wires now stuffed into my back pocket once warmed the field that stretches before me, I know they no longer work, because my ass is freezing. I mention this to Charlie. "Well," he says, "they never worked very well on the field either."

By game time the temperature has dropped to fourteen degrees, with a wind-chill of five degrees, and it's not just the tundra that is frozen. An icy slurry covers the concrete steps that rise through the stadium. As with all professional venues, the brightness of the field is a shock, and the players in their uniforms stand out against the background. The Pack is having a terrible season, they're 3–9, but the Lions, a divisional rival, are just as bad this year (2–10). The in-conference game — Favre's one hundredth at Lambeau — will be nationally televised, and the Pack actually has a chance to win. All of which charges the air with an extra bit of excitement.

But there is still a small-town feel, which is what separates Green Bay from most other NFL cities. As the pregame rolls on we meet the Ball Boy of the Week, the Packer Lucky Family of the Week (they watch from a couch in a special section), the Tee Retriever of the Week, and the Fortunate Fan of the Week. We learn that Sargento is the official cheese of Lambeau Field. All we're missing is the Homecoming Queen waving from the back of a convertible Mustang.

As at Michigan's Big House, the seats are nothing more than aluminum benches with numbers stenciled on top. At this time of year, that provides an added benefit in that everyone is huddled in tight, which makes it warmer and cozier, provided you don't mind snuggling up to your fellow beer-guzzling football fan. The downside: Aluminum gets really cold. The Packer faithful sit on just about anything to insulate their posteriors from the frigid metal: scarves, cardboard boxes, thick weekend newspapers. As an alternative, vendors rent seat cushions for $5 a pop. At $2.50 per cheek it seems like the best heating bargain I'm going to get all winter. Charlie and I spring for the deluxe model, which includes a backrest, and settle into our seats.

Kickoff passes and we throw ourselves into the game. It's not a pretty contest but it's fun and there's an added interest for me since I'm not here as a neutral observer; I've come to root for the Pack and I want them to win. As the game progresses I notice bursts of loud, thumping dance tunes over the speaker system. This has become so standard at sports events that I don't think twice about it until one of the guys sitting behind us says, "It seems kinda weird, them playing the strip club music in here." The moment he says it, I think, he's right, it sort of does. There is something refined about the place that makes dance tunes unfit. This is what's different about watching a game here; from the town to the fans to the aura of the team, there's a feeling that this is the kind of place where club music just doesn't fit.

The game is a close one, with the teams settling for a series of early field goals that puts Detroit ahead 6–3. The crowd is into the action, but people go for long stretches without moving much, as if they've huddled against the cold. Alternately, some people stand and stomp their feet, trying to keep the blood flowing. When something good happens, what follows is not the usual sound of applause but the muffled thunder of thousands of thick mittens pounding into one another. And the shouts bring up little bursts of steam as if seventy thousand smokestacks have all kicked on at once.

Detroit goes ahead 13–3 before the Packers strike big. In the second quarter, their unheralded rookie running back, Samkon Gado, breaks around the right side for a sixty-four-yard touchdown. The play is a relative of the classic Packer sweep, and as it develops in front of me I can see the often-played clip of Lombardi explaining the Xs and Os on a chalkboard ("We get a seal here, and a seal here . . .") and then Gado is streaming down the sideline. The crowd rises as one. Thousands of gloves begin pounding together, and as everyone shouts, "Go, Go!" the place is enveloped in a view-obscuring mist of steamy breath.

When Charlie and I go for a walk at halftime we see a row of four guys with big blocks of cheese on their heads and no shirts. Amateurs. It's all I can do to keep from clucking my tongue at them. In the second half, I concentrate on Favre. He is interesting to watch in that I've seen him on TV a hundred times but I never really got a feel for his over-the-top sling and exactly how hard he throws the ball. I can't imagine trying to catch one of his missiles in this weather.

Late in the fourth quarter, the Pack rallies for a game-tying field goal, providing just what everyone wants on a cold night in Wisconsin — overtime. (What was rule two? Don't complain about the weather. Check.) I go to take a sip of my beer, which has been sitting on the concrete. The bottom quarter of it is frozen solid. I realize that I'm not doing much better. When I stand I can't feel my feet. It's now eleven thirty. The temperature has dived into the single digits, and I've been outdoors since about four. I give in. In the downtime between the end of regulation and the start of overtime I head to the men's room and stand under the heater, hoping to regain some feeling in my feet. There are a few other guys doing the same thing and we make sure to have a loud conversation about how cold we are so that no one thinks we just like standing around while other guys use the urinal.

I make it back in time to see Favre complete two passes and the Pack kick a field goal to win. The crowd files out in frozen jubilation. That is the true magic of Lambeau. That despite the bitter cold and their frozen extremities, the fans are truly joyous, just as they would've been sick and disgruntled had their team lost. The power of their passion is enough to make the rest of us care, even if it's just a fraction of how much they do, which is why I, too, am happy.

★ The long walk back to the car is a familiar one. There is that odd sensation when the feeling begins to slowly return to my feet, when part of them is numb and part just hurts. I'm certain that if I kicked something, small cracks would spread across my foot and the whole thing would crumble and fall off. I know this sensation from my own days attending December games at Giants Stadium.

I remember one, in particular. It was a fierce divisional game between the Giants and the Eagles. The day was brutal, with winds gusting to 30 mph, on-and-off snow, and temperatures around twenty degrees, without factoring in the wind-chill. To make it worse, the Giants were getting killed. Philly dominated from the beginning, and it was ugly. My dad and sister were ready to go before halftime, but my brother and I refused. It wasn't an option. We'd never left a game with more than a few minutes remaining. We toughed it out until five minutes into the third quarter, then gave up, limping back to the car.

I was in college then, and it was the last time the four of us ever went to a game together. We were all starting to move in different directions, getting older, certainly too old for the cold. Personally, it was also about the time I started looking at sports differently. When I started thinking about them more than feeling them.

My son played soccer this year, too. Like my daughter had been the year before, he was in the skills league. In his case the problem was not winning and losing but quitting. He'd shown a disturbing tendency thus far in his young life to lose interest in things rather quickly. He already dropped tae kwon do, yoga, and music. He seemed to like soccer, though, and we were happy, because we'd begun to suspect that he was either impetuous or suffered from ADD, and we didn't like either possibility. So far we'd been willing to write it off to immaturity, but another early departure would have come dangerously close to setting a trend that even we as love-blind parents would be hard-pressed to ignore.

Then, about halfway through the season, we came upon a damp and cool Saturday morning. His sister was comfy on the couch. *Clifford* was playing on the small screen. I came in with his blue T-shirt (his team was the Blue Dragons) and cleats. When he saw me he declared that he didn't like soccer anymore and he didn't want to go. I tried to reason with him. Then to beg. He wasn't giving. I was frustrated. I knew it wasn't that he didn't want to play soccer, it was just that he was warm and comfy and pleasantly entertained, so he didn't feel like moving.

Then from my mouth sprang a speech that could not have been more perfect had I been reading from the script of an after-school special. He had to go, I said, because he made a commitment. When he joined the team, that was like making a promise to everyone that you'd come and try hard and have a lot of fun. If he didn't go his coach and his teammates would all be wondering where he was. They were expecting him. They were counting on him. If he didn't like soccer, that was okay; he didn't have to play next year. But this year he had to go.

It worked. In my head, every Pee Wee Football and Little League coach I ever had was cheering. It was one of the classic, if not clichéd, speeches we give kids and parents about the value of sports. They're not about petulant stars, drugs, guns, aggressive behavior toward women, greed, and any number of other maladies that dominate the headlines, but about teamwork, dedication, effort, commitment, focus, and self-esteem.

It occurs to me as I walk back to my car that the tingling sensation in my toes is the feeling of commitment and dedication. Of belonging to a team and showing up and giving your all because the rest of the team is counting on you. These are far different things than going to a game shirtless and with a piece of cheese on your head. The connection between the Packers and the people of Green Bay is much deeper than that. It is written on the names of the streets, and in the neighborhoods where the players lived. It's on those bicycles that kids and players ride together, it's in the little plaques and simple houses that people take time to find and remember. Their adoration is not the same as religion — they don't worship the Packers — but they have a religious devotion, a commitment, deeper and more meaningful than the one I encouraged between my son and his soccer team, but of the same type. They celebrate their holidays with the team, honor their dead through them, and share so many moments of joy and pain together.

What makes sports so great, so different from reading or politics, is the way it can become a whole-body encounter. It's not just in my head, but in my feet, in my flesh and bones. I don't have to take my shirt off and wear a silly hat to experience that. As I start my car and crank the heat, I think, that is a pretty good speech. I'll have to give it one day.

10 ★ Fenway Park, Opening Day

Boston Red Sox vs. Toronto Blue Jays

April 11, 2006

I'VE BEEN WAITING FOREVER, and by the time the T — Boston's subway — comes rattling into Copley Station, it's packed with so many people wearing Red Sox shirts it's almost impossible to get onboard. But I can't wait any longer, so I shove on, squeezing into a spot on the bottom step, pressed against the door. When the car stops at Kenmore Station, I'm shot out of the doors like toothpaste from a tube that's been sat on. Dozens of people mill in the streets. Police direct traffic, both pedestrian and vehicular, and celebrants spill out of a bar on the corner, taking up positions along the sidewalk.

I don't know where I'm going, but I follow the unshaven guys in red caps. We round a corner and head up a crowded city street. A girl hands out a special edition of the *Boston Herald* with the Sox on both the front and back covers. Outside a bank, a seven-piece jazz ensemble pumps out tunes while a bank manager right out of central casting — brown suit, thick black glasses — hands out balloons with the institution's name on them.

For some reason, I feel as though I need to hurry, so instead of strolling along with the traffic, I weave among the reams of gawkers, slow walkers, and scalpers. At another bar, even more people crowd onto an outdoor patio, drinking and laughing while a Dixieland quartet, complete with straw boaters and red-and-white-striped jackets, plink out classics. Several of the local pubs opened at nine this morning and plan to stay open all day, promising "seventeen hours of service." They hold my attention for a second, but not much longer, because as I approach, rising up behind them are the bleachers of Fenway Park.

Originally I wondered if the trips to Wrigley and Fenway would be too similar; some of the coincidences are startling. Fenway was built in 1912 and rebuilt after a fire in 1934. Wrigley was built in 1914 and rebuilt after a fire in 1937. Both are celebrated for intimate and quirky designs shoehorned into city neighborhoods. Wrigley has its ivy-covered brick, while Fenway has its thirty-seven-foot-high wall in left field, the infamous Green Monster, its odd zigzag cutout in center, and its deep right-field wall that curves around the foul pole. Both have hand-operated scoreboards, and both, the theory goes, recall a time of greater individuality and craftsmanship, unlike the mass-produced cookie-cutter designs that followed (Three Rivers, etc.) and the mass-produced faux-quirky stadiums that came after those (Camden Yards, etc.). Most of all, each was inhabited by a team bedeviled by a much-analyzed curse and harboring one of the longest championshipless streaks in sports, stretching more than eighty-five years, until the Sox finally won in '04.

But I knew in my heart they would be different, if for no other reason than I was going to each with dissimilar motivations. As I approach Fenway, I know I was right. From a distance, the little brick structure appears tucked in among the other buildings as if it were no more than just another warehouse, but up close it's a different story. In 2003 the Red Sox added four rows of seating above the left-field wall. The seats have rows of countertops in front of them, and when the Sox are on TV there's almost always a shot of people sitting at the tables, looking like volunteers at a telethon.

From Lansdowne Street, where I'm now walking, it appears quite different. What's not visible on TV are the huge steel support brackets affixed to the little brick wall that cantilever the bleachers over the street. When I stand against the wall and look up, the structure hangs over me. The place literally looms over the neighborhood.

Farther up the block I count ten TV trucks; some from national outlets like ESPN are joined by an armada of local and regional representatives from as far away as Rhode Island, New Hampshire, and Connecticut. It is Opening Day, but it's just one team, playing one of 162 regular-season games. I'm not certain, but I don't think there are many teams around the country creating quite such a fuss just for getting back to work. The team looms over all of New England.

It's a very un-Wrigley-like feel, partly because the place seems to cast a bigger shadow, figuratively speaking, and partly because it looks so different. Whereas Wrigley's not much to see from the outside, Fenway's brick surfaces and green stanchions are charming and quaint, like an old New England school, maybe. The atmosphere is also different. It's less casual and more energetic. No doubt that's partly because this is Opening Day, which always gives the crowd a boost. After a long winter, I must admit the blue skies and puffy white clouds have got my spirits soaring, too. This is the last stop on my excursion, and I think it's somehow appropriate to end with a beginning.

★ I expect something else will separate my experience at Fenway from my trip to Wrigley: history. This is a connecting thread to all the events on my list. Baseball dates to the mid-1800s. The Kentucky Derby and Wimbledon began in the 1870s, and the Michigan–Ohio State rivalry goes back to 1897. The NCAA Championship was born in 1939, although sixty-four-team March Madness didn't start until 1985. The Super Bowl has only been around for forty years, but the NFL is eighty years old. Which is why, when I was making up my list, history played such a big part. I went back and read about each event or place, and those that made it had the longest, strongest ties to the past, which in some way guarantees their ties to the future as well.

There is personal history, too. I grew up a Yankees fan, but not just any Yankees fan. Starting in about 1974, Yankees began to move to my hometown. As I remember it, the first was Catfish Hunter. I was only seven, but even I knew who Hunter was. Before long he was joined by Thurman Munson, Graig Nettles, and Mickey Rivers. Tommy John, Chris Chambliss, and Sparky Lyle all lived in neighboring towns.

Bobby Bonds lived in town during his short stint with the team in 1975 (I never met them, but I remember hearing stories about his sons, Bobby and Barry). Don Gullett lived in a little house on the same street as the school, so kids would sometimes see him in his yard on the way to class. On such mornings, talk of the sighting would buzz through the student body faster than word of a particularly lenient substitute.

Munson, the venerable captain, lived about five blocks from me, and a few years after he died in a plane crash, I had a paper route that included his former house. Nettles, though, was my personal favorite; I wore #9 and played third base, just like he did. His son was three years younger than I, and one day, when I was in seventh grade, I happened into the auditorium while one of the younger grades was putting on their annual play. I stopped and sat on a table in the back of the room to watch for a few minutes.

Moments later the back door opened and someone slipped into the room. The figure was backlit by the daylight streaming into the dark auditorium, so I didn't get a good look at him. Moments later, he settled in three feet away from me. I glanced over. It was Nettles! I had not intended to stay for the entire show, but I could not now make myself move. So there we sat until the curtain fell, Graig Nettles and me. Watching the play. When the lights were still down, and the kids were taking their bows, he slipped out as quietly as he'd come in. I never looked directly at him and never said a word to him.

Part of what accounted for that level of reverence was that in 1977 and '78 the Yanks won the World Series. So it wasn't just that we were living among our idols, sitting next to them at school plays, we were living among the best collection of baseball players on the planet. When I was a ten-year-old boy, my neighbors were kicking ass and taking names. It was great.

The ass they kicked most often and in the most dispiriting of ways was that of the Red Sox. When the Yanks and Sox faced off in a one-game playoff to decide who would represent the American League East in the '78 pennant, I somehow ended up watching at home alone with my dog. I was so addled by the tension of the game that about halfway through I convinced myself that things went better for the Yankees when the dog was in the room and worse when she left, so I forced the poor mutt to stay in front of the TV.

It worked. In the seventh inning, Bucky Dent hit a three-run shot over the Green Monster to put the Yanks ahead. I was ecstatic, but there was no one there to celebrate with, so I burst out my front door and ran around the house yelling. The dog was no doubt confused but happy to get out of the room, and so ran beside me all the way, jumping and yelping as we made our way around the yard. Together we paced the floor for the next two innings, the pooch nipping at the untied laces of my shoes, until it was finally over.

In that moment, though, I was not really a Red Sox hater. I didn't own a "Boston Sucks" T-shirt like some of my friends (one of whom was famously asked to turn his inside out when he showed up at school with it). I was an equal-opportunity vicarious asskicker; I wanted the Yankees to beat every team they played. It just so happened that they seemed to play Boston more than anyone else, and more often than not it was the Sox who stood between my team and my goals for them.

Fenway will be different because it means more to me. I have a deeper connection to it. I don't hate the Red Sox or their fans, but we do have a history.

★ Ignatius Giglio will balance me. Giglio is a local man with the distinction of being the longest-tenured season-ticket-holder of the Boston Red Sox. He bought his tickets in 1935 and never relinquished them. Born in Quincy, Mass., in 1915, to Francesco and Rosalie Giglio, who had emigrated from Sicily, Ignatius was the youngest of eleven children. Francesco had started and built a trucking company, and as they grew up most of the Giglio boys entered the family business. As a teen, Ignatius hung around the garage, cleaning up and running errands. He was given a baseball cap by a sales rep from Kelly Tires that had the company's name across it in green letters. Ignatius wore the hat so much that people started to call him Kelly, and for most of his life that's how he was known.

From early on, Kelly loved sports, especially baseball and football. So much so that he wanted to become a gym teacher. His mother wouldn't allow it. It was business school and trucking for Kelly. Well, maybe he couldn't say no to that, but when he hit twenty and had a few bucks in his pocket, he went out and bought season tickets to the Red Sox. For $2.75 a year he could go to the ballpark sixty or seventy times a season. That might not be the same as spending his life with a whistle around his neck amid the sound of thumping balls and squeaking sneakers, but it was pretty good.

There was always dinner before the game. An early dinner, because Giglio had to arrive in time to watch batting practice. He always watched batting practice. Just as he always parked at the same Shell station a few blocks from Fenway, where they came to know him so well, they saved a spot for him.

Even when he went off to fight during World War II, he held on to those tickets. When he returned home, in 1944, he married, but he didn't stop going to the games. His new wife, Dora, was not a baseball fan but quickly became one. The couple went to two or three games a week when the Sox were in town. Not just that first year, but every year, every week for sixty years. She didn't go on the weekends. That's when he'd take one of his four sons or maybe give the tickets to someone else. When the Sox were on the road, he'd watch on TV.

His original seats were up behind home plate, but a few years after the war he received a letter from the team telling him they were going to move him farther up and out along the third-base line. Giglio saw the seats and said no thanks. He didn't know what they had planned for his old seats, but he knew the park wasn't selling out, and if they were going to take him for granted after all those years, they could keep their tickets.

The Sox blinked. No, no, Mr. Giglio, they said, you're important to us. Where would you like to sit? Anywhere. You tell us.

Anywhere?

Anywhere.

Giglio pointed at a string of seats in the first row between the dugout and home plate. Well, the team said, we have to reserve those for dignitaries and special guests, but can we give you the same spot six rows back?

Deal. So from the early '50s on, that's where Giglio sat, seven rows off the on-deck circle, next to Joe Cronin, the former American League president, and the comedian Frankie Fontaine. From there he could watch red-and-white-clad ballplayers emerge from the dugout and take practice swats framed by the hand-operated scoreboard cut into the Green Monster. The players were so close, a shout not only got their attention, it told them if the shouter had put sauerkraut on that dog. A "Go get 'em" or "You can do it" might have brought a smile from Ted Williams, a wink from Jimmie Foxx, or a nod from Jim Rice.

Kelly never had anything bad to say. Carl Yastrzemski might have struck out for the fourth time in a game, and as he walked back the air would be filled with "You suck" and "You're a bum," but never from Giglio. "You'll get 'em next time, Yaz," he'd say, clapping softly. He'd instruct his sons to do the same. Always positive, always there.

It's where he watched the '46 Series, when Johnny Pesky double-clutched on a throw home, allowing the Cardinals to win Game Seven and the series. And he was there for the '67 Series, when they removed the seats next to him so that a wheelchair-bound Joe Kennedy could sit and watch with Teddy and Joan. He saw Ted Williams's final at bat, a majestic homer over the right-field wall, and he was there when Tony C. took one in the ear. He stood, leaning right, when Carlton Fisk wished his ball around the left-field foul pole to take Game Six of the '75 Series.

He saw it all, because Kelly Giglio always did one other thing: He stayed until the final out. Every time. Get there for batting practice, stay until the last pitch. Two or three times a week, every year, for seventy years.

★ Thousands of Red Sox faithful have gathered around Fenway. There's just one problem: The gates have not yet opened and won't for another twenty minutes. To get to my seat I have to enter on the far side of the park, which seems like a bummer at first, but it allows me to walk among the masses and get a feel for the place. The particularly exuberant or impatient are already lined up several hundred deep at every entrance. Thousands of their less-anxious brethren crowd the streets outside the little park — eating, drinking, buying ridiculously overpriced programs — and one street, Van Ness, which runs along the first-base side, is completely shut down. Guys dressed as players from the turn of the century, complete with flannel jerseys and faux handlebar mustaches, walk around on stilts, playing catch with people in the crowd.

When I reach the other side of the stadium, the Sox supporters are so thick I can't even get to the gate, so I'm forced to wait. The delicious smell of greasy food spices the air: sausage and peppers, burgers, and various things kabobbed sizzle away at a bevy of carts. It smells like exactly what it is, a ball game crossed with a street fair, and the aroma spurs my hunger. I watch for a few minutes as people stop and point when they notice the players' parking lot, located down the street and identifiable by the selection of rimmed-up, chromed-out custom SUVs and sleek Porsches spilling out of the gate.

I look up at the building itself. Fenway may have suffered a long championship drought, but the place started out on a tear. The Sox first played there in 1912 and won the World Series four times in the next six years — 1912, '15, '16, '18 — thanks to an ace pitching staff that included Babe Ruth. (The 1915 Series was played at the larger Braves Field.) Despite his key role in those triumphs, Ruth was traded to the Yankees for cash in 1920. The Red Sox didn't win again for eighty-four years, a span of time during which the Yanks racked up twenty-six titles, the most of any team in any professional sports. No wonder the Red Sox fans felt cursed by Ruth.

As at Wrigley, I can't help but think of all those fans. The people that have stood outside these gates waiting to get in, the day filled with possibility, and those who, so many times, have left disappointed. How many over all those years have passed through here? How many of them have I seen on my TV screen as I watched all those Yankees–Red Sox games?

Finally, noon approaches. As it does, the crowd breaks out in a New Year's–like countdown. *Three, two, one* . . . the gates swing open and we surge forward with a cheer. I'm swept along, and it is a good feeling.

The interior of the stadium is cavernous and echoey. Water (at least I hope it's water) drips onto the bare, cracked concrete floors. Hundreds of wires run willy-nilly through the rafters. The steel posts are a deep green that adds to the dark, dank feeling. They're chipped and uneven and I can see that they've been painted over dozens of times. On one post there's a drop box for the Jimmy Fund, a cancer charity the Sox have supported since the '50s. It's a simple red metal box with a slot in the top, like a tiny mailbox. Where the paint is nicked, little bits of rust show through. The Master Lock that secures the lid looks like it's been there so long, Ellis Kinder himself might have tried to pick it for drinking money.

Whereas Wrigley played to its own history, offering up a self-conscious nostalgia, Fenway seems unaware and unconcerned with its past. Instead of things that are made to evoke the feeling of the '50s, it's filled with things that are actually just old. I can't help but like the place.

★ Michael Giglio answers the door in a short-sleeve shirt and flip-flops. His goatee is surrounded by a day's worth of stubble. I'd first spoken to Michael the previous July, shortly after I returned from Wimbledon. A few weeks earlier, I'd called Kelly directly, and he seemed open to the concept of going to a Red Sox game with me, but said I should talk to his son, Michael, who arranged such things. Michael, who it turned out lives about a half hour away from me in New Jersey, also thought it was a great idea, but there was one problem. The previous week, his father had fallen and hurt his back. The senior Giglio was in the hospital for a brief recovery, but when he got out and was back on his feet, Michael would set something up. Call back in a few weeks, he said.

I called three weeks later, but received no return call. I called once a week for the next three weeks. Finally, in late August, Michael called me. He was sorry he hadn't been in touch sooner, but while his father was in the hospital for his back the doctors had discovered multiple myelomas. It was too late to do anything about them. It had all happened so quickly. Ignatius Giglio died on August 9, 2005.

He'd hung on to see his beloved Sox win, and a year and a half later, he was gone. I told Michael how sorry I was, and for a moment the phone was silent. I related to him how I'd lost my mother only a year earlier, and I knew how difficult it could be, how in some ways I was still dealing with it. "The truth is, Jim, it hurts," he said. "We're all sad, but he had a great run. He was ninety and he lived his whole life with his family around him, he had a successful business, and everything he could've wanted."

"It's great you have such perspective on it," I said.

"I've been thinking about you," he replied. "If you're still interested, I'd like to get together and share some of my dad's stories, show some pictures and things."

"That would be great," I said.

So Michael and I stayed in touch. We spoke on the phone perhaps a dozen times over the next nine months before we could finally arrange a meeting, and over the course of those conversations I came to know him. He is every bit the sports nut his dad had been. Besides the Sox tickets, which he doesn't use as much as he'd like to, the Boston College alum has sixteen seats for that school's football team and goes to not just the home games but some of the away games, too. He also goes to some BC basketball games, and since he's married to a Yankees fan and Penn State graduate, some of those teams' games as well. When we spoke, we'd start out talking about calendars and end up in long discussions about college football, college basketball, the old Big East, and of course the Yankees and Red Sox. Or, as he'd say, the Red Sox and Yankees.

What I enjoyed so much about the chats was that he was, like me, a guy who could take a step back and discuss his teams objectively and yet, more like the me I was trying to rediscover, he could also watch the games with passion. He told stories about watching Yankees-Sox games with his wife, the two of them taking turns yelling at the TV and threatening to choke their respective managers.

That is how I have come to arrive at his house one warm day. I notice immediately that he does not look like his father, who I'd seen beaming out of photos, a ruddy-faced man with bright white hair and dark eyes. Michael, fifty-three, has a rounder face and softer look, but like his old man, Michael conveys a robustness, not just with his firm grip and stout bearing, but through his voice, which is loud and clear.

After our initial greeting, we make our way into a back room, where his mother, Dora, who's visiting for a few days, sits on a couch watching *Dr. Phil.* As I look at her soft, broad face framed by a high wall of white hair streaked with black, I can't help but think: This is a woman who's probably been to more baseball games than most beat writers.

The three of us start to talk baseball and Kelly Giglio. Michael recalls the craziness of the '04 playoffs, when the Sox were three outs from elimination before rallying to win four straight games against the Yankees. He and his father spoke by phone after every half inning, watching with disbelief and joy as their team fought back from the brink, going speechless when they finally clinched it. During all those stressful moments, Michael never worried about his dad's heart giving out — "I was too busy worrying about my own."

His dad, he points out, never believed in the curse. The way he saw it, the Yankees had better teams. They deserved to win. The Sox didn't. Except 2003. "That one hurt," Michael says. "That year, the Sox were a better team." This leads to a discussion of Grady Little and his decision to leave Pedro Martinez on the mound late in a Game Seven the Sox were leading when it was obvious to everyone that the pitcher was tiring. "My wife and I were at that game," Michael says, "and she was crying for me. She said, 'I can't believe this is happening to you again.'"

Dora is right in on the baseball talk, sharing her thoughts and recollections, too. But what she remembers, more than anything, is the routine of it. Sure there were big games and famous people who sat nearby. When the Sox finally won it all, Kelly was ecstatic; the phone rang off the hook for days. Friends and family just showed up at their house to celebrate. And there was the day in 1985, when the Sox celebrated Kelly's longevity by allowing him to throw out the first pitch on Opening Day.

But more than any of that, it was the reassuring steadiness of going to the park two or three nights every week. First dinner, then batting practice, then the main event. They chatted with the people they knew around them; they listened to the familiar cadence of the game. The crowd had changed over the years — there was no beer and not nearly as much yelling in the old days — and the players had grown hair and beards to match the odd length of their pants, but Fenway was exactly the same. She could count on it as sure as she could count on Kelly coming through the door every day after work.

Baseball, along with family, had come to center their relationship; it was the heavenly body in whose gravitational pull they orbited. Now, one year after Kelly's death, Dora could talk about him freely, flip through photo albums and dredge the depths of her memory without pause or pain, but earlier in the year when a nephew had offered to take her to a spring training game during a trip to Florida, she'd turned him down. "Oh, it would've been too much," she says, waving a hand in front of her face. "I couldn't go to a ballpark without him."

I realize now why history had played such an important part in choosing events for my list. Besides tapping into my mother's penchant for travel and big-name happenings, my sports odyssey was also a response to the bout of nihilism brought on by her death. Sports, after all, have a history and a future. We know even if somewhat dimly what came before and we also know that those who come after us will read the books and watch the documentaries and have some sense of what we saw and heard and screamed for. From Ruth to Aaron to Bonds, the stories, good or bad, will be retold over and over and linked not just with each other but with those of future home-run kings who threaten their records. Whenever the crowd sings the national anthem or "My Old Kentucky Home" or "Take Me Out to the Ball Game," their voices become the voices of all those who have sung it before them and those who have yet to join the choir. In that way, sports trumps death.

★ From the dugout, the field is a sliver of green under a patch of blue broken up by the multicolored jumble of the crowd. Cut off by the edge of the roof and the top of the steps, the view is like that of a letterbox movie, a long narrow expanse framed by dark edges.

I've wandered in here off the field, during a lull in the Blue Jays' batting practice. The field, unlike Wrigley's in August, was a perfect toupee of thick grass fiber, plush and soft and just long enough to provide a satisfying squish when I stepped on it. A few Jays had stood around the cage taking swipes at the air and giving each other shit. Other players loitered in small clusters in the outfield, gabbing like schoolgirls until one or two of them would lope off to track a fly ball.

Around me the grounds crew was setting up for some sort of Opening Day ceremony. Two crusty, older members of the crew passed behind me. "Djou look up the first-base line?" one asked. "Doesn't nobody go to school no more?" As I glanced up the line there were in fact hundreds of kids leaning out over the fence, trying to snag either an autograph or a foul ball, if not both. They had no doubt skipped school, although they were a long way from *Little Rascals*–type truants. Standing there with their parents, they appeared to be a well-heeled bunch (considering ticket prices, they'd have to be), and despite their unexcused absences I doubt any of them would use the "nobody . . . no more" construction.

Most were wearing mitts, and I think of a young Michael Giglio, who, he told me, always brought his mitt to the game. I brought mine too when I was a kid. Being a sports fan is a truly hopeful endeavor.

Out behind the kids, the stands were filling up, and for a moment I allowed myself to envision the place packed to the gills with screaming fools. I somehow melded the video clips in my head of an overflowing and raucous Fenway as I've seen it on those October nights when the Yankees were in town with the reality of the half-full, sunlit stadium before me. For the briefest second I could make it work. I could turn the stoic seatbacks that were staring at me into a crowd prodded to their feet by high drama and pure excitement, but it was fleeting and ultimately unsatisfying. I couldn't fully conjure the sound or replicate the internal state that would accompany such a moment — the magical hyperreality of adrenaline, pressure, stress, focus, and skin-tingling anticipation that only competition can arouse.

Instead, like the benchwarmer that I've become, I spotted the dugout. It was empty, and the long wooden seat glinted with a varnished warmth that spoke to me. I trotted down the steps, half expecting someone to stop me, and slid onto the bench. The long green pad is stiff but comfy, and I take a moment to check out the old-fashioned black phone that hangs in a metal box, and think about calling out the bullpen to get a lefty up. I sit down and lean back, taking in the view from the dark, womblike interior, the same view Red Sox players have been drinking in for ninety years.

Around the infield, the grounds crew brushes the base lines, trowels smooth the dirt around the bases, and hoses the base paths to keep the dust down and to make them look better on TV. There's something comforting about the ritual of such preparations. The tradition. Like some ancient priests preparing a sacrifice.

Fenway's intimacy and quirkiness are evident from here. Everything is close at hand and the seats crowd the playing surface. The sides of the grandstands rise quickly and, with their corrugated roofs, seem to overhang the field. There are entire sections of seats in the center that don't face the field. Instead, a person sitting in one of them, staring straight ahead, would find himself looking at an area just beyond first base.

As I make my way back through the park, there's an odd energy. The crowd is large and perky, but very casual. The sense of anticipation and tension accompanying so many of the other events on my list is not as palpable. When I pass through the press box, the TVs are tuned to a soap opera. Even after the game starts, the energy flags. I wonder if this is because it's Opening Day, a Super Bowl–like happening that draws a not quite as dedicated and knowledgeable crowd out to the park.

I wander out to one of the brand-new seating areas at the top of the grandstands on either side; this is their public debut. Like the new seating above the Monster, these areas have rows of seats with countertops in front of them, and the top row is just a counter with a large standing-room area behind it. It's there that I take up a position among hundreds of other fans. The seating, or lack of seating, adds to the sense of relaxed nonchalance. Without the strictures of assigned seating, there's more of a party atmosphere. Guys jockey for position at the counter, talking trash with their buddies and checking their BlackBerrys. The action on the field becomes less of a focal point. It's a familiar feeling, the beer, the high-fives, the constant undertow of chatter as the game flashes by in the background. For all the intimacy and character the stadium can provide, standing here is like . . . like watching a game in a sports bar.

At the same time, I think, This is the next step. The coming generations of sports fans will still come to the game, but they'll enjoy them in new ways, and that continuum, no matter how it changes, will connect them to me just as it connects me to the men who stood outside the gates wearing fedoras on Opening Day ninety-four years ago.

★ The Sox, who've led for most of the game, add a run in the seventh to pad their lead, and when they do, the crowd stands up and takes note, cheering as loud and hard as anyone anywhere. By the bottom of the eighth the home team has all but sealed it. I lean against the rail and wait for the final out. I stay there even after the game is over, watching as the backslapping masses file past. Then I make my way down to Section 16, Box 31, Row H, Seats 1 and 2. Kelly Giglio's seats.

I don't sit, though. I turn and face the field. The grounds crew is pulling up the bases and dragging the field. I can hear the jostling of bats in the dugout. Shades of the past are everywhere. The chairs, the field, the scoreboard. Old black-and-white images of Ted Williams, washed out by the afternoon sun, loop through my head. Visible too is the future. The new pavilions, the bleachers above the Green Monster, the Boston skyline in the distance. How much has that changed since 1935? An entire city blossomed, like minerals crystallizing above the right-field wall, as Giglio sat watching.

I sit. It snowed only a week ago and while there's still a chill in the air there is the definite scent of spring on the breeze. My year of sports (fourteen months, actually) is over, and I'm trying to assess what I'm left with. I don't want to draw the obvious conclusion, reach for the easy reductive answer about how all the pieces relate, and what, in retrospect, it all means.

I know a few things. I know that I love sports as much as ever, and I know that I'm ready to sink myself back into them. Maybe I'll have to pick my spots more carefully, pare down the number of teams I devote myself to, but I want to ride the roller coaster again. I want to experience the highs and lows. I want to give myself up to it and let it take me where it will. And I want to share it. With my friends, the old ones I no longer see enough and the new ones I see more often, and with my father and brother and my kids, too. Even if the results aren't what we want, we'll have gotten something from it that we will always have. Without question, the best events were the ones I shared with other people, whether that was an RV full of race fans or my wife and good friends.

As far as the ten events, I don't know what connects them, beyond the obvious. Maybe it's that through either the absence or presence of whatever attributes I encountered they showed me what I was seeking.

There is something else, though. Ignatius Giglio had no doubt been here when Bucky Dent hit that moonball over the Green Monster, sending an eleven-year-old boy and his confused dog, watching two hundred miles away, for a lap around the house. And so at this moment I am connected to him not just by the seat of my pants, firmly planted on the spot his had occupied for all those years, but also by the incidents that overlapped our lives and by the widening circle of connections that envelope us: his Red Sox, my Yankees, his son, my friend, his wife, my mother, his season tickets, my journey.

For almost the entirety of the seventy years he held those tickets, for eighty-six of the ninety years he lived, the Red Sox did not win. I think of all the days and nights he spent right here. All those moments, the brilliant to the banal. The pitching duels, the longball blowouts, the rain delays, and the doubleheaders. Always clapping, always positive, from batting practice to the final out. Like a boy in the bleachers wearing a mitt, it is an incredible act of hope — a word that envelopes all those other ones I'd been wrestling with, passion, commitment, romance, friendship, community, the future, and even the past.

Through this man I have never met and never will meet, I have come to see sports as both immense and minuscule. These games are both terribly important and unbearably trivial, and within their measured lines incredible doses of the human condition are on display. Neither the quantity of events nor the caliber of them matters. Whether I fly to New Delhi for the India-Pakistan cricket match or drive across town two or three times a week to see the local team take the field, it matters only that what is on the field engages me in the moment and in the world around me. It matters only that, win or lose, I can get up the next day and approach the stadium with hope. That is the *one* thing every sports fan must do.

ACKNOWLEDGMENTS: I would like to thank: Terry McDonell, David Bauer, and Jim Herre at *Sports Illustrated* for allowing me to take on this project. All the friends and colleagues who helped — whether successfully or not — with everything from credentials to inside tips to photography: Adena Ellis, Farrell Evans, Stan Grossfeld, Gina Houseman, Carolyn Koshnick, Albert Lin, Bruce Madej, Miriam Marseau, Bob Martin, Rick McCabe, Erick Rasco, Cheryl Spain, Sarah Thurmond, L. Jon Wertheim, and, especially, Gene Menez. The cast of characters who offered their hospitality, shared their wit, and sacrificed their time to bring color and life to my excursions: the entire Bateh family, especially Albert, Jonan, and Essa, the irrepressible Carlos, Cliff Christl, Jason and Carrie Dombrowski, Doug Drouillard and family, the entire Giglio family, especially Michael, Dalne Hasse, David Ingmire, Diane Ingmire, Jimmy Keirlan, Ron and Becky McCartney, Matt Mazoffa, Sue and Joe Malecki, Charles Plueddeman, Mike Stankowski, and Ted and Karen Walsh. The little agent that could, Matthew Carnicelli. Dick Friedman for his insights and feedback. Maura Fritz, whose editorial guidance went above and beyond the call of duty. Susan Canavan and Will Vincent and everyone at Houghton Mifflin. Most of all, my crazy, sports-loving family: my sister, Denise, my brother, Alex, and my father, George. My two wonderful children (who as always shall remain nameless in print, although they'll probably hate me for that someday), and my editor-, proofreader-, support system-, and inspiration-in-chief, the lovely and beautiful Karin Anne Henderson.